Lipsmackin' Vegetarian Backpackin'

Lipsmackin' Vegetarian Backpackin'

Christine and Tim Conners

ThreeForks™

GUILFORD, CONNECTICUT
HELENA, MONTANA

AN IMPRINT OF THE GLOBE PEQUOT PRESS

We dedicate this book to the memory of Dr. David E. Yount, loving father, brilliant scientist, and a steadfast source of encouragement during the compilation of our first backpacking cookbook, *Lipsmackin' Backpackin'*.

We miss you Dad . . .

Text design: Nancy Freeborn
Photos by Tim Conners

Library of Congress Cataloging-in-Publication Data
Conners, Christine.
Lipsmackin' vegetarian backpackin' / Christine and Tim Conners. –1st ed.
p. cm.
Includes index.
ISBN-13: 978-0-7627-2531-1

1. Vegetarian cookery. 2. Outdoor cookery. I. Conners, Tim. II. Title.
TX837.C597 2004
641.5'636–dc22

2004040513

Manufactured in the United States of America
First Edition/Seventh Printing

Contents

Acknowledgments vii

Introduction 1

Using This Book 5

Recommendations and Tips 8

Breakfast 13

Lunch 45

Dinner 81

Breads 139

Snacks and Desserts 153

Drinks 169

Acknowledgments Reprise 185

Appendix A: Dehydrophobia 186

Appendix B: Sources of Dried Foods and Other Ingredients 189

Appendix C: Measurement Conversions 191

About Our Contributors 194

Index 206

About the Authors 214

Packable Trailside Cooking Instructions 215

A Song of Ascents

I will lift up my eyes to the mountains;
From where shall my help come?
My help comes from the Lord,
Who made heaven and earth.

Psalm 121 : 1-2 (NASB)

Acknowledgments

A number of years ago, we lived in California's Tehachapi Mountains near the Pacific Crest Trail (PCT). Before we had children, we spent a great deal of time together along the local stretch of the PCT. We loved the trail; and while Christine was mostly sidelined due to her first two pregnancies during our last three years in the Golden State, Tim became a volunteer trail maintenance coordinator to help keep the chaparral-choked PCT passable in the Tehachapi and Piute Mountains.

Through our close involvement with the PCT, as well as the Pacific Crest Trail Association through whom Tim volunteered his time, we frequently would meet up with backpackers walking from Mexico to Canada as they passed through the Mojave-Tehachapi area along Highway 58. We occasionally had the opportunity to shuttle them between the PCT and town, sometimes taking them back to our home for a short break from trail life. Word got out; and it wasn't long before it became a regular occurrence to have several backpackers staying at our home at any one time during the peak hiking season.

We can genuinely say that these were some of the most interesting and enjoyable people we ever had the pleasure of meeting. To this day, we remain in contact with many of these once-strangers, now friends. It was during those years that Christine first had the idea of putting together a book of our trail guests' favorite backpacking recipes.

Well, Christine is tenacious, and it was only a matter of time before a publisher would have to say yes . . . either that, or face endless badgering. As first-time authors, we were very fortunate to have Falcon Press acquiesce to our repeated requests. With a publisher on board and a wonderful core group of initial contributors, many of whom were our guests during their long-distance PCT treks, the recipes began to pour in; and, before long, *Lipsmackin' Backpackin'* became a reality.

It was in 2001 that Falcon-Globe Pequot Press asked us if we'd be interested in compiling a sequel, this time filled exclusively with vegetarian recipes. We were elated! By then, we had moved far from the high trails of the west. Working on a second book gave us the opportunity to live the wilderness trail life vicariously while we otherwise focused on raising our now three small children.

Flyin' Brian Robinson, who walked all 7,400 miles of the Pacific Crest, Continental Divide, and Appalachian National Scenic Trails in 2001, was the first contributor to *Lipsmackin' Vegetarian Backpackin'*. We were off to a great start. Subsequent and significant help came from trail organizations, rangers, park attendants, Web masters, and bulletin board operators as they helped spread the word of our new need for input. The list of people to whom we are indebted is almost endless. We wish that we could recognize all of you by name. In lieu of this, please accept our collective thank you!

But, of course, we reserve our greatest and most sincere appreciation for our contributors, without whom neither our first or second book would exist. Despite having tested, adapted, and refined hundreds upon hundreds of trail recipes over the years, we continue to be amazed at the innovative ideas coming from these people.

It is their diverse and creative approaches to food preparation that make the *Lipsmackin'* books unique. If we are considered experts in the subject of backpack cooking, it is only because we have been taught by the experts themselves.

The contribution process was sometimes a bit arduous as each recipe was tested and often retested for suitability. Most contributors were contacted numerous times as we worked through the nuances of their submissions. Some contributors found the process more than they bargained for, and withdrew from the foray. For those who stuck with us, we are especially grateful for your patient assistance and good humor. And, as is obvious during a quick glance through the book, sometimes we've given your recipes somewhat wacky names. For this, we appreciate your forgiveness! Special thanks go to Laurie Ann March and Ken Harbison for answering the call at the last minute to test and refine several of the recipes. Your skill and precision made the difference.

Finally, we would like to thank our children, James, Michael, and Maria, for being on the front line in sampling the very large array of victuals that resulted from the testing process. As any parent knows, appealing to a young child's palate is one of the most difficult challenges to conquer. And, trust us, they were tough critics, especially considering the often unique aesthetics associated with the recipes. On those evenings when kitchen testing failed, cereal was often the backup plan. Thanks, kids, for putting up with Mom and Dad as we raced to meet the publishing deadline. You were real troopers!

Introduction

Lipsmackin' Vegetarian Backpackin' is the sequel to *Lipsmackin' Backpackin': Lightweight Trail-tested Recipes for Backcountry Trips.* Just like the original, our latest book contains a unique collection of more than 150 favorite recipes from highly experienced backpackers. Once more, we've extensively queried the outdoor community to find all-new approaches to food preparation. And, once again, we've thoroughly tested hundreds of recipes and included only those that we believe to be the best of the best.

In short, we've built this book according to the same principles used to create *Lipsmackin' Backpackin'*. However, in addition to all-new recipes, there is one other obviously significant difference relative to our first book: While about two-thirds of the recipes in *Lipsmackin' Backpackin'* were vegetarian, *Lipsmackin' Vegetarian Backpackin'* is completely meat-free. Despite this rather large change in focus, we believe that we've succeeded in making this book a solid complementary companion to the original by retaining those features of the first that have proven to be particularly helpful to readers and improving upon those that were less so.

Why Lipsmackin' Vegetarian?

Having convenient meat-free food preparation choices available at the grocery store is a tremendous asset on the home front, where time tends to be at an ever-increasing premium for most people. When dining out, many restaurants are adding to the number of innovative and tasty vegetarian items that they place on the menu. Having these types of expanded options available can make it much easier to adhere to a more strict vegetarian discipline or to reduce the frequency in which some might otherwise "fall off the wagon" due to a lack of adequate food choices. That philosophy is the underlying reason for this book: to increase the food options available to the hiking and backpacking community by providing exceptional meat-free menu selections.

Meeting the Diverse Needs of Unique Individuals

There are several different classes of vegetarianism and probably an almost endless number of reasons and opinions why folks choose to avoid animal products. There are those who tend to not eat any meat, dairy, or egg products—vegans; those who will not consume meat products but are comfortable eating dairy and eggs—ovo-lacto vegetarians; and there are, of course, shades and variations in between.

Complicating all of this are the reasons why people choose vegetarianism. Some desire to lessen the impact that their food choices have on the environment; many are interested in retaining or improving their health; others believe it to be unethical to exploit or kill animals or abhor the conditions in which they are often raised within the factory farming industry. Still others choose vegetarianism because of religious doctrine.

This book does not try to persuade the reader toward any particular argument regarding vegetarianism. That said, it is probably worth stating what this book is not. This is not a vegan cookbook, although vegans will indeed find a large selection of recipes to choose from. This is not a health book, although the reader will certainly discover a great number of very nutritious selections. And although every recipe can be classified as at least suitable for ovo-lacto vegetarians, this book isn't even meant to be strictly for vegetarians: Any hiking omnivore would have a tough time turning their nose up at the great-tasting recipes found in these pages.

Obviously, we've made every attempt to eliminate meat products from our book. Considering the manner in which food is processed in these modern times, it is possible that something offensive may be lurking deep behind a scientific label that few can pronounce. If this is the case, allow us to apologize in advance. We can't claim to know the source of every compound in processed foods; but when we came across a recipe that clearly contained a meat by-product, either we found a suitable work-around, or it was no longer considered for the book.

Meeting the Needs of the Long-Distance Backpacker

The requirements of the long-distance backpacker are obviously quite different from those of the overnighter or weekender. The distance packer often walks much farther each day and sometimes travels as long as a week or more without the opportunity for resupply. The body's ever-increasing caloric demands under such conditions further complicate the logistics associated with the menu-planning aspects of the trip. The long-distance backpacker must also overcome far greater psychological challenges that can threaten the completion of the journey. All of these difficulties, if not properly addressed, can easily lead to an aborted trip, physical injury, nutritional deficiencies, or, at the least, a nasty disposition.

One of the most important elements in the distance hiker's backpack for combating these deleterious issues is plenty of great-tasting food that can stand up to the extreme rigors and tough requirements of life on the long trail. To this end, all recipes in *Lipsmackin' Vegetarian Backpackin'* had to meet the same strict standards that we developed for those in the first book according to the following criteria:

Weight

Hikers obviously must keep their pack weight to a minimum to reduce risk of musculoskeletal injury and to maximize daily mileage. Food comprises a significant percentage of the overall pack weight at the trailhead. We've selected recipes that offer exceptional nutritional qualities for their weight.

Taste

Backpacking is often a very difficult way of life. Food is essential during a rough day, not only to restore one's physical vitality but to nurture the spirit as well. The power of food to make or break a long trip is often underestimated. Agreeable flavor is critical to keeping you on the trail, and the characteristic of good taste was essential for our recipes. If we didn't think it tasted good, we didn't include it.

Nutritional Value

Just as a pack full of bland food can cut short a long trip as surely as a twisted ankle, so can nutritionally defunct food eaten days on end. While some of our recipes are "comfort foods," included as an option to provide that needed psychological boost occasionally, they comprise only a small percentage of the book. You'll find many nutritious options designed to keep you running with a full head of steam.

Variety

Food boredom can quickly sap the pleasure from eating. Although there are some people who can happily eat the same meal day after day for months on end while on the trail, this is definitely the exception, not the rule. Large amounts of the same food can quickly become revolting. This is a surprisingly common contributing factor for many aborted backcountry trips since it isn't long before the mind begins to repeatedly ask the hiker, "Why are you doing this?" We offer a very wide range of food choices as well as a number of unique approaches to food preparation, all specifically geared to help you avoid this problem.

Simplicity

Although the degree of required at-home preparation varies from page to page, all recipes in this book requiring on-trail preparation have easy final instructions for the backcountry. For those that require heat from a stove, never more than a single pot is required for preparation. This should be welcome news to most hikers since less-than-ideal cooking situations tend to be the rule. Most recipes have been designed to produce individual servings on the trail.

Durability

We've focused on recipes that can hold up well in the pack by resisting crushing and crumbling and that have reasonably long shelf-lifes before spoiling. Provided that a thorough job is conducted throughout the dehydration process and during packaging, and as long as temperatures are kept reasonable during shipping and storage, the recipes in this book should easily handle the rigors of resupply and trail life.

Eating Ugly Food

One of the more obvious differences between backpacking foods and those that you set on the kitchen table is the appearance. You'll notice that aesthetics are not on our list of the needs of the long-distance backpacker and so were of little interest to us. It may look like it came straight from the sawmill, but, trust us, it really does taste terrific.

Unlike health-focused cookbooks that treat fats, sodium, carbs, and calories like the plague, we realize that these nutritional metrics are all vital in proper measure to the well-being of the long-distance backpacker, so you'll find a wide range of each as you peruse the recipes. We've included pertinent nutritional information for each recipe to assist you in planning a trail menu that's right for your situation.

Terminus

Even if you do not consider yourself a vegetarian, we are confident you'll find that the recipes in this book produce fantastic food for the trail: hearty, nutritious, and loaded with flavor, easily rivaling their omnivorous counterparts. There really isn't anything strange or mysterious about this stuff. For those of you who are vegetarian, we are pleased to be able to expand your horizons and make it that much easier for you to pursue a better way of living. Regardless of who you are, our most sincere desire is that our book might help you enjoy your time in the backcountry even more.

Here's hoping that our family will have the opportunity to share a meal with you somewhere down the trail.

Using This Book

Lipsmackin' Vegetarian Backpackin' has been arranged based on the same format used in *Lipsmackin' Backpackin'*.

Lurking behind the apparent subjectivity with which we've categorized the recipes lies a measure of logic. All breakfast recipes were selected for ease of preparation to allow you to break camp more quickly in the morning. To make your midday breaks more convenient, none of the lunch recipes require the use of a cookstove. Recipes requiring a combination of longer-period rehydration and cooking were typically reserved for dinner, when the majority of backpackers tend to take the most time to relax for the day. On the other hand, you'll find that the bread, drink, and snack recipes cover the gamut as to which times of day each is most appropriate. No matter what level of objectivity we've used, we realize that one person's dinner would nevertheless be another's lunch; so if you do not see what you are looking for in one meal group, try searching another.

Oftentimes, the contributor provided an interesting anecdote related to his or her experience with a particular, often favorite, recipe. If so, we've included the story, as well. We believe that you will find this information enjoyable and will more fully appreciate the recipe in light of the circumstances in which it has been used in the past. The contributor's name and hometown can be found at the bottom of each recipe. At the back of the book, a biographical sketch introduces you to each of our contributors, often focusing on that person's outdoor experience.

Novel food preparation ideas, valuable for general use, can be found in the chapter titled "Recommendations and Tips." Additional preparation ideas are scattered in individual recipes throughout the book. To further assist you in the kitchen, standard measurement conversions and typical weights of dried foods can be found at the back of the book as well.

While a significant fraction of the recipes in *Lipsmackin' Vegetarian Backpackin'* require dried ingredients, many of these items can be found commercially, eliminating the need for the reader to own a dehydrator for more than four-fifths of the recipes. For this reason, we've included in the back of the book a comprehensive list of national suppliers of dried food products and unique ingredients that might otherwise be difficult to locate in your community.

If you have never dried your own food before and break out in a cold sweat just thinking about the prospect of doing so, turn immediately to Christine's appendix on dehydrophobia. You'll find helpful information for your problem.

Using the Recipes

Ingredient Lists and Food Preparation Instructions

Within each recipe, a thorough ingredient list is provided. Complete preparation instructions are grouped according to whether they require completion "At home" before the trip begins or once "On the trail." Note that while the instructions are comprehensive, it is assumed that the reader maintains a basic operating knowledge of the use of standard kitchen appliances as well as a food dehydrator for those recipes that require one.

On-trail instructions are duplicated at the back of the book in a tear-out format that allows the reader to take them along in the backpack to eliminate any guesswork during the final steps of preparing the food. To spare the appearance of the book, these instructions are also available on-line in PDF format at www.falconbooks.com/lipsmackin.

Note that any recipe that calls for water during on-trail preparation assumes that it will be thoroughly filtered or otherwise properly treated prior to its use in the recipe.

Serving Sizes

We have estimated how many average servings each recipe will produce. Of course, the definition of "average" is subjective, and our use of serving units was intended only as a roughly consistent reference between recipes. You should carefully consider your own individual appetite and nutritional needs. If you will be on the trail for many days or weeks, your appetite will probably change significantly with time. For some, what would be a satisfying meal at the beginning of the trip might only be the first course days later.

For exceptionally high-caloric-density foods, a serving has often been set to the smallest convenient unit, one "Energy Ball" for instance. In breaking these types of recipes down to the lowest common denominator, we believe that menu and nutritional planning will be simplified since what constitutes a serving in these cases can vary enormously from person to person. One hiker may pop just a couple of Energy Balls following a main course at lunch, whereas another could very well eat an entire bag of them as their main meal.

Weight Values

For each recipe, a weight value is given for each individual serving as well as for the recipe in its entirety. The reader should translate these values as necessary to any customized serving size. The weight value represents pack-ready ingredients. It does not include the weight of listed optional ingredients or water that may be required for final on-trail preparation.

Note that weight data are approximate subject to the accuracy of a standard kitchen spring-scale. Variations in brands used, drying temperature, and drying times will all affect the actual final weight. Weight values in each recipe have been rounded to the nearest ounce.

Nutritional Information

The nutritional information included in this book is intended to serve as a starting point for evaluating the overall dietary value of a particular menu. Calorie, protein, carbohydrate, sodium, fiber, fat, and cholesterol data are included for each recipe in order to help the reader balance each according to individual nutritional requirements. You must be knowledgeable of your own backcountry needs so that you do not shortchange critical nutrients on your trip.

Keep in mind that even though you may strike a good balance between the seven nutritional parameters mentioned above, your body also requires a large number of vitamins, minerals, and micronutrients. Although supplements can help meet the body's daily requirements for these nutrients, a menu rich in vegetables and fruits, dehydrated or fresh, is advisable. The demands of long-distance trekking are so great on the body that top-quality food must be the rule and not the exception.

Note that the nutritional information presented in this book is on a per-serving basis and will vary depending on the reader's choice of product brands, ingredient substitution, or the inclusion of optional ingredients.

Caution Regarding the Use of Ziplock Bags with Hot Water

While trail cooking is obviously fraught with a number of fire- and heat-related dangers that must be carefully controlled, the use of ziplock food storage bags with heated water introduces an additional hazard that the reader must be aware of and exercise due caution with in order to avoid serious burns or damage to gear.

Some recipes in *Lipsmackin' Vegetarian Backpackin'* call for the pouring of hot, sometimes boiling, water into a ziplock bag for the final step of on-trail food preparation. The value of this method is that it greatly simplifies meal preparation and the clean-up process, and it often eliminates the need to use precious water for washing cook pots and utensils because the final cooking instrument and serving plate are the bag itself. However, the method also requires extreme care to prevent accidental burning from the hot food contents.

The specific concern involves the softening of the plastic that can occur at temperatures consistent with boiling water. To provide additional margin against bag burst and skin burns, use high-quality, thick, freezer-type bags for this type of application. Once the hot water has been introduced to the bag, do not place it in a position where the hot contents will spill on you should the bag tip over or burst open. We recommend setting the bag within a cook pot before adding hot water. The pot will help stabilize the bag when the water is poured and while the food rehydrates. Keep the bag within the pot until the temperature of the food drops to a safe level, as the pot will contain the contents should the bag unexpectedly rupture.

The chemical stability of plastics used in ziplock bags is well documented for temperatures at which food is typically prepared. There is no demonstrated toxic effect in using quality ziplock bags for food temperatures at and below that of boiling water.

We have never experienced a problem using this cooking method. With proper caution, you shouldn't either.

Recommendations and Tips

Food-Planning and Preparation Tips

The following list of food-planning and preparation tips and recommendations contains the more valuable lessons we've learned over the years. Some we've stumbled upon ourselves while others came from our contributors. Whether you've been at it for years, or are new to the trail, we hope that you learn something here that makes life easier the next time you head for the backcountry.

- Premix ingredients to the maximum extent possible at home. This will reduce waste and simplify your food preparation in the field.
- Carry a plastic container that doubles as a measuring cup. If graduations are not included on the container, make your own prior to the trip by etching the container for appropriate measurements such as a quarter, half, and full cup.
- Learn to approximate one teaspoon and one tablespoon using your pack spoon.
- When packaging a meal, label the container or storage bag with a description of the contents. Either carry final preparation instructions on a small sheet of paper along with the recipe or write the instructions on the container or bag.
- If using boxed store-bought food on the trail, transfer the contents of the box to a less voluminous container if possible. Be sure to cut the directions from the box and include them for use while on the trail.
- If the ingredients in a particular recipe are foreign to you, test the recipe at home before using it on a long trip.
- Dried or powdered drink mixes should typically be added to the container following the water in order to prevent clotting.
- Carry a well-rounded selection of spices with you on every trip. Experiment with the spices and tailor your collection to fit your own taste. Besides salt and black pepper, some of the more common spices include cinnamon, oregano, curry, garlic, cumin, basil, cayenne pepper, and thyme.
- Collect condiment packages for your upcoming trips. They provide an easy way to liven up a meal. Ketchup, mustard, mayonnaise, and relish are often readily available, but soy sauce, Parmesan cheese, dried red peppers, and hot sauce can also be found. Be careful that the condiments don't spoil. Some, such as mayonnaise, have a relatively short shelf life.

- Butter is available in packages that resemble oversized condiment packs. While retaining the taste, Butter Buds make for a more convenient, less costly, and lower-fat replacement for butter.

- For vegans, soy milk powder can often be exchanged in like amounts for dairy milk powder. Olive oil typically can also be substituted for butter, ounce for ounce.

Additional guidance and suggestions regarding the selection of particularly useful kitchen appliances and on-trail cook gear can be found in *Lipsmackin' Backpackin'*.

Drying and Rehydrating Recommendations

Many individuals enjoy dehydrating their own foods for the trail. It is a simple process and takes little time for one to become proficient at it. Pound for pound, home-dried food products usually cost much less than their commercially available dehydrated counterparts and can be produced fresh in custom-tailored quantities. And when it comes to taste, there is no comparison between dehydrated foods and similar items that have been ravaged through the process of freeze-drying. A home dehydrating unit also allows the backpacker to produce dried foods that are not available on the market: tailored leathers made with exotic fruits, vegetarian chili blends, spaghetti sauce based on your mom's secret recipe, fruit smoothies, cold trail salads. The list is truly endless.

Regardless of your opinion regarding home dehydrating, the recipes in *Lip smackin' Vegetarian Backpackin'* were carefully selected to provide all readers with a wide range of options. Less than one-fifth of the recipes in this book absolutely require the use of a home dehydrator. An additional one-fifth call for the use of a dehydrator in the At-home directions, although the dried products in those recipes, typically vegetables or fruits, can also be found commercially. See the list of sources of dried foods located at the back of this book.

If dehydrating appeals to you already, then fire up your unit and get ready to lay out some great-tasting food blends on those dryer trays. And keep reading because all dehydrator operators need to remain familiar with the following list of tips and cautions!

- To reduce the risk of bacterial contamination of the food, always clean and rinse your hands, work area, dehydrator, and utensils thoroughly before drying.

- Food that is under-dried will contain more moisture and therefore will spoil more quickly than if it has been dried thoroughly. For an enjoyable trip, and for your own health and safety, it is important that you dry your food properly.

- Ensure that products containing eggs and dairy are thoroughly cooked prior to drying. Salting the final product will help keep the food preserved. It is recommended that these types of food be kept frozen until you are ready for your trip.
- Store dried food tightly in moisture-proof containers or sealed bags and place them in a cool, dry, and dark place. Heavy-duty freezer-type ziplock plastic bags work well for both storage and trail use. If moisture does enter, the food may begin to rehydrate and will spoil much faster if so. *Never use food that looks or smells rancid in any way.*
- Food dried at home can generally be stored at room temperature for up to two months, in a refrigerator for up to six months, and in a freezer for up to one year.
- It is better to store and carry dehydrated foods in individual meal-size bags and containers. Avoid storing multimeal amounts of food in a single container or bag, as the repeated openings and closings could compromise the seal, allowing the remaining food to spoil more quickly.
- When packaging dried food in bulk, identify each item as it is bagged, along with the date that it was dried. Make sure to eat the food that has been stored for the longest period first. While packing for your trip and before cooking in the field, ensure that your dehydrated food hasn't spoiled. This is especially critical for foods containing dairy or eggs.
- Foods that are chopped and sliced more thinly and to a consistent size will dry more rapidly and evenly and will rehydrate more readily on the trail.
- Place pieces of cut food on the drying trays so that air will pass between and around the food. Minimize overlap; otherwise, the drying may be inconsistent among the pieces.
- Check food on an hourly basis when you are first learning the nuances of your dehydrator. Some dehydrators may require rotating the food pieces or trays in order to speed the drying process or to prevent uneven drying.
- A blender can easily reduce chili, smoothie mixes, spaghetti and noodle sauces, bean dishes, and other chunky foods to a smooth consistency that produces thin rolls of uniformly dried leathers that quickly rehydrate on the trail.
- Avoid mixing different aromatic foods when drying; otherwise, unpleasant surprises could result that may not be discovered until out on the

trail. For example, if spaghetti sauce were to be dried with peaches, the flavor of the sauce would be transferred to the peaches and vice versa.

- When drying very aromatic foods, your house will be completely filled with the aroma. This is something to consider before you load your dehydrator with chopped horseradish roots.
- Cook pasta, beans, and rice at home and dehydrate them before your trip. They will rehydrate more quickly on the trail and require far less time and fuel to heat. Or forget the stove, and simply rehydrate without heat to make a cold pasta and bean salad.
- Small food items, such as rice or grains, and thick liquids or pastes can be dried on dehydrator trays lined with parchment paper. We used to recommend plastic wrap in this role, but we've found that parchment paper generally works much better. Dried foods tend to avoid clinging to it; and the paper itself is breathable, which leads to a more rapid and even drying process.
- When drying liquids and pastes, the depth of the pool should be kept to less than 1/4 inch, with the center of the pool even thinner, to permit more uniform drying.
- When drying fresh vegetables, ensure that they are ripe, clean, and free of bruises. Prior to drying, blanching should be performed on most vegetables to stop an enzymatic action that can cause spoilage. This is accomplished by steaming the vegetables until slightly tender, but not fully cooked. Stir the vegetables frequently during the blanching process. Onions, mushrooms, and tomatoes do not require blanching. Vegetables will normally feel somewhat brittle when dried.
- Cooking certain families of vegetables, such as legumes, corn, and roots, prior to drying will reduce the time required for rehydration and cooking on the trail.
- When drying fresh fruit, ensure that it is ripe, clean, and free of bruises and pits. To minimize browning during the drying process, first soak the fruit for five minutes in a mixture of ¼ cup lemon juice to one quart water. Dried fruits will normally have a leathery texture and be somewhat chewy.
- We have had difficulty rehydrating generic brands of quick or instant rice in certain situations. Our results have been far better using name-brand rice, such as Uncle Ben's.

The range of dehydrators available on the market, and the nuances in the operating procedures between them, make it impossible for us to give even general instructions regarding drying temperatures and times. So, particularly if you're new to drying, practice using your dehydrator and become proficient in adapting it to new recipes before you first use it to prepare a backpack full of trail food for a long-distance trip.

Breakfast

Sasquatch Scones

SUZANNE ALLEN
SEATTLE, WASHINGTON

AT HOME:

- **1 1/2 cups all-purpose bleached wheat flour**
- **1/3 cup sugar**
- **2 teaspoons baking powder**
- **1/2 teaspoon baking soda**
- **1/4 teaspoon salt**
- **1 tablespoon nonfat powdered milk**
- **1/4 cup chopped walnuts**
- **1/2 cup currants**
- **1/4 teaspoon nutmeg**
- **1/4 teaspoon cinnamon**

In a bowl, combine and mix all dry ingredients. Divide evenly into 2 ziplock quart-size freezer bags. Dried fruit, such as cranberries or blueberries, can be added to the scone mix.

ON THE TRAIL:

- **4 teaspoons vegetable oil per serving**
- **1/4 cup water per serving**

To make 1 serving, add 1 teaspoon of oil and 1/4 cup of water to 1 bag of scone mix. Knead the bag until the dough becomes stiff. Warm 1 tablespoon of oil in a nonstick pan at low heat. Spoon 3-inch blobs of dough into the pan and cook on very low heat until the bottoms are browned and the tops begin to lose their shine. Flip and continue cooking until the bottom sides are lightly browned.

Ground cloves or cardamom make good spice alternatives. Dried lemon peel adds zing. Soy milk powder may be substituted for powdered dairy milk.

TOTAL WEIGHT: 1 POUND
Weight per serving: 8 ounces
Total servings: 2

Nutritional information per serving:

Calories:	825
Protein:	13 g
Carbohydrates:	134 g
Sodium:	902 mg
Fiber:	4 g
Fat:	24 g
Cholesterol:	0 mg

AUTHORS' NOTE:

In the Pacific Northwest they call him Bigfoot, in the Himalayas, Yeti. Mentioned in several Native American tales, Sasquatch is the Indian name for the legendary "hairy giant," said to roam the dark woods, standing up to 9 feet tall and weighing up to 900 pounds. If he does exist, it's safe to assume that he's hungry. These scones are packed with lots of calories just in case one of these big, hairy guys decides to join you for breakfast.

Jenkins Journey Cakes

"Versions of this cornbread recipe are known to date back to more than two hundred years ago. Frequently referred to as 'Johnny cakes,' it is thought that the original name may have actually been 'journey cakes,' as this was perfect bread for a long expedition.

"We further amended the recipe's title in honor of Jim Jenkins, explorer, author, ranger, and conservationist who worked tirelessly to communicate the wonder and beauty of the Southern Sierra and to preserve and protect the California mountains that he loved. We have spent much time wandering the trails of this region and relied heavily on Jim's precise and wonderfully written guidebook materials to find our way and to appreciate more fully the history, geography, flora, and fauna in those many areas that we visited. He passed away at a young age, but his legacy lives on for those, like us, who also love his mountains. Mount Jenkins, at 7,921 feet, lies just north of Walker Pass along the Pacific Crest Trail, and was named by the Bureau of Land Management in memory of Jim."

CHRISTINE AND TIM CONNERS
SAVANNAH, GEORGIA

TOTAL WEIGHT: 1 POUND 4 OUNCES
Weight per serving: about 7 ounces
Total servings: 3

Nutritional information per serving:

Calories:	470
Protein:	11 g
Carbohydrates:	102 g
Sodium:	434 mg
Fiber:	8 g
Fat:	5 g
Cholesterol:	96 mg

AT HOME:

2 cups cornmeal
1/4 cup all-purpose bleached wheat flour
3 tablespoons King Arthur dried whole egg powder
1/3 cup Nido whole milk powder
1/2 cup brown sugar
1/2 teaspoon salt
1/2 teaspoon ginger

In a large bowl, combine and thoroughly mix all dry ingredients. Divide mixture evenly between 3 ziplock quart-size bags, about 1 heaping cupful each.

ON THE TRAIL:

1/3 cup water per serving
1 tablespoon butter per serving

To prepare 1 serving, add 1/3 cup of water to 1 bag of cake mix. Knead contents thoroughly. Melt 1 tablespoon of butter in a pan. Cut a corner from the bottom of the bag and squeeze several dollops of the mixture into the pan. Cook both sides as you would a pancake.

Ketchikan Couscous

AT HOME:

1/3 cup Fantastic Foods whole wheat couscous
2 tablespoons nonfat powdered milk
2 tablespoons chopped dates or dried fruit of your choice
1/2 tablespoon brown sugar
1/16 teaspoon salt
1/8 teaspoon cinnamon
2 tablespoons chopped walnuts or nuts of your choice

Combine all dry ingredients and package in a ziplock bag.

ON THE TRAIL:

2/3 cup water
Optional: add butter to taste for a creamier flavor

To prepare 1 serving, heat 2/3 cup of water to boiling. Stir in the mix and cook for 2 minutes. Remove from heat. Allow the pot to stand covered until the liquid is absorbed and the couscous is tender, approximately 5 minutes.

CAROLE AND KEN HARBISON
SAN FRANCISCO, CALIFORNIA,
AND ROCHESTER, NEW YORK

Weight per serving: 5 ounces
Total servings: 1

Nutritional information per serving:

Calories:	500
Protein:	14 g
Carbohydrates:	78 g
Sodium:	450 mg
Fiber:	11 g
Fat:	11 g
Cholesterol:	2 mg

Chewonki Morning Bulgur

RACHEL JOLLY /
CHEWONKI FOUNDATION
BURLINGTON, VERMONT

Weight per serving: 6 ounces
Total servings: 1

Nutritional information per serving:

Calories:	503
Protein:	17 g
Carbohydrates:	66 g
Sodium:	800 mg
Fiber:	8 g
Fat:	21 g
Cholesterol:	15 mg

AT HOME:

1/2 cup bulgur wheat
1 tablespoon dried onion
1/4 teaspoon salt
1/4 teaspoon pepper
1/4 teaspoon oregano
1/4 teaspoon cumin
1/4 teaspoon garlic
1 (1-ounce) stick string cheese

Combine all ingredients except cheese in a quart-size ziplock freezer bag. Carry cheese separately.

ON THE TRAIL:

1 cup water
1 tablespoon olive oil

For optimum hydration, presoak the single serving of bulgur mix in 1 cup of water beginning the prior evening. In the morning, warm a pan and scramble the bulgur mix in 1 tablespoon of olive oil. Remove from heat and add small pieces of the stick of string cheese to the top of the mixture, allowing the cheese to melt into the scramble before serving.

Trailside Breakfast Rice

HEATHER BURROR
MARTINEZ, CALIFORNIA

Weight per serving: 8 ounces
Total servings: 1

AT HOME:

- **1 cup instant brown Minute Rice**
- **1/2 (1.7-ounce) package vanilla instant pudding (about 1/4 cup)**
- **2 tablespoons nonfat powdered milk**
- **1/4 teaspoon cinnamon**
- **1/4 cup dried mixed berries**
- **2 tablespoons chopped honey-roasted peanuts**

Place 1 cup of rice into a ziplock bag. Seal and set aside. Combine the remainder of the dry ingredients in a separate ziplock bag.

ON THE TRAIL:

- **1 3/4 cups water**

To make 1 serving, bring 1 3/4 cups of water to a boil. Add the bag of rice and heat for approximately 10 minutes until rice is fully cooked. Next, add the bag of mix containing the pudding. Remove from heat. Stir and serve.

Nutritional information per serving:

Calories:	362
Protein:	7 g
Carbohydrates:	80 g
Sodium:	395 mg
Fiber:	4 g
Fat:	3 g
Cholesterol:	1 mg

Cheesy Breakfast Grits

"Here's a fast recipe that won't hold you back in the morning."

KEN HARBISON
ROCHESTER, NEW YORK

Weight per serving: 5 ounces
Total servings: 1

Nutritional information per serving:

Calories:	520
Protein:	33 g
Carbohydrates:	56 g
Sodium:	1,160 mg
Fiber:	3 g
Fat:	19 g
Cholesterol:	56 mg

AT HOME:

- **2/3 cup Quaker Original Flavor Instant Grits (or two 1-ounce packets)**
- **1/3 cup nonfat powdered milk**
- **1/16 teaspoon garlic powder**
- **1 tablespoon dried egg white powder**
- **2 ounces jack or cheddar cheese**

Combine grits, powdered milk, garlic, and dried egg in a ziplock bag. Carry cheese separately.

ON THE TRAIL:

- **1 cup water**

To make 1 serving, stir the contents of the bag into 1 cup of water and heat to boiling while stirring. Remove from heat and add cheese, chopped into small pieces. Continue to stir until blended, then serve.

A quick breakfast idea: Combine a handful of dehydrated fruits (apples, peaches, bananas, raisins, pineapple, cranberries—whatever is available) in a pot with just enough water to cover. Bring to a boil and simmer to rehydrate. Add brown sugar to sweeten to taste.

SHERRY BENNETT
ROCHESTER, NEW YORK

Saucy Summer Breakfast Burritos

HEATHER BURROR
MARTINEZ, CALIFORNIA

TOTAL WEIGHT: 9 OUNCES
Weight per serving: about 5 ounces
Total servings: 2

Nutritional information per serving:

Calories:	435
Protein:	86 g
Carbohydrates:	41 g
Sodium:	2,222 mg
Fiber:	8 g
Fat:	22 g
Cholesterol:	333 mg

AT HOME:

1 (16-ounce) jar mild salsa
6 tablespoons whole egg powder
2 large flour tortillas

Dry the salsa in a dehydrator. When ready, tear the salsa leather into small pieces and place in a quart-size ziplock freezer bag. Place the egg powder in a separate ziplock bag. Carry the tortillas separately.

ON THE TRAIL:

1 1/2 cups water
1 tablespoon butter or vegetable oil
2 ounces (1/2 cup) shredded cheese

To make 2 servings, add 3/4 cup of boiling water to the salsa bag to rehydrate. Next, add 3/4 cup of cold water to the egg mix and shake well to reconstitute. Melt 1 tablespoon of butter or pour 1 tablespoon of vegetable oil in a warmed pan and add both the rehydrated salsa and the egg mix. Scramble. Shred 2 ounces of cheese (about 1/2 cup) and divide onto each of the 2 tortillas. Add scrambled-egg mix to both. Roll and serve.

Caution: See the "Using This Book" section regarding the use of ziplock bags with hot water.

Four-Corners Fiesta Burritos

HEATHER BURROR
MARTINEZ, CALIFORNIA

TOTAL WEIGHT: 12 OUNCES
Weight per serving: 6 ounces
Total servings: 2

Nutritional information per serving:

Calories:	495
Protein:	22 g
Carbohydrates:	50 g
Sodium:	1,779 mg
Fiber:	6 g
Fat:	22 g
Cholesterol:	333 mg

AT HOME:

1 (16-ounce) package frozen stir-fry vegetables
6 tablespoons whole egg powder
1 (1.25-ounce) pack Taco Bell taco seasoning mix
2 large flour tortillas

Chop stir-fry vegetables into small pieces and dry in a dehydrator. Place vegetables into a quart-size ziplock freezer bag. In another ziplock bag, place the powdered egg and taco seasoning mix. Carry tortillas separately.

ON THE TRAIL:

1½ cups water
1 tablespoon butter or vegetable oil
2 ounces (½ cup) shredded cheese

To make 2 servings, add ¾ cup boiling water to the bag of dried vegetables to rehydrate. Next, add ¾ cup cold water to the egg mix and shake well to reconstitute. Melt 1 tablespoon of butter or pour 1 tablespoon of vegetable oil in a warmed pan and add both the rehydrated vegetables and the egg mix. Scramble. Shred 2 ounces of cheese (about ½ cup) and divide onto each of the 2 tortillas. Add scrambled-egg mix to both. Roll and serve.

Mountain Muesli

AT HOME:

4 cups Quaker Old Fashioned Oats
1/2 cup wheat germ
1/2 cup shredded coconut
1 cup chopped honey-roasted peanuts
1 cup honey
1 cup dried cherries (or your favorite dried fruit)

Preheat oven to 200°F. In a large bowl, combine all the ingredients except the cherries. Spread mixture over a large tray and toast in the oven for 30 minutes. Remove, cool, and add dried cherries. Store in gallon-size ziplock freezer bags.

ON THE TRAIL:

Dairy or soy milk powder to taste

Add 1 cup of muesli mix to your favorite dairy or soy milk powder and water.

HEATHER BURROR
MARTINEZ, CALIFORNIA

TOTAL WEIGHT: 2 POUNDS 7 OUNCES
Weight per serving: about 4 ounces
Total servings: 10

Nutritional information per serving:

Calories:	540
Protein:	16 g
Carbohydrates:	95 g
Sodium:	70 mg
Fiber:	5 g
Fat:	12 g
Cholesterol:	0 mg

Kalalau Quinoa Cereal

Jason Rumohr on innovative survival techniques: "On one of my first backpacking trips, a friend and I didn't realize how much work hiking in the heat would be. We hadn't packed any snacks or lunch. About eight miles in, we crashed on a shady bridge over a roaring creek, where we fell asleep. When we woke up, we saw an elderly man sitting at the other end eating a sandwich. We were delirious and later wondered if we had just imagined him. Then the hard part came: climbing up a high ridge in 90-degree heat without any water. We became tired and weak. Soon I was so thirsty that I drank my friend's contact lens saline solution. It was salty, but it quenched my thirst for a bit."

AT HOME:

2 cups quinoa
1 cup raw sunflower seeds
1 cup raisins (or your favorite dried fruit)
4 tablespoons brown sugar
1 teaspoon cinnamon
Optional: salt to taste

Add the quinoa to 4 cups of water and bring to a boil. Cover and reduce heat. Continue to cook until all the water is absorbed, usually an additional 10 to 15 minutes. When finished, dry the cereal on parchment-lined dehydrator trays. Once dried, combine and mix with the remainder of the dry ingredients in a large bowl. Divide evenly among 5 individual quart-size ziplock freezer bags (about 1 cup each).

Optional: You can forgo the raisins if you'll be hiking in blueberry country while they are ripe. This cereal is very tasty as is, but fresh, wild blueberries make it heavenly.

ON THE TRAIL:

3/4 cup water per serving

To make 1 serving, bring 3/4 cup of water to a boil and add to the bag of cereal mix. Allow the contents to rehydrate for several minutes before serving.

JASON RUMOHR
SEATTLE, WASHINGTON

TOTAL WEIGHT: 1 POUND 8 OUNCES
Weight per serving: about 5 ounces
Total servings: 5

Nutritional information per serving:

Calories:	552
Protein:	14 g
Carbohydrates:	87 g
Sodium:	12 mg
Fiber:	9 g
Fat:	18 g
Cholesterol:	0 mg

Caution: See the "Using This Book" section regarding the use of ziplock bags with hot water.

Blue Bear Mush

HEATHER BURROR
MARTINEZ, CALIFORNIA

AT HOME:

1 cup Arrowhead Mills Bear Mush
1/2 cup dried blueberries
2 tablespoons brown sugar
1/4 teaspoon salt
1/3 cup nonfat powdered milk

Mix all dry ingredients together in a bowl. Divide evenly into 2 ziplock quart-size freezer bags (about 1 cup each).

ON THE TRAIL:

1 1/2 cups water per serving
Optional: 1 tablespoon butter per serving

For each serving, bring 1 1/2 cups of water to a boil and add to the bag of cereal mix. Stir and let cool before serving.

Caution: See the "Using This Book" section regarding the use of ziplock bags with hot water.

TOTAL WEIGHT: 11 OUNCES
Weight per serving: about 6 ounces
Total servings: 2

Nutritional information per serving:

Calories:	435
Protein:	12 g
Carbohydrates:	103 g
Sodium:	358 mg
Fiber:	7 g
Fat:	0 g
Cholesterol:	3 mg

Mule Fuel

AT HOME:

- 1 (1-serving) packet spiced apple cider mix
- 1 cup Quaker Old Fashioned Oats
- 1/4 cup slivered almonds
- 1/4 cup cranberries, currants, raisins, or other chopped dried fruit
- 1/2 teaspoon cinnamon

Mix all dry ingredients together and store in a ziplock freezer bag.

ON THE TRAIL:

- 1 cup water

To prepare 1 serving, add 1 cup of hot or cold water to the cereal mix and serve.

BARBARA HODGIN
"MULE 2"
SACRAMENTO, CALIFORNIA

Weight per serving: 7 ounces
Total servings: 1

Nutritional information per serving:

Calories:	679
Protein:	17 g
Carbohydrates:	107 g
Sodium:	34 mg
Fiber:	12 g
Fat:	23 g
Cholesterol:	0 mg

Omega Breakfast

"I make this in big batches and eat it almost daily on or off the trail. The dried fruits and nuts can, of course, be varied to your taste."

RICHARD HALBERT
"RANGER RICK"
TRAVERSE CITY, MICHIGAN

AT HOME:

Main ingredients list:

1 cup rolled oats
1 cup rolled rye
1 cup Post Grape-Nuts
1 cup sunflower seeds
1 cup dried cranberries
1 cup raisins
1 cup date pieces
1 cup soy nuts
1 cup walnut pieces
1/2 cup pumpkin seeds
1/2 cup sesame seeds

In a very large bowl, mix all items in the main ingredients list. Add 1 cup of the resulting cereal mixture to each of 9 ziplock quart-size freezer bags.

To each single-serving bag also add:

1/3 cup nonfat powdered milk
1/2 teaspoon cinnamon
1/2 teaspoon nutmeg
1 tablespoon ground flaxseed

Add powdered milk, cinnamon, nutmeg, and ground flaxseed according to the single-serving list to each of the 9 bags. Flaxseed can be ground at home using a coffee grinder.

ON THE TRAIL:

1 cup water per serving

Bring 1 cup of water to a boil and pour into a single-serving bag. Seal and let stand for 5 minutes before eating.

TOTAL WEIGHT: 4 POUNDS 4 OUNCES
Weight per serving: about 8 ounces
Total servings: 9

Nutritional information per serving:

Calories:	657
Protein:	21 g
Carbohydrates:	85 g
Sodium:	88 mg
Fiber:	14 g
Fat:	31 g
Cholesterol:	0 mg

Caution: See the "Using This Book" section regarding the use of ziplock bags with hot water.

Crimson Skies Oatmeal

AT HOME:

1/2 cup Quaker Old Fashioned Oats
1/4 cup Ocean Spray Craisins
2 tablespoons orange drink powder
1/4 cup chopped walnuts
2 tablespoons Better Than Milk soy powder mix

Combine all dry ingredients in a ziplock bag.

ON THE TRAIL:

1 1/4 cups water

Bring 1 1/4 cups of water to a boil. Add mix from the single-serving ziplock bag and reduce heat. Cook for a few additional minutes, stirring occasionally, then cover and remove from heat. Let stand momentarily before serving.

RICHARD HALBERT
"RANGER RICK"
TRAVERSE CITY, MICHIGAN

Weight per serving: 7 ounces
Total servings: 1

Nutritional information per serving:

Calories:	613
Protein:	11 g
Carbohydrates:	90 g
Sodium:	250 mg
Fiber:	6 g
Fat:	24 g
Cholesterol:	0 mg

North Woods Oatmeal

AT HOME:

3/4 cup quick oats
1 teaspoon white or brown sugar
1/16 teaspoon salt
1/3 cup nonfat powdered milk
2 tablespoons dried blueberries
1 (2-bar) package Oats 'N Honey Nature Valley Granola

Combine oats, sugar, salt, powdered milk, and dried blueberries in a quart-size ziplock freezer bag. Carry granola bars separately.

ON THE TRAIL:

1 1/2 cups water

To prepare 1 serving, add bag of oat mix to 1 1/2 cups of boiling water and stir. Remove from heat and allow to stand for 5 minutes. Crumble up 2 granola bars and sprinkle on top before serving.

KEN HARBISON
ROCHESTER, NEW YORK

Weight per serving: 5 ounces
Total servings: 1

Nutritional information per serving:

Calories:	550
Protein:	20 g
Carbohydrates:	99 g
Sodium:	420 mg
Fiber:	10 g
Fat:	10 g
Cholesterol:	5 mg

Adirondack Apricot Oatmeal

AT HOME:

3/4 cup quick oats
1 teaspoon brown sugar or maple sugar
1/16 teaspoon salt
1/3 cup nonfat powdered milk
2 apricots, dried and chopped
3 tablespoons cashew nut pieces

Package all dry ingredients in a quart-size ziplock freezer bag.

ON THE TRAIL:

1 1/2 cups water

Add 1 1/2 cups of boiling water to the single-serving bag of oatmeal mix and stir. Allow to stand for 5 minutes before serving.

Caution: See the "Using This Book" section regarding the use of ziplock bags with hot water.

KEN HARBISON
ROCHESTER, NEW YORK

Weight per serving: 4 ounces
Total servings: 1

Nutritional information per serving:

Calories:	510
Protein:	21 g
Carbohydrates:	74 g
Sodium:	370 mg
Fiber:	7 g
Fat:	17 g
Cholesterol:	6 mg

Olympus Oatmeal

RAMONA HAMMERLY
ANACORTES, WASHINGTON

Weight per serving: 7 ounces
Total servings: 1

Nutritional information per serving:

Calories:	620
Protein:	20 g
Carbohydrates:	124 g
Sodium:	165 mg
Fiber:	12 g
Fat:	6 g
Cholesterol:	5 mg

AT HOME:

1/2 cup dried fruit pieces
1 cup Quaker Old Fashioned Oats
1/3 cup nonfat powdered milk

Carry fruit, oats, and milk powder separately.

ON THE TRAIL:

2 cups water
Optional: sugar, butter, cinnamon, allspice, wheat germ, or salt to taste

To make 1 serving, add dried fruit to 2 cups of water and bring to a boil. Add oats when the water begins to boil vigorously. Stir and simmer for 5 minutes. Add powdered milk and any optional ingredients. Stir and serve. Note that adding oats to the water before it is really boiling can result in a gluelike texture that tastes flat.

A fatty condiment, such as butter, makes a good addition in cold weather.

Kearsarge Pass Oatmeal

"A go-light, premixed-at-home concoction, which, when out on the trail, requires only the addition of some hot water to create a nourishing breakfast with little effort and minimal cleanup."

AT HOME:

1/2 cup nonfat powdered milk
3/4 cup Quaker Old Fashioned Oat Flakes
1/4 cup Kretschmer Original Toasted Wheat Germ
2 tablespoons raisins
1 tablespoon brown sugar

Mix all the dry ingredients together and transfer to an appropriate container for your backpack. I personally prefer hard plastic containers with tight covers. Do not use instant or quick oats or your breakfast will become pasty!

ON THE TRAIL:

Slightly more than 1 cup water

For 1 serving, bring a little more than 1 cup of water to a boil. Remove from the stove and pour over the dry mix. Stir. You should strive for the consistency of ordinary cooked oatmeal, but don't cook *this* mix! You will be wasting your time and reduce the texture to mush.

BILL ALBRECHT
LANCASTER, CALIFORNIA

Weight per serving: 7 ounces
Total servings: 1

Nutritional information per serving:

Calories:	525
Protein:	28 g
Carbohydrates:	90 g
Sodium:	193 mg
Fiber:	11 g
Fat:	7 g
Cholesterol:	6 mg

Desert Gruel

"This recipe is an adaptation of one from the amazing Carol Anderson of Tucson, a truly inspired cook at home who can't comprehend why anyone would spend much time cooking in the great outdoors.

"The funny thing about this recipe is how popular it is with other backpackers. Jack and I did a four-day trip in Paria Canyon with two friends, one of whom brought along some really exotic food. I was a little embarrassed the first time we poured up the gruel, but we ended up having to share for the rest of the hike!"

AT HOME:

- **1 tablespoon nutritional yeast**
- **1 tablespoon Just Whites dried egg whites**
- **2 tablespoons sesame seeds**
- **1 (2-ounce) package Fantastic Foods Split Pea Soup**
- **1/4 cup quinoa flakes**
- **1/4 cup rice flour**
- **1/4 cube Rapunzel Vegan Vegetable Bouillon**

Mix all dry ingredients together and store in a ziplock bag.

ON THE TRAIL:

- **1 tablespoon olive oil**
- **1 1/2 cups water**

To prepare 1 serving, mix dry ingredients together in a cook pot along with 1 tablespoon of olive oil and 1 1/2 cups of water. Heat, ensuring that the bouillon cube dissolves before serving.

The gruel can be made even tastier if you toast the seeds and quinoa prior to packaging. Chopped nuts can be substituted for the sesame seeds.

JACK YOUNG AND JO CRESCENT
WINTERS, CALIFORNIA

Weight per serving: 8 ounces
Total servings: 1

Nutritional information per serving:

Calories:	481
Protein:	27 g
Carbohydrates:	70 g
Sodium:	1,197 mg
Fiber:	13 g
Fat:	11 g
Cholesterol:	0 mg

Pikes Peak Pineapple Pancakes

AT HOME:

1 (20-ounce) can Dole Crushed Pineapple
1 1/2 cups Arrowhead Mills Multigrain Pancake Mix

Dry pineapple along with its juice on a parchment-lined dehydrating tray. Once pineapple is dry, divide evenly into 2 separate ziplock bags. Add 3/4 cup of pancake mix to each bag and seal.

ON THE TRAIL:

2/3 cup water per serving
1/2 tablespoon vegetable oil per serving
Optional: syrup or powdered sugar to taste

To make 1 serving, add 2/3 cup of water to 1 bag of pineapple pancake mix. Knead the mix inside the bag to eliminate large chunks from the batter. Wait approximately 20 minutes, giving the pineapple a chance to rehydrate. Heat 1/2 tablespoon of vegetable oil in a pan. Cut a corner from the bottom of the bag and squeeze pancake batter onto pan. Cook as you would plain pancakes. Serve with syrup or powdered sugar if desired.

CHRISTINE AND TIM CONNERS
SAVANNAH, GEORGIA

TOTAL WEIGHT: 13 OUNCES
Weight per serving: about 7 ounces
Total servings: 2

Nutritional information per serving:

Calories:	337
Protein:	4 g
Carbohydrates:	64 g
Sodium:	303 mg
Fiber:	5 g
Fat:	7 g
Cholesterol:	0 mg

Chuckwalla Chocolate Chip Pancakes

AT HOME:

2/3 cup Aunt Jemima or Hungry Jack Pancake Mix
2 tablespoons mini chocolate chips or chopped regular chips

Place pancake mix and chocolate chips into a ziplock freezer bag.

ON THE TRAIL:

1/2 cup water
1 teaspoon vegetable oil
3 tablespoons maple or pancake syrup

Add 1/2 cup of cold water to the dry ingredients in the single-serving bag. Knead the mixture well enough to break up the larger lumps. Do not overwork the batter as this will make the pancakes less tender. Grease a pan with 1 teaspoon of vegetable oil. Warm the pan on medium heat until drops of water sizzle and disappear quickly. Pour or spoon approximately 1/4 of the batter at a time into the heated pan. Cook until the top bubbles and the bottom is golden brown. Flip with a spatula and cook until the remaining side becomes golden brown as well. Add additional oil to the skillet, if needed, for subsequent pancakes. Serve with syrup.

CAROLE AND KEN HARBISON
SAN FRANCISCO, CALIFORNIA,
AND ROCHESTER, NEW YORK

Weight per serving: 6 ounces
Total servings: 1 (4 pancakes per serving)

Nutritional information per serving:

Calories:	690
Protein:	10 g
Carbohydrates:	125 g
Sodium:	1,000 mg
Fiber:	2 g
Fat:	18 g
Cholesterol:	20 mg

Arapaho Apple Pancakes

AT HOME:

1 1/2 cups Arrowhead Mills Multigrain Pancake Mix
3 ounces dried apple rings, finely chopped
1 (1-serving) packet spiced apple cider mix

In a bowl, blend pancake mix, apple pieces, and apple cider mix. Divide mixture evenly into 2 separate quart-size ziplock bags (about 1 heaping cup each).

ON THE TRAIL:

1 tablespoon oil per serving
1/2 cup water per serving

To prepare 1 serving, place 1 tablespoon of oil on a frying pan and warm over low heat. To 1 bag add 1/2 cup of water. Knead the mixture by breaking apart large clumps. Cut a hole in 1 corner of the bag and squeeze enough batter into the pan to make 1 manageable pancake. Fry and flip the pancake once it is browned on the bottom. Brown the other side and serve. Repeat for the remainder of the batter.

CHRISTINE AND TIM CONNERS
SAVANNAH, GEORGIA

TOTAL WEIGHT: 15 OUNCES
Weight per serving: about 8 ounces
Total servings: 2

Nutritional information per serving:

Calories:	620
Protein:	12 g
Carbohydrates:	110 g
Sodium:	985 mg
Fiber:	12 g
Fat:	16 g
Cholesterol:	0 mg

Wood Gnome Cobbler

"My great-grandmother, Nana Effie, was a pioneer who had a love of the outdoors that she passed on to her children. As a missionary in the early 1900s, she lived on a reservation in spartan conditions for several years. She was a very strong-willed woman, which contrasted sharply with her tiny physical dimensions of less than 5 feet tall and only about 100 pounds in weight. She lived to be ninety-seven, at which time she was still walking a mile each day to the store to buy her quart of milk or loaf of bread. She was a very good cook and readily able to adjust to any situation. This recipe is something she prepared for the kids in a single pot, and I easily adapted it to backpacking."

AT HOME:

1/2 cup dried mixed berries
2 tablespoons sugar
1 teaspoon cornstarch
1 pinch nutmeg
1/2 cup Bisquick

Combine dried berries, sugar, starch, and nutmeg in a ziplock storage bag. Place Bisquick in another.

ON THE TRAIL:

1 cup and 3 tablespoons water

To prepare 1 serving, bring 1 cup of water to a boil and add the bag of fruit mix. Place 3 tablespoons of water in the bag of Bisquick and knead the mixture. Cut a bottom corner from the Bisquick bag and drop spoonful-size dollops into the soup, pushing down the dumplings so that they are immersed. Cover the pot to steam the mixture for about 5 to 7 minutes, with the heat just high enough to keep the liquid boiling. Check occasionally, adding more water if needed to prevent scorching. The cobbler is ready once the dumplings are fully cooked.

TRACI MARCROFT
ARCATA, CALIFORNIA

Weight per serving: 7 ounces
Total servings: 1

Nutritional information per serving:

Calories:	620
Protein:	6 g
Carbohydrates:	130 g
Sodium:	744 mg
Fiber:	4 g
Fat:	10 g
Cholesterol:	0 mg

AUTHORS' NOTE:
While it sounds like it would make a great after-dinner dessert, which it does, Wood Gnome Cobbler really shines as a fantastic warm breakfast.

Niagara Bars

SHERRY BENNETT
ROCHESTER, NEW YORK

AT HOME:

- **2⅔ cups Quaker Old Fashioned Oats**
- **½ cup plus 1 tablespoon whole wheat flour**
- **6 tablespoons all-purpose bleached wheat flour**
- **½ cup sesame seeds**
- **½ cup brown sugar**
- **¼ teaspoon cinnamon**
- **1½ teaspoons salt**
- **⅓ cup nonfat powdered milk**
- **½ cup vegetable oil**
- **¾ cup honey**
- **2 teaspoons vanilla extract**

Preheat oven to 325°F. In a bowl, mix all dry ingredients together. Heat oil, honey, and vanilla in a pan, then add to the dry ingredients in the bowl. Stir well. Pat batter into a 9x13-inch parchment-lined pan. Bars should be about ½-inch thick. Cook for 30 minutes. Cool, then slice into 32 bars. Place in plastic food wrap for the trail.

TOTAL WEIGHT: 2 POUNDS
Weight per serving: 1 ounce
Total servings: 32 (1 bar per serving)

Nutritional information per serving:

Calories:	113
Protein:	2 g
Carbohydrates:	15 g
Sodium:	117 mg
Fiber:	1 g
Fat:	5 g
Cholesterol:	1 mg

Ol' Kooger's Mountain High Granola

EMMETT AUTREY
"OL' KOOGER"
AMARILLO, TEXAS

AT HOME:

- **6 cups rolled oats**
- **1 cup wheat bran**
- **2 cups wheat germ**
- **1/2 cup shredded sweetened coconut**
- **1 cup brown sugar**
- **1 1/2 cups chopped pecans**
- **1 cup honey**
- **1/4 cup vegetable oil**
- **1 tablespoon vanilla extract**
- **1 1/2 cups dried fruit (raisins, apricots, and dried cranberries, or your choice)**
- **4 2/3 cups nonfat powdered milk**

Preheat oven to 325°F. In a large mixing bowl, thoroughly blend the oats, bran, wheat germ, coconut, brown sugar, and pecans. In a separate pan, heat the honey, vegetable oil, and vanilla extract to a slight boil. Continue to simmer on very low heat for 10 minutes. Pour the liquid mix onto the dry mix in the bowl and stir thoroughly with a large spoon. Pour the mixture onto a cookie sheet previously treated with nonstick vegetable spray. Place sheet in the preheated oven for 30 minutes, stirring periodically until light golden brown. Remove and cool. Place in a large bowl and stir in the dried fruit. Place 1 cup of granola into each of 14 quart-size ziplock freezer bags. To each bag add 1/3 cup powdered milk.

ON THE TRAIL:

- **1 cup water per serving**

Add 1 cup of hot or cold water to 1 serving of cereal and serve.

TOTAL WEIGHT: 4 POUNDS 10 OUNCES
Weight per serving: about 5 ounces
Total servings: 14 (1 cup per serving)

Nutritional information per serving:

Calories:	587
Protein:	19 g
Carbohydrates:	96 g
Sodium:	141 mg
Fiber:	9 g
Fat:	17 g
Cholesterol:	5 mg

Koolau Ridge Granola

"I grew up in Hawaii and spent a great deal of time hiking in the Koolau Mountains of Oahu. The range runs north-south for almost the entire length of the island, offering a diversity of hiking experiences including majestic waterfalls and breath-taking views. I created this recipe to reflect the unique flavors of the islands."

—Christine

AT HOME:

- **1/4 cup canola oil**
- **1 (12-ounce) jar Smucker's Pineapple Preserves**
- **1 cup chopped, lightly salted macadamia nuts**
- **1 (16-ounce) bag Bob's Red Mill 5-Grain Rolled Hot Cereal**
- **1/2 cup shredded sweetened coconut**
- **6 ounces dried mango slices, chopped**

In a large pot, heat oil and preserves until thin. Chop macadamia nuts and add to pot along with the cereal and coconut. Stir until liquid has covered the mixture evenly. Spread in a nonstick jelly roll pan. Bake at 250°F for 1½ hours. Stir periodically. Cut mango slices into small pieces. Once cooled, add mango pieces and stir. Store in large ziplock bags for the trail.

ON THE TRAIL:

Optional: dairy or soy milk powder to taste

To make 1 serving, mix 1 cup of cereal with milk or soy powder and water, or eat straight out of the bag. Serve either hot or cold.

CHRISTINE AND TIM CONNERS
SAVANNAH, GEORGIA

TOTAL WEIGHT: 2 POUNDS 6 OUNCES
Weight per serving: about 5 ounces
Total servings: 7 (1 cup per serving)

Nutritional information per serving:

Calories:	618
Protein:	11 g
Carbohydrates:	104 g
Sodium:	44 mg
Fiber:	12 g
Fat:	21 g
Cholesterol:	0 mg

Orange Sky Granola

"If you are looking for a granola with unique flavor, Orange Sky is it!"

CHRISTINE AND TIM CONNERS
SAVANNAH, GEORGIA

TOTAL WEIGHT: 2 POUNDS 10 OUNCES
Weight per serving: about 4 ounces
Total servings: 10 (1 cup per serving)

Nutritional information per serving:

Calories:	605
Protein:	12 g
Carbohydrates:	89 g
Sodium:	19 mg
Fiber:	5 g
Fat:	23 g
Cholesterol:	0 mg

AT HOME:

1/4 cup canola oil
1 (18-ounce) jar Smucker's Orange Marmalade
1 (16-ounce) bag Bob's Red Mill 5-Grain Rolled Hot Cereal
16 ounces chopped hazelnuts
1 cup shredded sweetened coconut
1 1/2 cups dried cranberries

In a large pot, heat canola oil and marmalade until thin. Add cereal, nuts, and coconut. Stir until liquid has covered the mixture evenly. Spread in a nonstick jelly roll pan. Bake at 225°F for 2 hours. Stir periodically. Allow granola to cool after baking. Add cranberries to mixture. Store in large ziplock bags for the trail.

ON THE TRAIL:

Optional: dairy or soy milk powder to taste

To make 1 serving, mix 1 cup of cereal with milk or soy powder and water, or eat straight out of the bag. Serve either hot or cold.

Grizzly Berry Granola

AT HOME:

1/4 cup canola oil
1 (18-ounce) jar Smucker's Blackberry Jelly
2 cups chopped, lightly salted cashews
1 (16-ounce) bag Bob's Red Mill 5-Grain Rolled Hot Cereal
1 cup shredded sweetened coconut
1 ounce Just Blueberries–brand dried blueberries
1 ounce Just Strawberries–brand dried strawberries
1 ounce Just Blackberries–brand dried blackberries

In a large pot, heat oil and jelly until thin. Chop cashews and add to pot along with the cereal and coconut. Stir until liquid has covered the mixture evenly. Spread in a nonstick jelly roll pan. Bake at 225°F for 2 hours. Stir periodically. Allow granola to cool after baking. Once cooled, add dried fruit. Store in large ziplock bags for the trail.

ON THE TRAIL:

Optional: dairy or soy milk powder to taste

To prepare 1 serving, mix 1 cup of cereal with milk or soy powder and water, or eat straight out of the bag. Serve either hot or cold.

CHRISTINE AND TIM CONNERS
SAVANNAH, GEORGIA

TOTAL WEIGHT: 2 POUNDS 9 OUNCES
Weight per serving: about 3 ounces
Total servings: 12 (1 cup per serving)

Nutritional information per serving:

Calories:	473
Protein:	10 g
Carbohydrates:	69 g
Sodium:	65 mg
Fiber:	8 g
Fat:	19 g
Cholesterol:	0 mg

Rockhouse Basin Apple Granola

"I probably would still be sitting in front of the TV had it not been for my friend and coworker Drew Yuhas. On Columbus Day, 1992, Drew almost had to forcefully drag me from my sheltered ways, out the door, and along with him on a group day hike that he had coordinated. Our destination was the Rockhouse Basin region of the Domeland Wilderness in the Southern Sierra. While I had day hiked a few times in my life before then, I had never ventured into such a remote area, and I really had no interest to do so on the morning of that day, either.

"Before the area burned years later in the huge Manter Fire, the Rockhouse Basin region was especially beautiful, and that warm fall day made it all the more so. Even I had to admit to this once we arrived. We spent the afternoon wandering southward along the east bank of the Kern River. My attention was constantly pulled toward the strikingly mysterious high granite domes miles beyond the far side of the Kern. They demanded additional exploration, and I was actually sad that we didn't have the time or equipment to do so. A thought came to me that I wasn't entirely comfortable with at first: If I really wanted to get close and personal with this great wilderness, I'd need to shoulder a heavy pack and plan on spending a few days on the trail.

"But something magical happened that day. As the afternoon wore on, not only did I accept the fact that I had to return, but also, I couldn't wait to do so. And several weeks later, I did just that, accompanied by my trail mentor and friend Terry Larson. It was my first multiday trip; and while I made virtually all the mistakes that a novice can, the die was cast and I was hooked. In the Domeland Wilderness of autumn 1992, I became a backpacker."

—Tim

AT HOME:

- **1/4 cup canola oil**
- **1 (18-ounce) jar apple jelly**
- **1 (16-ounce) bag Bob's Red Mill 5-Grain Rolled Hot Cereal**
- **1 1/2 cups pecan pieces (6 ounces)**
- **1 cup shredded sweetened coconut**
- **5 ounces dried apple rings, chopped**

In a large pot, heat canola oil and apple jelly until thin. Add cereal, nuts, and coconut. Stir until liquid has covered the mixture evenly. Spread in a nonstick jelly roll pan. Bake at 225°F for 2 hours. Stir periodically. Allow granola to cool after baking. Chop apples into small pieces and add to cooled granola. Store in large ziplock bags for the trail.

ON THE TRAIL:

Optional: dairy or soy milk powder to taste

To prepare 1 serving, mix 1 cup of cereal with milk or soy powder and water, or eat straight out of the bag. Serve either hot or cold.

CHRISTINE AND TIM CONNERS
SAVANNAH, GEORGIA

TOTAL WEIGHT: 2 POUNDS 8 OUNCES
Weight per serving: 4 ounces
Total servings: 10 (1 cup per serving)

Nutritional information per serving:

Calories:	480
Protein:	8 g
Carbohydrates:	77 g
Sodium:	121 mg
Fiber:	8 g
Fat:	19 g
Cholesterol:	0 mg

Lunch

[illegible]balls

HANNAH MORRIS
BURLINGTON, VERMONT

TOTAL WEIGHT: 1 POUND
Weight per serving: 1 ounce
Total servings: 16 (1 ball per serving)

[illegible]tter
1/2 cup Quak[illegible] [illegible]uick Oats
1/2 cup chocolate chips, crushed
1/2 cup flaked sweetened coconut

Combine and mix peanut butter, oats, and crushed chocolate chips in a bowl. Form 16 balls and roll each in coconut, thoroughly coating the exterior. Package in a ziplock bag for the trail.

Nutritional information per serving:

Calories:	153
Protein:	5 g
Carbohydrates:	10 g
Sodium:	69 mg
Fiber:	2 g
Fat:	11 g
Cholesterol:	0 mg

Northville-Placid Trail Balls

SHERRY BENNETT
ROCHESTER, NEW YORK

TOTAL WEIGHT: 1 POUND
Weight per serving: less than 1 ounce
Total servings: 24 (1 ball per serving)

AT HOME:

1/2 cup peanut butter
1/2 cup honey
1 cup nonfat powdered milk
1 cup Quaker Old Fashioned Oats
1/4 cup toasted wheat germ

Combine peanut butter and honey. Add milk powder and oatmeal. Thoroughly mix, then shape into balls. Roll the pieces in wheat germ. Let them stand for several hours before packaging. Wrap individually in wax paper or plastic wrap. Can be stored in a ziplock bag or a plastic container for use on the trail.

Nutritional information per serving:

Calories:	78
Protein:	3 g
Carbohydrates:	11 g
Sodium:	36 mg
Fiber:	1 g
Fat:	3 g
Cholesterol:	1 mg

Spirit Lifters

"I like recipes that you can look forward to, that lift your spirit when you're tired. This recipe goes a long way in doing that. Kind of like the feeling you get on a bitter cold, windy day, when someone puts a hot cup of tea in your hands!"

AT HOME:

1/2 cup whole wheat flour
1/2 cup all-purpose bleached wheat flour
1/2 cup brown sugar
1/2 cup quick-cooking oats
1/4 cup wheat germ
1 tablespoon grated orange rind
1/2 cup butter, softened
2 eggs
1 cup slivered almonds
1/4 cup raisins
1/4 cup flaked coconut
1/2 cup semisweet chocolate chips

Preheat oven to 350°F. In a large bowl, combine flour, sugar, oats, wheat germ, and orange rind. Beat in the butter, eggs, almonds, raisins, coconut, and chocolate chips. Line a 9x9-inch pan with parchment paper. Pour in the batter and bake for 35 minutes. Cool and cut into 16 bars.

SHERRY BENNETT
ROCHESTER, NEW YORK

TOTAL WEIGHT: 1 POUND 12 OUNCES
Weight per serving: about 2 ounces
Total servings: 16 (1 bar per serving)

Nutritional information per serving:

Calories:	193
Protein:	4 g
Carbohydrates:	19 g
Sodium:	86 mg
Fiber:	2 g
Fat:	12 g
Cholesterol:	42 mg

Trekin' Fuel

"The advantage of using candy corn in this recipe, instead of chocolate or carob, is that it doesn't melt and provides lots of short-term energy. I also use this mix for breakfast by just adding a little powdered milk to it, hot or cold. Gets me on the trail quickly with a burst of energy."

AT HOME:

1 (28-ounce) box Quaker Honey & Raisins 100% Natural Oats Granola

1 (6-ounce) bag Cape Cod dried cranberries

1 (7-ounce) bag Sun Maid apricots, chopped

1 (10-ounce) container Sunsweet chopped dates

1 (12-ounce) bag candy corn

2 cups salted peanuts

In a large bowl, mix all ingredients together. Package in ziplock freezer bags for the trail.

ON THE TRAIL:

Eat straight out of the bag like gorp or add milk to make a cereal. Serving size is 1 cup.

TED AYERS
"TREKIN' TED"
RAPID CITY, SOUTH DAKOTA

TOTAL WEIGHT: 4 POUNDS 8 OUNCES
Weight per serving: about 5 ounces
Total servings: 15 (1 cup per serving)

Nutritional information per serving:

Calories:	547
Protein:	7 g
Carbohydrates:	74 g
Sodium:	99 mg
Fiber:	8 g
Fat:	16 g
Cholesterol:	0 mg

AUTHORS' NOTE:

Ted, coworker Marty Brenner, and I hiked the length of the John Muir Trail through the High Sierra together during three weeks in 1993. I was still very new to backpacking and would sometimes make ridiculous multipot meals over the stove even at lunch time. On the other hand, Ted, an experienced outdoorsman, would often just eat a handful of gorp or a PowerBar and then have to wait for me to finish up with my mealtime fiasco. He knows how to keep things light and simple, and I learned much from that experience. Of course, after twenty-one days of PowerBars, he swore he'd never be able to eat another one. Marty, on the other hand, had an interesting dessert recipe while we were on the Muir. It involved a half-dozen caffeinated coffee bags, boiled in water, as a nightcap. But that's a story too uncouth for a sophisticated book such as this.

—Tim

Horse Thief Gorp

AT HOME:

2 pounds roasted and salted mixed nuts
12 ounces dried apricots, chopped
12 ounces dried pears, chopped
12 ounces raisins
6 ounces roasted and salted sunflower seeds
10 ounces carob chips

Combine all ingredients and store in plastic ziplock bags for the trail.

MATTHEW FARNELL
WOODLAND, WASHINGTON

TOTAL WEIGHT: 6 POUNDS
Weight per serving: 4 ounces
Total servings: 24 (approximately 1 cup per serving)

Nutritional information per serving:

Calories:	466
Protein:	12 g
Carbohydrates:	41 g
Sodium:	124 mg
Fiber:	6 g
Fat:	29 g
Cholesterol:	0 mg

Oregon Rain Gorp

AT HOME:

1 cup dried cranberries
1 cup roasted hazelnuts
1 cup semisweet chocolate chips

Combine ingredients together. Package all ingredients in a 1-gallon-size ziplock bag or place 3/4 cup of gorp mix into each of 4 ziplock quart-size bags.

BETH MURDOCK
PORTLAND, OREGON

TOTAL WEIGHT: 1 POUND
Weight per serving: 4 ounces
Total servings: 4 (¾ cup per serving)

Nutritional information per serving:

Calories:	559
Protein:	6 g
Carbohydrates:	69 g
Sodium:	1 mg
Fiber:	3 g
Fat:	30 g
Cholesterol:	0 mg

Just Gorp

"There are so many versions of gorp. This is one of my favorites. It's tasty and provides quick energy."

AT HOME:

1 cup low-fat granola

1 cup plain M&Ms

1 cup dry-roasted lightly salted peanuts

1 cup raisins

Combine ingredients together. Package all ingredients in a 1-gallon-size ziplock bag or place 1 cup of gorp mix into each of 4 ziplock quart-size bags.

LIZ BERGERON
SACRAMENTO, CALIFORNIA

TOTAL WEIGHT: 7 OUNCES
Weight per serving: about 2 ounces
Total servings: 4 (1 cup per serving)

Nutritional information per serving:

Calories:	593
Protein:	13 g
Carbohydrates:	83 g
Sodium:	179 mg
Fiber:	8 g
Fat:	24 g
Cholesterol:	5 mg

Logger's Gorp

"We sometimes ate this like popcorn in the evening at home when I was a kid. Dad learned the recipe growing up in logging camp. Takes some chewing, so it's good for killing time if you're stuck in your tent. An easy way to eat it is to simply lap it up with your tongue."

AT HOME:

- **1/2 cup raisins, fresh and a bit sticky**
- **1 cup uncooked Quaker Old Fashioned Oats**

Mix the ingredients together in a bowl and transfer 1 cup of the resulting gorp to each of 2 ziplock bags. Note that slightly fresh and sticky raisins work best because the oatmeal will cling to them more readily.

RAMONA HAMMERLY
ANACORTES, WASHINGTON

TOTAL WEIGHT: 6 OUNCES
Weight per serving: 3 ounces
Total servings: 2 (1 cup per serving)

Nutritional information per serving:

Calories:	280
Protein:	6 g
Carbohydrates:	58 g
Sodium:	10 mg
Fiber:	6 g
Fat:	3 g
Cholesterol:	0 mg

Hula Gorp

CHRISTINE AND TIM CONNERS
SAVANNAH, GEORGIA

AT HOME:

6 ounces dried mango, torn into bite-size pieces
8 ounces dates, chopped
6 ounces dried pineapple pieces
1 cup sweetened shredded coconut
2 cups roasted and salted macadamia nuts

Combine ingredients. Package 1 cup of gorp mix into each of 7 ziplock quart-size bags, or carry it all in a gallon-size ziplock bag.

TOTAL WEIGHT: 2 POUNDS 3 OUNCES
Weight per serving: 5 ounces
Total servings: 7 (1 cup per serving)

Nutritional information per serving:

Calories:	605
Protein:	7 g
Carbohydrates:	81 g
Sodium:	183 mg
Fiber:	9 g
Fat:	32 g
Cholesterol:	0 mg

On cold nights, put hot water in your water bottle, seal it tightly to ensure that it doesn't leak, and put it at the bottom of your sleeping bag to warm your feet at night. This also keeps the water warmer than it would if it was left out in the cold all night, so in the morning it doesn't take as much fuel to boil water for a hot breakfast.

REBECCA SPENCER
ALBANY, CALIFORNIA

Zion Gorp

"We were backpacking in Zion National Park one Christmas. Gloria weighed about 105 pounds at the time. We had almost topped a ridge to a fantastic view point when we met another couple on the trail headed the opposite direction. We exchanged greetings, had a short visit, and continued on our way. As we departed, the lady in the other group was overheard to exclaim something to the effect, 'Did you see that little tiny lady with that great big backpack?' We attributed Gloria's endurance and strength to Zion Gorp."

LARRY AND GLORIA BRIGHT
JOHN DAY, OREGON

AT HOME:

1 cup pumpkin seeds (pepitas)
1 cup salted peanuts
1 cup unsalted sunflower kernels
1 cup carob chips
1 cup soy nuts
2 cups raisins

Mix ingredients together and package in sturdy ziplock bags for the trail.

"We start all of our gorp recipes with this base version and adjust it when we want a different taste."

TOTAL WEIGHT: 2 POUNDS 8 OUNCES
Weight per serving: about 6 ounces
Total servings: 7 (1 cup per serving)

Nutritional information per serving:

Calories:	682
Protein:	24 g
Carbohydrates:	70 g
Sodium:	172 mg
Fiber:	11 g
Fat:	37 g
Cholesterol:	0 mg

Spiderman Gorp

AT HOME:

- 1 (16-ounce) jar lightly salted peanuts
- 24 dried apricots, halved (about 8 ounces)
- 5 ounces dried apples
- 1 (9-ounce) box raisins
- 1 (21-ounce) bag M&Ms
- 2 cups granola cereal

In a large bowl, mix all ingredients together. Place 1 cup of gorp into each of 12 snack-size ziplock bags.

MIKE AND SUE REYNOLDS
"SPIDERMAN" AND "GROUND CONTROL"
COLUMBUS, INDIANA

TOTAL WEIGHT: 3 POUNDS 8 OUNCES
Weight per serving: about 5 ounces
Total servings: 12 (1 cup per serving)

Nutritional information per serving:

Calories:	670
Protein:	15 g
Carbohydrates:	81 g
Sodium:	256 mg
Fiber:	9 g
Fat:	30 g
Cholesterol:	6 mg

Coins

lered a form of currency on the trail, these 'coins' have the

AT HOME:

1/2 cup butter, softened

2 cups finely grated sharp cheddar cheese

1/2 tablespoon vegetarian Worcestershire sauce

1 tablespoon sesame seeds

1 cup all-purpose bleached wheat flour

Combine butter, cheese, sauce, and sesame seeds in a bowl. Add flour a little at a time while kneading. Form into a long roll, 1 inch in diameter. Cut into 1/4-inch slices. Bake at 350°F for about 15 minutes. Let cool, then package for the trail.

SHERRY BENNETT
ROCHESTER, NEW YORK

TOTAL WEIGHT: 15 OUNCES
Weight per serving: less than 1 ounce
Total servings: 60 (1 coin per serving)

Nutritional information per serving:

Calories:	36
Protein:	1 g
Carbohydrates:	2 g
Sodium:	41 mg
Fiber:	<1 g
Fat:	3 g
Cholesterol:	8 mg

No self-respecting backpacker or paddler should be without a home dehydrator. They are worth their weight in gold!

SHERRY BENNETT
ROCHESTER, NEW YORK

Red Husky

"The name of this recipe was inspired by my dog, a red husky named Quinn."

AT HOME:

2 ounces sharp cheddar cheese
1/4 cup raw almonds

Package ingredients separately for the trail.

ON THE TRAIL:

To make 1 serving, cut 2 ounces of cheese into bite-size pieces. Combine with 1/4 cup of almonds and eat.

ROBERT LAUTERBACH
"RED HUSKY"
ROCHESTER, NEW YORK

Weight per serving: 4 ounces
Total servings: 1

Nutritional information per serving:

Calories:	390
Protein:	20 g
Carbohydrates:	6 g
Sodium:	180 mg
Fiber:	3 g
Fat:	33 g
Cholesterol:	30 mg

AUTHORS' NOTE:

Here's a very simple midday recipe that makes for a striking taste combination.

Bear Bait

AT HOME:

1/2 cup honey

1/2 cup cashew butter

Combine ingredients and carry in a plastic squeeze tube or container.

ON THE TRAIL:

Eat straight from the tube or use on crackers, tortillas, or pita bread.

RICHARD HALBERT
"RANGER RICK"
TRAVERSE CITY, MICHIGAN

TOTAL WEIGHT: 10 OUNCES
Weight per serving: about 1 ounce
Total servings: 8 (2 tablespoons per serving)

Nutritional information per serving:

Calories:	150
Protein:	2 g
Carbohydrates:	22 g
Sodium:	0 mg
Fiber:	1 g
Fat:	8 g
Cholesterol:	0 mg

AUTHORS' NOTE:

Honey and nut butters make a wonderful combination that packs an energy wallop: carbs for the near term and fat for the long haul. I remember buying a tube of honey, a jar of peanut butter, and a pack of tortillas in Mammoth Lakes during a resupply stopover on my John Muir hike. Man, did that hit the spot once we were back on the trail. Ten years later, I can still taste it!

Honey has the interesting property of sticking to anything that you might even think about touching. Premixing with the oily nut butter will help reduce this annoying tendency.

—Tim

Mud

"Last summer, I was leading a small group of women on a weekend canoe trip in the Adirondacks. One of the ladies, the only one that I didn't know, asked what kind of food she should bring. Well, as much as I like cooking and preparing food, I said, half-joking, half-serious, 'Don't worry about the food. Just bring the wine, and I'll see to it that no one goes hungry.' This girl brought six bottles of wine and there were only four of us!"

SHERRY BENNETT
ROCHESTER, NEW YORK

AT HOME:

- **1/4 cup Quaker Old Fashioned Oats**
- **1/4 cup nonfat powdered milk**
- **1/4 cup sunflower seeds**
- **1/4 cup raisins**
- **1/4 cup chopped walnuts**
- **1/4 cup mini chocolate chips**
- **1/2 cup peanut butter**
- **1/2 cup honey**

Mix all ingredients and place in a container for use on the trail.

ON THE TRAIL:

Eat straight from the container or use as a delicious spread on crackers or bagels.

Optional: Use peanut butter chips in place of chocolate chips.

TOTAL WEIGHT: 1 POUND 2 OUNCES
Weight per serving: about 1 ounce
Total servings: 20 (2 tablespoons per serving)

Nutritional information per serving:

Calories:	108
Protein:	3 g
Carbohydrates:	13 g
Sodium:	46 mg
Fiber:	1 g
Fat:	6 g
Cholesterol:	<1 mg

Grunch

AT HOME:

- 1 cup crunchy peanut butter
- 1/2 cup honey
- 1/2 cup finely crushed graham cracker crumbs
- 1/4 cup nonfat powdered milk
- 3 tablespoons cinnamon
- 1 tablespoon ground cloves

Combine all ingredients. Pack in a container for use on the trail.

ON THE TRAIL:

Eat straight from the container or use as a spread on crackers or bread.

SHERRY BENNETT
ROCHESTER, NEW YORK

TOTAL WEIGHT: 1 POUND 2 OUNCES
Weight per serving: about 1 ounce
Total servings: 20 (2 tablespoons per serving)

Nutritional information per serving:

Calories:	112
Protein:	4 g
Carbohydrates:	11 g
Sodium:	63 mg
Fiber:	1 g
Fat:	7 g
Cholesterol:	<1 mg

Whole-Food Granola Bars

"This is a very flexible recipe as there are numerous ways to modify it. Applesauce can be replaced with bananas, and the combinations of dried fruit are endless. Have fun!"

MATTHEW FARNELL
WOODLAND, WASHINGTON

AT HOME:

2 cups raw almonds
1 cup applesauce
1½ teaspoons cinnamon
1½ cups water
1½ cups dried apricots
½ cup dried cranberries
½ cup chopped walnuts
½ cup ground flaxseed
½ cup whole wheat flour
5 cups Quaker Old Fashioned Oats
Optional: honey or other natural sweetener to taste

Soak almonds in water for at least 6 hours. Drain. In a blender, combine the almonds, applesauce, cinnamon, and 1½ cups water. Thoroughly process the mixture in the blender, then pour into a large mixing bowl. Add the remainder of the ingredients to the bowl and mix. Take ¼ cup of dough and plop onto parchment-lined dehydrator trays. Flatten each to about ½-inch thick. This should form approximately 26 bars. Dry until the bars are hard. Package for the trail.

TOTAL WEIGHT: 3 POUNDS
Weight per serving: about 2 ounces
Total servings: 26 (1 bar per serving)

Nutritional information per serving:

Calories:	192
Protein:	6 g
Carbohydrates:	26 g
Sodium:	8 mg
Fiber:	5 g
Fat:	7 g
Cholesterol:	0 mg

Cabin Fever Cookies

AT HOME:

- **1/2 cup rye flour**
- **1/2 cup Quaker Old Fashioned Oats**
- **1/2 teaspoon salt**
- **1/2 teaspoon xanthan gum or baking powder**
- **3/4 cup chopped walnuts**
- **1/3 cup vegetable oil**
- **1 cup brown sugar**
- **1 teaspoon vanilla extract**
- **2 eggs**

Preheat oven to 350°F. Combine rye flour, oats, salt, xanthan gum, and walnuts. In a separate bowl, beat oil, sugar, vanilla, and eggs. Add the dry ingredients and mix. Pour into a greased 9x9-inch pan. Bake for approximately 30 minutes. The cooked dough should pull away from the edges of the pan, and the surface should be somewhat resistant when poked. Set pan aside to cool before cutting the cookie dough into 8 bars.

RAMONA HAMMERLY
ANACORTES, WASHINGTON

TOTAL WEIGHT: 1 POUND
Weight per serving: about 2 ounces
Total servings: 8 (1 bar per serving)

Nutritional information per serving:

Calories:	286
Protein:	6 g
Carbohydrates:	28 g
Sodium:	172 mg
Fiber:	3 g
Fat:	18 g
Cholesterol:	60 mg

Lembas Waybread

AT HOME:

1 cup plain yogurt

3 cups Quaker Old Fashioned Oats

1/2 teaspoon salt

1/2 teaspoon baking soda

1 1/2 cups sifted all-purpose bleached wheat flour

1/2 cup olive oil

Preheat oven to 375°F. Mix the yogurt and oats thoroughly and let stand. In a separate bowl, mix the salt, baking soda, and flour. Next, add oil to the flour mix, followed by the now-soggy oatmeal. Knead the mixture. Add water if needed to give the consistency of pie dough. Divide the dough in half, forming two smooth, flat rounds. Place each in the middle of an ungreased cookie sheet and roll the dough out until it is about 1/8-inch thick. Score the dough into 2x2-inch squares. A serrated pizza cutter works well for this. Place in oven and bake for about 15 minutes or until a golden brown. Remove from oven and allow to cool. Reduce oven temperature to about 170°F, corresponding roughly to the lowest heat setting. Cut the bread along the serrated lines and break into squares. Separate the pieces and, once the oven reaches the lower temperature, dry for an additional 3 hours, leaving the oven door slightly ajar. Once dry, let cool. If you have difficulty finding large, elven leaves, package the waybread instead in a ziplock bag for the trail.

RAMONA HAMMERLY
ANACORTES, WASHINGTON

TOTAL WEIGHT: 1 POUND 6 OUNCES
Weight per serving: about 4 ounces
Total servings: 6

Nutritional information per serving:

Calories:	420
Protein:	10 g
Carbohydrates:	53 g
Sodium:	330 mg
Fiber:	4 g
Fat:	20 g
Cholesterol:	3 mg

AUTHORS' NOTE:

In JRR Tolkien's "Lord of the Rings," Galadriel gave packages of the elven food lembas, wrapped in protective leaves, to Frodo and Sam to help sustain them on their difficult journey to Mordor. Whether your journey is life-changing or a cakewalk, be sure to carry versatile, great-tasting lembas!

Dodie-Kakes

"After several years of being pen pals, Jack and I finally arranged to get acquainted and planned a two-night backpacking trip in southern New Mexico, where I was living at the time. When I picked him up at the airport, I shamefacedly confessed that, although I had scouted a location with dependable water, I had not done *any* food prep despite the fact that we were heading out the next morning. No problem though! To my amazement, Jack cheerfully toured me through the aisles of a local supermarket, putting together a complete three-day menu in less than an hour. Not only that, but he prepared an amazing meal that he cooked over an open fire our first night out on the trail. Needless to say, I fell madly in love, and we've been backpacking together ever since! Sigh... my backpacking hero!"

JACK YOUNG AND JO CRESCENT
WINTERS, CALIFORNIA

TOTAL WEIGHT: 1 POUND 3 OUNCES
Weight per serving: about 2 ounces
Total servings: 8 (1 bar per serving)

Nutritional information per serving:

Calories:	244
Protein:	8 g
Carbohydrates:	24 g
Sodium:	41 mg
Fiber:	6 g
Fat:	13 g
Cholesterol:	0 mg

AT HOME:

- **1/2 cup roasted pumpkin seeds, chopped**
- **1/2 cup raisins**
- **1/2 cup quinoa flakes**
- **2 tablespoons flaxseeds**
- **2 tablespoons whole grain quinoa**
- **2 tablespoons sesame seeds, toasted**
- **2 tablespoons honey**
- **1 tablespoon rice bran**
- **1 tablespoon red pepper flakes**
- **1 tablespoon Just Whites–brand egg whites**
- **1/2 teaspoon xanthan gum**
- **1/3 cup flour (your choice)**
- **4 tablespoons hummus mix**
- **6 tablespoons tahini**
- **6 tablespoons water**

Preheat oven to 325°F. Mix together all the ingredients, form into a loaf, and slice into 8 bars. Place bars on a greased cookie sheet and bake for 20 minutes. Pack in ziplock bags for the trail.

"These bars are more of a meal than a treat, although they are very tasty. In addition, they pack well. For the flour, we use a mixture of rice and rye."

Baja Burritos

MARA NABER
MOUNTAIN RANCH, CALIFORNIA

Weight per serving: 4 ounces
Total servings: 1

Nutritional information per serving:

Calories:	418
Protein:	17 g
Carbohydrates:	78 g
Sodium:	1,215 mg
Fiber:	22 g
Fat:	4 g
Cholesterol:	0 mg

AT HOME:

- **1⁄4 cup Ortega Mild Salsa**
- **1 cup fresh coleslaw vegetable mix**
- **1⁄2 onion, diced**
- **1⁄2 cup Fantastic Foods Refried Beans**
- **2 corn tortillas**

Pour salsa onto a parchment-lined dehydrator tray and dry. Combine coleslaw mix and diced onion and dry on a second parchment-lined dehydrator tray. Place dried coleslaw-onion mix in a quart-size ziplock freezer bag. Place the dry refried beans and salsa patty in another. Carry tortillas separately.

ON THE TRAIL:

- **3⁄4 cup water**

To prepare 1 serving, pour 1⁄2 cup of boiling water into the bag of beans and salsa early in the day. Add 1⁄4 cup of cool water to the vegetable mix. By midday, the foods will be rehydrated and ready to eat. Cut a corner from the ziplock bag containing the rehydrated bean and salsa mix. Squeeze 1⁄2 of the contents onto 1 tortilla. Next, add 1⁄2 of the coleslaw mix to the tortilla and roll it up to serve. Repeat for the other tortilla.

Caution: See the "Using This Book" section regarding the use of ziplock bags with hot water.

Greek Wayfaring Tortilla

KATARINA SENGSTAKEN
"KATGIRL"
HOLLIS, NEW HAMPSHIRE

Weight per serving: 5 ounces
Total servings: 1

AT HOME:

10 sun-dried tomato halves
1 teaspoon dried basil
3 ounces feta cheese
1 taco-size whole wheat tortilla

Cut sun-dried tomatoes into small pieces and place in a sandwich-size ziplock bag along with the basil. Carry feta cheese separately. Wrap tortilla in foil and carry that separately as well.

ON THE TRAIL:

1 tablespoon olive oil

To prepare 1 serving, crumble the feta cheese. Add it, along with 1 tablespoon of olive oil, to the bag of dried tomato-basil. Shake the bag, then place the mixture on the tortilla. Roll and serve.

Nutritional information per serving:

Calories:	614
Protein:	21 g
Carbohydrates:	49 g
Sodium:	1,670 mg
Fiber:	6 g
Fat:	38 g
Cholesterol:	45 mg

Fresh veggies make a meal real. Garlic, kale, and carrots pack well, last a long time, and are delicious.

JASON RUMOHR
SEATTLE, WASHINGTON

Tapenade

KEN HARBISON
ROCHESTER, NEW YORK

Weight per serving: 8 ounces
Total servings: 1

Nutritional information per serving:

Calories:	680
Protein:	21 g
Carbohydrates:	86 g
Sodium:	825 mg
Fiber:	6 g
Fat:	29 g
Cholesterol:	120 mg

AT HOME:

1/2 ounce sun-dried tomatoes
1/2 teaspoon dry Italian seasoning
Optional: 1/4 ounce Just Bell Peppers–brand dried bell peppers
3 ounces cream cheese
2 whole wheat pita bread shells

Place sun-dried tomatoes, seasoning, and optional bell peppers, if desired, in a ziplock bag. Freeze for 10 minutes, then chop in a blender or food processor. Package for the trail in a ziplock bag. Carry the cheese and pita shells separately.

ON THE TRAIL:

2 tablespoons water

Preferably several hours before lunch, but no less than 15 minutes prior, add 2 tablespoons of water to the 1-serving bag of dry mix and knead into a thick paste. Spread the cheese into the pita shells, then add the now-rehydrated tapenade and serve.

Cheeses can often be found at the grocery store in small, sealed 1-ounce packets that carry well on the trail.

Anasazi Trail Food

"In 1994, the Veterans Administration sent me, a nurse, to help with disaster relief following the Northridge earthquake. One late afternoon I saw a group of hawks riding the thermals upward in great, swirling circles. At the time I was in Santa Clarita, below the San Gabriel Mountains. I knew that the PCT was somewhere up above where the hawks were headed. 'Someday, I'll be up there,' I said. Hiking the PCT was something I had wanted to do for decades. In 1998 my husband and I stopped for lunch near Mt. Gleason on the PCT just to the north of Santa Clarita. As we ate our bean dip and crackers, I realized that we were looking down to where I had been looking up four years earlier, without the slightest hope that I would be hiking the trail so soon. We hiked 1,000 miles along the PCT that summer.

"We use rehydrated bean dips for our lunches when we hike. While we were on our thousand-mile PCT hike, we had a bag of dehydrated tomatoes in every resupply box. We used mostly cherry tomatoes, which were great when added to the bean dips. We also used almost every kind of beans and peas to make our dips. You can add different veggies, seeds, and nuts to make your own unique version."

BETH MURDOCK
PORTLAND, OREGON

TOTAL WEIGHT: 8 OUNCES
Weight per serving: 4 ounces
Total servings: 2

Nutritional information per serving:

Calories:	440
Protein:	22 g
Carbohydrates:	73 g
Sodium:	1,288 mg
Fiber:	23 g
Fat:	17 g
Cholesterol:	0 mg

AT HOME:

1 cup dry Anasazi beans, washed
1 tablespoon vegetable oil
1 onion, finely chopped
1 clove garlic, minced or pressed
1 (15-ounce) can diced tomatoes
1 teaspoon dried oregano
1 teaspoon dried cumin
1/2 to 1 chipotle chili in adobo sauce, mashed
1 teaspoon salt

In a pot, barely cover the beans with water, then bring to a boil. Reduce heat and simmer until fully cooked. Sauté the onion and garlic in the oil over moderate heat until softened and translucent. Add the tomatoes, seasonings, chili, and the beans along with a little of the water that they were cooked in, putting aside the remainder of the water used to cook the beans. Simmer over very low heat to blend the flavors. Next, run through a food processor until chopped but not pureed. Add bean cooking water if the mixture is too thick to pour. Spread the mixture on parchment paper. Dry, then divide evenly between 2 ziplock quart-size bags.

ON THE TRAIL:

1 cup water per serving

To rehydrate 1 serving, cover the contents of the bag with about 1 cup of water. Hike on for a couple of miles, then stop and serve your bean dip. Anasazi Trail Food goes great naturally with crackers or tortillas.

Chainsaw's No-Longer-Secret Method for Vacuum-Sealing Oils and the Like: Make small 1-inch by 3-inch packages using the seal strip on your vacuum sealer. Seal one narrow end and both longer sides. Set a bunch of them, open end up, in the flatware holder in your dishwasher. Fill each with a tablespoon of oil or slightly heated ghee. Place them in the freezer, still upright and still unsealed. Once the oil is solid, or very viscous, you can seal it using your sealer without the vacuum sucking the oil out of the package.

DAVE HICKS
"CHAINSAW"
DUBLIN, VIRGINIA

Basic Backpacker's Sushi

"Special thanks to Marc Sherman with Outdoor Gear Exchange at gearx.com and Brandon Stone, who helped create this recipe."

CHRISTINE AND TIM CONNERS
SAVANNAH, GEORGIA

TOTAL WEIGHT: 1 POUND
Weight per serving: 4 ounces
Total servings: 4

Nutritional information per serving:

Calories:	424
Protein:	10 g
Carbohydrates:	86 g
Sodium:	160 mg
Fiber:	3 g
Fat:	5 g
Cholesterol:	0 mg

AT HOME:

2 cups sushi rice
1/4 cup sugar
1/4 cup rice vinegar
1/2 teaspoon salt
1/4 cup sesame seeds
8 sheets Nori dried seaweed
Optional: Cucumber, pickled burdock, pickled radish, dried carrots, pickled ginger, pickled mango, soy sauce, powdered wasabi, miso soup powder

Prepare sushi rice according to the directions on the package. In a large bowl, combine the sugar, rice vinegar, salt, and sesame seeds. Once rice is ready, add it to the liquid and stir until the rice is evenly coated by the seasoning. If you'd like to include optional ingredients, process those that are vegetables, fruit, or roots in a food grinder, then add to the rice mixture at this time. Place mixture on parchment-lined dehydrator trays and dry. Next, break apart the clumps and place about 1 cup of the dried rice mixture into each of 4 separate ziplock quart-size freezer bags. Carry sheets of seaweed separately. Optional soy sauce and powdered condiments should be packaged separately for the trail.

ON THE TRAIL:

1 cup water per serving

To make 1 serving, bring 1 cup of water to a boil early in the day. Pour it into 1 bag of sushi rice mixture. Carefully knead the bag to further break apart remaining clumps of rice mix. Insulate the bag to retain heat as long as possible, and place it in your pack. By midday the rice should be fully rehydrated.

At lunchtime, lay 1 sheet of nori flat with the shiny side down and the perforations running perpendicular to you. Moisten lightly with your fingers. Scoop half of the rice from your bag and place on the sheet of nori. Form a band of rice side to side across the length of the sheet about 1 inch from the end closest to you. Carefully roll the nori away from you as you might a fat cigar. The roll can be cut into traditional sushi slices or served like a burrito.

Optional: There are other approaches for preparing sushi on the trail. To avoid home drying, you can instead prepare instant rice on the trail and add a small amount of dried sushi seasoning, available in Oriental food stores. You could also add any fresh ingredients that you may have in your pack at the time. And sushi doesn't necessarily need to be rolled. You can place the rice and your favorite ingredients on top of a nori sheet, fold it up, and pop it into your mouth.

Caution: See the "Using This Book" section regarding the use of ziplock bags with hot water.

AUTHORS' NOTE:

If you really want to impress your friends, and avoid ugly looking sushi, a traditional bamboo mat can be used to roll your sushi. Ultralight backpackers might frown at the additional weight of such a device (about 3½ ounces). However, when you think about all the alternate applications for such a mat, the additional weight seems minimal; use it as a sun shade, a bug swatter, a hand fan, or a place mat for your utensils! In an emergency situation you could even burn it as kindling on a wet night. Or how about this: Use it like a fig leaf in the event you're caught naked in the woods. Now that's versatility!

Black Bear Hummus

AT HOME:

1 (7-ounce) box Fantastic Foods Instant Black Beans
1/4 cup sesame seeds
1 teaspoon lemon pepper
1/4 teaspoon garlic powder
1/2 teaspoon onion powder
1/4 teaspoon cumin

Combine and mix all dry ingredients. Into each of 4 ziplock quart-size freezer bags add 1/2 cup of mixture.

ON THE TRAIL:

1/2 cup water per serving
Optional: 1 teaspoon vegetable oil per serving

To make 1 serving, bring 1/2 cup of water to a boil early in the day and add to the bean mixture, along with 1 teaspoon of optional oil, if desired. Knead the mixture in the bag and stash away in your pack until lunch. When you stop later in the day, eat the hummus as is or add as a topping to your favorite crackers.

Caution: See the "Using This Book" section regarding the use of ziplock bags with hot water.

SUZANNE ALLEN
SEATTLE, WASHINGTON

TOTAL WEIGHT: 10 OUNCES
Weight per serving: about 3 ounces
Total servings: 4

Nutritional information per serving:

Calories:	237
Protein:	13 g
Carbohydrates:	35 g
Sodium:	579 mg
Fiber:	9 g
Fat:	6 g
Cholesterol:	0 mg

Heavenly Hummus

"A great dip for carrots, celery, or crackers!"

MARA NABER
MOUNTAIN RANCH, CALIFORNIA

Weight per serving: 4 ounces
Total servings: 1

Nutritional information per serving:

Calories:	369
Protein:	13 g
Carbohydrates:	55 g
Sodium:	1,656 mg
Fiber:	7 g
Fat:	12 g
Cholesterol:	0 mg

AT HOME:

1 cup fresh coleslaw vegetable mix
1 tablespoon chopped fresh chives
1/2 sweet red pepper, chopped
1/4 cup Ortega Mild Salsa
1/2 cup Fantastic Foods Original Hummus mix

Mix together coleslaw, chives, and chopped red pepper. Place this vegetable mix on a parchment-lined dehydrator tray and dry. Pour salsa onto a separate, parchment-lined dehydrator tray and dry as well. Package the dried vegetable mix into a quart-size ziplock freezer bag and the hummus mix and dried salsa in another.

ON THE TRAIL:

3/4 cup water
Optional: condiment packets of mustard

To make 1 serving, pour 1/2 cup boiling water into a bag of hummus-salsa mix early in the day. Add 1/4 cup cool water to the vegetable mix. By midday the foods will be rehydrated and ready to eat. Combine the vegetable mix with the hummus. Can be served as is or used as a dip for crackers, celery, or carrots. Optional mustard adds some zing.

! Caution: See the "Using This Book" section regarding the use of ziplock bags with hot water.

Boundary Waters Hummus on Rye

"Hummus and rye crisp will forever remind me of a sunny lunch by a waterfall in the middle of a long portage in the Boundary Waters Canoe Area Wilderness."

AT HOME:

1 (6-ounce) package Fantastic Foods Original Hummus

1 (9-ounce) package rye crispbread

Into each of 3 separate bags, place 1/3 cup firmly packed hummus mix. If you are planning on using all 3 servings during the same trip, place the unopened package of crispbread into a gallon-size ziplock bag. This will help protect the crispbread and prevent crumbs once the bread package is opened. For single servings, place 3 ounces of bread (about 6 pieces) into each of 3 ziplock quart-size bags.

ON THE TRAIL:

1/2 cup water per serving

To prepare 1 serving, add 1/2 cup cool water to 1 bag of hummus and knead the mixture in the bag. Let stand for a few minutes. Snip the corner from the bottom of the bag and squeeze the hummus onto each of your 6 pieces of crispbread.

RAMONA HAMMERLY
ANACORTES, WASHINGTON

TOTAL WEIGHT: 15 OUNCES
Weight per serving: 5 ounces
Total servings: 3

Nutritional information per serving:

Calories:	495
Protein:	15 g
Carbohydrates:	84 g
Sodium:	1,067 mg
Fiber:	14 g
Fat:	9 g
Cholesterol:	0 mg

Carter Notch Coleslaw

KEN HARBISON
ROCHESTER, NEW YORK

TOTAL WEIGHT: 7 OUNCES
Weight per serving: about 2 ounces
Total servings: 4

Nutritional information per serving:

Calories:	160
Protein:	2 g
Carbohydrates:	36 g
Sodium:	300 mg
Fiber:	3 g
Fat:	0 g
Cholesterol:	0 mg

AT HOME:

- **1/2 cup lemon juice**
- **1 cup vinegar**
- **1 1/2 cups sugar**
- **1 teaspoon salt**
- **1 teaspoon ground mustard seed**
- **1 teaspoon celery seed**
- **1 (16-ounce) bag fresh coleslaw vegetable mix**
- **1 carrot, shredded**
- **1 cup chopped sweet onion**
- **1/2 cup chopped green pepper**

Optional:

- **1/4 teaspoon caraway seed**
- **1/2 teaspoon prepared horseradish**

Heat liquids, sugar, and spices, stirring to dissolve the sugar. Immediately remove from heat once the syrupy mixture reaches boiling. Combine the shredded vegetables in a heavy-duty plastic bag or bowl and cover with the hot syrup. Refrigerate, covered, for at least 8 hours, mixing at least once during the period. Drain, then spread the vegetable mixture thinly and evenly onto parchment-lined dehydrator trays. Dry, breaking up any lumps partway through the drying process. When ready, distribute the slaw mixture evenly between 4 ziplock quart-size freezer bags (about 2/3 cup each).

ON THE TRAIL:

- **2/3 cup water per serving**

To make 1 serving, add 2/3 cup of water to 1 bag of slaw. Allow to rehydrate for at least 30 minutes.

Add the contents of a fast-food packet of vinegar for additional tang.

Cleo's Coleslaw

"This recipe is named after Cleo's Bath, a beautiful waterfall at Pinecrest Reservoir. My youngest came up with the name. She has fond memories of this place as it is where we took her and her older sister on their first backpack trip. She was seven years old and her sister eight at the time."

AT HOME:

1 1/2 cups fresh coleslaw vegetable mix
1 tablespoon chopped fresh chives
1 tablespoon chopped fresh mint leaves
1 tablespoon chopped fresh dill
2 tablespoons Brianna's Blush Wine Vinaigrette Dressing (or your favorite Italian dressing)

Mix all the ingredients together in a bowl. Dry the mixture on a parchment-lined dehydrator tray. When ready, package in a quart-size ziplock freezer bag.

ON THE TRAIL:

1/3 cup water

For 1 serving, add 1/3 cup of cool water to rehydrate. Allow to stand 10 minutes before serving.

A squirt of lemon juice, such as from a condiment pack, makes for a nice variation to the recipe.

MARA NABER
MOUNTAIN RANCH, CALIFORNIA

Weight per serving: less than 1 ounce
Total servings: 1

Nutritional information per serving:

Calories:	70
Protein:	1 g
Carbohydrates:	11 g
Sodium:	200 mg
Fiber:	2 g
Fat:	3 g
Cholesterol:	0 mg

Tabouli Salad

AT HOME:

1/2 cup Fantastic Foods Tabouli
1/2 cup Near East Couscous
2 tablespoons chopped dried tomatoes
1 teaspoon dried cilantro

Combine all ingredients into a quart-size ziplock bag.

ON THE TRAIL:

1 cup water

Add 1 cup of cold or warm water to the ziplock bag and allow the contents to rehydrate for about 15 minutes before serving. Can be eaten straight from the bag. Makes 1 serving.

RAMONA HAMMERLY
ANACORTES, WASHINGTON

Weight per serving: 7 ounces
Total servings: 1

Nutritional information per serving:

Calories:	672
Protein:	32 g
Carbohydrates:	145 g
Sodium:	1,149 mg
Fiber:	16 g
Fat:	2 g
Cholesterol:	0 mg

Why stand on tradition? Nori (dried seaweed) can be used as a wrapper for nontraditional fillings, such as polenta and sun-dried tomatoes. Traditional fillings, such as rice and veggies, can be spiced in new ways using nori.

BRANDON STONE "ULUHEMAN"
HONOLULU, HAWAII

Walking Carrot Salad

"The Walking Carrot Salad was inspired by an old tried-and-true family favorite carrot and raisin salad. Eat with a handful of soy nuts or peanuts, and you have a complete meal."

ROSALEEN SULLIVAN
HUDSON, MASSACHUSETTS

TOTAL WEIGHT: 1 POUND 1 OUNCE
Weight per serving: about 1 ounce
Total servings: 12

AT HOME:

2 cups grated carrot
2 cups applesauce
1 cup raisins
1 cup chopped walnuts
2 tablespoons Now-brand agar-agar powder
1 teaspoon cinnamon
1/4 cup honey

Combine all ingredients, except honey, in a saucepan. Allow the mixture to sit for about 5 minutes to allow the agar-agar powder to congeal. Next, cook over medium heat until the carrots begin to soften and the mixture thickens. Remove from heat and add honey. Applesauce and carrots can differ in sweetness depending on the brand or batch, so you may want to adjust the amount of honey used accordingly, keeping in mind that the dehydrated product will have a more concentrated sweetness. Place individual 1/4-cup dollops onto parchment-lined dehydrator trays and flatten. Dry to a leathery state, ensuring that no soft moisture pockets remain. Package for the trail, each piece representing 1 serving.

Vary the quantity or kind of nuts, maybe a spice other than cinnamon, or different fruits, such as pineapple in lieu of some or all of the raisins.

Nutritional information per serving:

Calories:	163
Protein:	2 g
Carbohydrates:	25 g
Sodium:	70 mg
Fiber:	2 g
Fat:	6 g
Cholesterol:	0 mg

AUTHORS' NOTE:

You probably haven't seen anything quite like this before, a unique type of veggie-fruit "leather" that tastes great and makes for an easy and nutritious meal. If you're having trouble finding it, agar-agar powder is a pure vegetable gelatin substitute that can be found at your local health-food store.

Teriyaki Tofu Jerky

PHIL HEFFINGTON
"SCODWOD"
EDMOND, OKLAHOMA

TOTAL WEIGHT: 3 OUNCES
Weight per serving: about 2 ounces
Total servings: 2

AT HOME:

- **1 cup Kikkoman teriyaki sauce**
- **1/2 cup pineapple juice**
- **1/4 cup brown sugar**
- **1 tablespoon ginger powder**
- **1 teaspoon garlic powder**
- **12 ounces extra-firm tofu**

In a bowl, combine all ingredients except the tofu to make the marinade sauce. Cut tofu into small pieces about 1/4-inch thick and add to the bowl of marinade, ensuring that all tofu pieces are coated. Place in your refrigerator overnight. The next day, dry the marinated tofu on parchment-lined dehydrator trays. It is ready once the tofu becomes chewy. Divide the dried tofu into 2 servings and package for the trail.

Nutritional information per serving:

Calories:	180
Protein:	14 g
Carbohydrates:	6 g
Sodium:	874 mg
Fiber:	0 g
Fat:	6 g
Cholesterol:	0 mg

Bragg's Tofu Jerky

MARA NABER
MOUNTAIN RANCH, CALIFORNIA

TOTAL WEIGHT: 3 OUNCES
Weight per serving: about 2 ounces
Total servings: 2

AT HOME:

1 cup Bragg's Liquid Aminos
1 tablespoon garlic powder
1 teaspoon ginger powder
12 ounces extra-firm tofu

In a bowl, combine Liquid Aminos and spices to make the marinade sauce. Cut tofu into small pieces about 1⁄4-inch thick and add to the bowl of marinade, ensuring that all tofu pieces are coated. Let stand for 1 to 2 hours, keeping in mind that the flavor will become stronger the longer the tofu marinates. Next, dry the marinated tofu on parchment-lined dehydrator trays. It is ready once the tofu becomes chewy. Divide the dried tofu into 2 servings and package for the trail.

Nutritional information per serving:

Calories:	100
Protein:	16 g
Carbohydrates:	5 g
Sodium:	1,380 mg
Fiber:	0 g
Fat:	5 g
Cholesterol:	0 mg

Try substituting kohlrabi, a member of the cabbage family, for tofu when making your favorite jerky recipe. Kohlrabi makes a great jerky because of its meatlike texture. Kohlrabi is also an excellent source of vitamins B and C, calcium, iron, phosphorous, carbohydrates, potassium, and fiber.

MATTHEW FARNELL
WOODLAND, WASHINGTON

Dinner

Triple Crown Curry Couscous

AT HOME:

- 1/2 cup couscous
- 1/4 cup cashew halves
- 1/4 teaspoon curry powder
- 2 tablespoons Mayacamas Chicken-Flavored Vegetarian Gravy Mix
- 2 tablespoons olive oil

Combine all dry ingredients together in a ziplock bag. Carry olive oil and water separately.

ON THE TRAIL:

- 1 1/2 cups water

To prepare 1 serving, bring 1 1/2 cups of water to a boil. Stir in all ingredients, remove from heat, cover, and let stand until liquid is absorbed. Let cool, then fluff the dish before serving.

On my Triple Crown trip, I used a homemade alcohol stove and ate straight out of the pot. I carried just the stove, one pot, and a spoon.

BRIAN ROBINSON "FLYIN' BRIAN"
MOUNTAIN VIEW, CALIFORNIA

BRIAN ROBINSON
"FLYIN' BRIAN"
MOUNTAIN VIEW, CALIFORNIA

Weight per serving: 5 ounces
Total servings: 1

Nutritional information per serving:

Calories:	787
Protein:	18 g
Carbohydrates:	82 g
Sodium:	420 mg
Fiber:	5 g
Fat:	45 g
Cholesterol:	0 mg

AUTHORS' NOTE:

While many of us dream about hiking a single long trail end to end in one season, Flyin' Brian knocked off all three of the Appalachian, Pacific Crest, and the Continental Divide Trails in 2001, becoming the first person to hike in a single year what has come to be known as the "Triple Crown." In this section you'll find several of Brian's favorite recipes that helped power him into history.

Pine Valley Couscous

AT HOME:

1 (10-ounce) package Near East couscous
1 cup sun-dried tomatoes
1/2 cup dried shiitake mushrooms
1/2 cup pine nuts
1 teaspoon parsley
1 teaspoon oregano
1 teaspoon basil
1 teaspoon turmeric
1 teaspoon garlic salt

Combine and thoroughly mix all dry ingredients in a bowl. Divide evenly into 3 ziplock quart-size freezer bags (approximately 1 heaping cup of mixture each).

ON THE TRAIL:

1 cup water per serving

To prepare 1 serving, place 1 cup of boiling water directly into a ziplock bag of Pine Valley Couscous mix. Allow to rehydrate for 10 minutes before serving.

Caution: See the "Using This Book" section regarding the use of ziplock bags with hot water.

CAROLYN HIESTAND
SEATTLE, WASHINGTON

TOTAL WEIGHT: 15 OUNCES
Weight per serving: 5 ounces
Total servings: 3

Nutritional information per serving:

Calories:	511
Protein:	20 g
Carbohydrates:	90 g
Sodium:	103 mg
Fiber:	7 g
Fat:	17 g
Cholesterol:	0 mg

Cedar Grove Couscous Risotto

AT HOME:

1 (16-ounce) bag frozen vegetable mix

1 (1.4-ounce) package Knorr Vegetable Soup Mix

1 cup unflavored textured vegetable protein

1 (10-ounce) package couscous

Thaw, chop, and dehydrate the frozen vegetables. Next, combine the dried vegetables, soup mix, and textured vegetable protein in a bowl. Divide the mix evenly into each of 2 ziplock quart-size freezer bags. Label these "Risotto A." Divide the couscous into each of 2 different ziplock bags and label these "Risotto B."

ON THE TRAIL:

3 cups water per serving

To make 1 serving, bring 3 cups of water to a boil. Add the mix from 1 bag labeled "Risotto A." Return to a boil and allow vegetables to become tender. Next, add 1 serving of couscous from a bag labeled "Risotto B." Stir, then cover and remove from heat. Let stand for about 5 minutes before serving.

HEATHER BURROR
MARTINEZ, CALIFORNIA

TOTAL WEIGHT: 1 POUND 4 OUNCES

Weight per serving: 10 ounces

Total servings: 2

Nutritional information per serving:

Calories:	890
Protein:	52 g
Carbohydrates:	162 g
Sodium:	1,613 mg
Fiber:	22 g
Fat:	3 g
Cholesterol:	0 mg

Absaroka Sweet & Sour

AT HOME:

- 3/4 cup instant white rice
- 1/4 cup Just Carrots–brand dried carrots
- 1/4 cup chopped candied pineapple tidbits
- 2 tablespoons bell pepper flakes
- 1 tablespoon dried minced onion
- 2 tablespoons chopped sun-dried tomato
- 1 tablespoon brown sugar
- 1/2 (7/8-ounce) packet Sun Bird– or Sun Luck–brand sweet and sour sauce mix

Thoroughly mix all dry ingredients and store in a ziplock bag.

ON THE TRAIL:

- 1 1/2 cups water

To prepare 1 serving, bring 1 1/2 cups of water to a boil. Add dry mixture to water. Cook for 5 minutes, stirring occasionally, before serving.

KEN HARBISON
ROCHESTER, NEW YORK

Weight per serving: 7 ounces
Total servings: 1

Nutritional information per serving:

Calories:	760
Protein:	15 g
Carbohydrates:	140 g
Sodium:	704 mg
Fiber:	11 g
Fat:	14 g
Cholesterol:	0 mg

AUTHORS' NOTE:

Some instant rice-based recipes are surprisingly sensitive to the brand of rice used. If you end up with poor results, try switching brands. We have had consistently good results with Uncle Ben's Instant. Also, the sweet and sour mix itself forms the foundation of this recipe, and so it is important that either Sun Bird or Sun Luck brands be used. If you do substitute another brand, bear in mind that the ingredients list in this recipe as well as the preparation instructions will probably require modification accordingly. Sun Bird and Sun Luck brands are readily available and can be found in the international foods section of your grocery store or in specialty food stores.

Thunder & Lightning Stir-Fry

"This recipe is simple to make and easy to rehydrate. And best of all, it's real food that tastes great!"

CHRIS IBBESON
"FLATFOOT"
HEMET, CALIFORNIA

TOTAL WEIGHT: 2 POUNDS 10 OUNCES
Weight per serving: 6 ounces
Total servings: 7

AT HOME:

1 (32-ounce) bag brown rice (about 5 cups)
1 bunch broccoli (about 4 stalks)
2 medium zucchini squash
2 pounds carrots
1 head cauliflower
2 medium onions
1 (15-ounce) bottle Kikkoman Teriyaki Sauce
1/4 cup brown sugar
1 teaspoon powdered ginger
1 teaspoon powdered garlic

Cook brown rice. Chop all vegetables and steam lightly. Return veggies to cutting board and chop further, keeping in mind that smaller pieces will dehydrate and rehydrate more readily. Place vegetables and rice together in a large bowl. In a separate bowl, mix the teriyaki sauce with the brown sugar, ginger, and garlic. Now add the sauce mix to the veggie-rice bowl and mix well. Place 3 cups of mixture onto each of 7 parchment-lined dehydrator trays. Each tray will produce 1 serving. Once dried, place the stir-fry mix from each tray into separate quart-size ziplock freezer bags.

ON THE TRAIL:

2 1/4 cups water per serving

To make 1 serving, bring 2 1/4 cups of water to a boil. Add hot water to the ziplock bag and wait 10 to 15 minutes for the mixture to rehydrate. Can be eaten directly from the bag.

Nutritional information per serving:

Calories:	685
Protein:	22 g
Carbohydrates:	137 g
Sodium:	2,741 mg
Fiber:	12 g
Fat:	5 g
Cholesterol:	0 mg

Caution: See the "Using This Book" section regarding the use of ziplock bags with hot water.

Green Dragon Pad Thai

BARBARA HODGIN
"MULE 2"
SACRAMENTO, CALIFORNIA

Weight per serving: 7 ounces
Total servings: 1

AT HOME:

1 teaspoon garlic flakes or bits
1 tablespoon sugar
4 tablespoons crushed raw peanuts
1/8 teaspoon cayenne pepper
1 teaspoon dried cilantro
3 tablespoons shredded raw coconut
1 (0.13-ounce) packet unsweetened lime Kool-Aid powder
1 tablespoon dried chives
1/4 cup dried vegetables
1/4 cup powdered eggs
3 1/2 ounces Thai Kitchen thin rice noodles

Place all dry ingredients except egg powder and noodles into a quart-size ziplock freezer bag. Label the bag "Green Dragon Sauce Mix." Carry egg powder and noodles separately in their own storage bags.

ON THE TRAIL:

1 pot water

To make 1 serving, add 1/4 cup of cold water to the bag of egg powder and knead into a batter. Bring a pot of water to a boil. Pour 1/4 cup of the hot water into the bag labeled "Green Dragon Sauce Mix" and knead until an even consistency. Add Thai noodles to the remaining water in the pot and cook for 2 minutes. Drain noodles. Next, pour both the reconstituted sauce and egg batter into the noodle pot. Stir, cover, and let sit for 3 to 4 minutes before serving.

Caution: See the "Using This Book" section regarding the use of ziplock bags with hot water.

Nutritional information per serving:

Calories:	860
Protein:	36 g
Carbohydrates:	122 g
Sodium:	432 mg
Fiber:	6 g
Fat:	28 g
Cholesterol:	0 mg

AUTHORS' NOTE:

Be prepared for a visual surprise when you add the water to the sauce mix! It will be readily evident how this dish came by its name.

Fuji Feast

AT HOME:

1 medium-size eggplant, peeled and diced
1 onion, diced
3 cloves garlic, pressed
4 ounces fresh mushrooms, diced
1 ounce fresh ginger, grated
1/3 cup low-sodium soy sauce
8 ounces somen noodles

Pare skin from eggplant. Chop vegetables into small pieces using a food processor. In a large bowl or resealable bag, mix together all vegetables, mushrooms, and spices. Add soy sauce, then mix, allowing the sauce to saturate all the vegetables. Let soak for about 20 minutes. Drain excess liquid. Place 2 cups of mixture onto each of 2 parchment-lined dehydrator trays. Each tray will produce 1 serving. When the mixture is dry, divide between 2 ziplock quart-size freezer bags. Carry noodles separately.

ON THE TRAIL:

1 pot water

To make 1 serving, bring a pot of water to a boil. Pour 1 cup of hot water into the vegetable-mushroom-spice-mix bag and allow contents to rehydrate. In the meantime, bring 4 ounces of noodles to a boil in the remaining water. Once the noodles are thoroughly cooked, drain water and add the eggplant mixture from the ziplock bag. Stir thoroughly and serve.

Caution: See the "Using This Book" section regarding the use of ziplock bags with hot water.

MARA NABER
MOUNTAIN RANCH, CALIFORNIA

TOTAL WEIGHT: 12 OUNCES
Weight per serving: about 10 ounces
Total servings: 2

Nutritional information per serving:

Calories:	585
Protein:	21 g
Carbohydrates:	121 g
Sodium:	2,228 mg
Fiber:	14 g
Fat:	3 g
Cholesterol:	0 mg

AUTHORS' NOTE:
Bragg's Liquid Aminos can be substituted for the low-sodium soy sauce, but at the expense of additional salt. If you are in need of a higher-calorie dinner, vegetable oil can be added on the trail.

Miso Madness

BRANDON STONE
"ULUHEMAN"
HONOLULU, HAWAII

Weight per serving: 6 ounces
Total servings: 1

AT HOME:

1 1/4 cups Uncle Ben's Instant Brown Rice
2 packets Kikkoman Instant Red Miso Soup mix
1/2 cup chopped dried shiitake mushrooms
1/4 cup hijiki or wakame seaweed
1/4 cup dried carrots and peas
1 teaspoon sesame seeds
1 garlic clove or 1/8 teaspoon garlic powder

Place dry ingredients and the garlic clove or garlic powder into a quart-size ziplock freezer bag. Makes 1 large serving.

ON THE TRAIL:

2 1/2 cups water

To make 1 serving, bring 2 1/2 cups of water to a boil. If using a garlic clove, cut into small pieces and toss back into the bag. Carefully pour the hot water into the bag and allow to stand 8 to 10 minutes, kneading occasionally to help ensure that all ingredients are evenly hydrated. Serve straight from the bag.

Caution: See the "Using This Book" section regarding the use of ziplock bags with hot water.

Nutritional information per serving:

Calories:	729
Protein:	20 g
Carbohydrates:	150 g
Sodium:	1,755 mg
Fiber:	15 g
Fat:	8 g
Cholesterol:	0 mg

Vegan Super Hero Burritos

"I cooked this meal on the Low Divide Trail one night. I was so hungry. When I took a bite, I leaned back from my sitting position in contentment but accidentally fell off an embankment into a creek."

BEN HAHN
"THE VEGAN SUPER HERO"
CORVALLIS, OREGON

AT HOME:

2 cups dried corn

1 package Zatarain's Red Beans and Rice mix

4 whole wheat tortillas

Package ingredients separately for the trail.

ON THE TRAIL:

1 tablespoon vegetable oil

3¼ cups water

To make 2 servings, add 2 cups of corn, 1 package of rice mix, and 1 tablespoon of vegetable oil to 3¼ cups of water and bring to a boil for 5 minutes. Reduce heat, cover, then simmer. Once fully cooked, scoop onto 4 tortillas, fold, and serve.

TOTAL WEIGHT: 1 POUND 3 OUNCES
Weight per serving: aboout 10 ounces
Total servings: 2

Nutritional information per serving:

Calories:	860
Protein:	26 g
Carbohydrates:	166 g
Sodium:	2,710 mg
Fiber:	14 g
Fat:	14 g
Cholesterol:	0 mg

Burrito Olé for Two

"The serving sizes are large. Thru-hiker appetites are voracious!"

AT HOME:

4 burrito-size flour tortillas
8 ounces sharp cheddar cheese
1 (4.5-ounce) package Lipton Spanish Rice
1 (7-ounce) package Fantastic Foods Refried Beans

Leave everything in the original packaging except for the refried beans. The beans should be sealed in a strong ziplock bag.

ON THE TRAIL:

4 cups water
Optional: hot sauce condiment packs

To prepare 2 servings, bring 4 cups of water to a boil. Pour 1¾ cups of the boiling water into a bowl containing the beans. Mix and let sit. Pour rice into the remainder of the boiling water and let simmer until fully rehydrated. Once the beans and rice are ready, fill 4 tortillas. Add 8 ounces of cheese and optional hot sauce.

To reduce weight, Knorr cheese powder may be used as a substitute for the cheddar cheese.

RICH SIMMONS
"RICHMAN-POORMAN"
PLYMOUTH, MICHIGAN

TOTAL WEIGHT: 1 POUND 14 OUNCES
Weight per serving: 15 ounces
Total servings: 2

Nutritional information per serving:

Calories:	1,405
Protein:	65 g
Carbohydrates:	182 g
Sodium:	2,381 mg
Fiber:	29 g
Fat:	50 g
Cholesterol:	120 mg

EZ Ed's Burritos

"This recipe turned out to be my favorite on my PCT thru-hike attempt in 2002. I ate it every fifth trail day. In my humble opinion, it is tasty, provides ample energy, and is easy to prepare. It has wheat, corn, rice, beans, and soy-based TVP—a good mix of carbs. The recipe generally makes enough so that I can save at least one burrito for breakfast the next day. Typically, I would stay inside my sleeping bag in the morning and nosh on the leftover burrito. One word of warning however: Make sure the mixture is well hydrated! This is a code-red gas alert. You could probably take Bean-O, but making sure the mix is well hydrated seems to do the trick."

AT HOME:

1 (5.6-ounce) package Lipton 5-Minute Spanish Rice and Sauce mix
1/4 cup Fantastic Foods Refried Beans
1 cup dehydrated black bean soup mix, any brand
1 (1.9-ounce) cup Health Valley Sweet Corn Chowder Soup mix
1/4 cup dried chopped onions
3 tablespoons textured vegetable protein
2 tablespoons dried cilantro
1 teaspoon red pepper flakes, or season to taste
1 (1.3-ounce) package Knorr Creamy Cheddar Sauce mix
8 flour tortillas

Except for the tortillas, combine and stir all dry ingredients in a bowl. Place 1 cup of mixture into each of 4 separate quart-size ziplock freezer bags. Carry tortillas separately.

ED MOLASH
"EZ ED"
OLYMPIA, WASHINGTON

TOTAL WEIGHT: 2 POUNDS
Weight per serving: 8 ounces
Total servings: 4

Nutritional information per serving:

Calories:	629
Protein:	25 g
Carbohydrates:	117 g
Sodium:	2,124 mg
Fiber:	15 g
Fat:	10 g
Cholesterol:	4 mg

ON THE TRAIL:

1 1/2 cups water per serving

Optional: hot sauce condiment packets

Bring 1 1/2 cups of water per serving to a boil. Pour water into a 1-serving ziplock bag. Knead the mixture thoroughly. Insulate so that the bag will hold the heat. Allow to sit at least 10 minutes, continuing to periodically knead the contents. Once ready, cut off 1 corner of the bag and squeeze the contents into each of 2 tortillas. Roll to form burritos.

Caution: See the "Using This Book" section regarding the use of ziplock bags with hot water.

A great addition to Italian or Mexican recipes are dried tomato chunks. Drain a number-ten can of tomato chunks, then dump them onto a parchment-lined dehydrator tray. Dry for 5 to 8 hours. They are reduced to large flakes that will rehydrate back into chunks very easily. They taste delicious. I add about a tablespoon of them per serving.

MARION DAVISON "LLAMALADY"
APPLE VALLEY, CALIFORNIA

Mountain Goat Quesadillas

AT HOME:

1 medium onion, chopped

1 (8-ounce) package fresh mushrooms, chopped

1 teaspoon olive oil

1 tablespoon vegetarian Worcestershire sauce

8 sun-dried tomatoes, chopped into small pieces

4 ounces goat cheese

4 flour tortillas

Chop the onions and mushrooms into small pieces. Sauté together with the olive oil and Worcestershire sauce. Place on a parchment-lined dehydrator tray and dry. Once ready, place mixture into a ziplock freezer bag along with the sun-dried tomatoes. Carry goat cheese and tortillas separately.

ON THE TRAIL:

¼ cup water

2 tablespoons olive oil

To make 2 servings, add ¼ cup of boiling water to the dry mix and allow to rehydrate for a couple of minutes. Add ¼ of the cheese and ¼ of the rehydrated vegetable mix to 1 tortilla shell. Fold the shell to enclose the mix and cheese. Put ½ tablespoon of oil on each tortilla shell. Fry on both sides of the tortilla until the cheese has melted. Repeat for the remaining 3 tortillas.

RACHEL JOLLY
BURLINGTON, VERMONT

TOTAL WEIGHT: 10 OUNCES
Weight per serving: 5 ounces
Total servings: 2

Nutritional information per serving:

Calories:	581
Protein:	20 g
Carbohydrates:	73 g
Sodium:	1,104 mg
Fiber:	10 g
Fat:	41 g
Cholesterol:	30 mg

AUTHORS' NOTE:

Goat cheese is delicious, but it does not keep long if it remains unrefrigerated. So use early in the trip or substitute with a more durable hard cheese.

Time-Traveler's Tamale

BRANDON STONE
"ULUHEMAN"
HONOLULU, HAWAII

Weight per serving: 8 ounces
Total servings: 1

Nutritional information per serving:

Calories:	636
Protein:	30 g
Carbohydrates:	128 g
Sodium:	797 mg
Fiber:	25 g
Fat:	6 g
Cholesterol:	0 mg

AT HOME:

- **1⁄2 cup cornmeal**
- **1 (2.4-ounce) cup Fantastic Food Cha-Cha Chili**
- **1 teaspoon chili powder**
- **1⁄4 cup Just Corn–brand dried corn**
- **1 clove garlic or 1/8 teaspoon garlic powder**
- **Optional: 1/4 cup chopped sun-dried tomatoes**

Place dry ingredients and the garlic clove or powder into a quart-size ziplock freezer bag.

ON THE TRAIL:

- **13⁄4 cups water**

To prepare 1 serving, bring 13⁄4 cups of water to a boil. If using a garlic clove, cut into small pieces and toss back into the bag. Carefully pour the hot water into the bag and allow to stand 8 to 10 minutes, kneading occasionally to help ensure that all ingredients are evenly hydrated. Serve straight from the bag.

Caution: See the "Using This Book" section regarding the use of ziplock bags with hot water.

Pacific Crest Tortillas

AT HOME:

1 (4.4-ounce) package Fantastic Foods Taco Filling
1 (7-ounce) package Fantastic Foods Instant Refried Beans
1/2 (1.25-ounce) package Ortega Taco Seasoning mix
6 flour tortillas (2 per serving)

Combine dry ingredients in a bowl. Divide mixture evenly between 3 ziplock freezer bags. Carry tortillas separately.

ON THE TRAIL:

1 cup water per serving

To make 1 serving, bring 1 cup of water to a boil and add to a bag of bean and seasoning mix. Seal bag and carefully knead contents. Once rehydrated, cut a corner from the bag and squeeze onto 2 tortillas. Roll them up and serve.

Caution: See the "Using This Book" section regarding the use of ziplock bags with hot water.

LIZ BERGERON
SACRAMENTO, CALIFORNIA

TOTAL WEIGHT: 1 POUND 9 OUNCES
Weight per serving: about 8 ounces
Total servings: 3

Nutritional information per serving:

Calories:	713
Protein:	40 g
Carbohydrates:	117 g
Sodium:	2,567 mg
Fiber:	25 g
Fat:	13 g
Cholesterol:	0 mg

Black Mountain Potatoes

AT HOME:

1 cup dried potato flakes
1/4 cup Kraft Parmesan cheese
1/4 teaspoon garlic salt
1 (2-ounce) package Health Valley Zesty Black Bean Soup mix

Combine potato flakes, Parmesan, and garlic salt in a ziplock bag. Carry bean soup separately in original packaging.

ON THE TRAIL:

2 1/2 cups water

To prepare 1 serving, bring 2 1/2 cups of water to a boil. Pour about 1 cup of the boiling water into the soup cup (don't fill it to the top!). Stir the soup and let sit 5 minutes. Add potato-cheese-garlic blend to the remaining water in the pan. Stir until the mix fully thickens. Once the bean soup is ready, pour it on top of your potato mountain and serve.

RICHARD HALBERT
"RANGER RICK"
TRAVERSE CITY, MICHIGAN

Weight per serving: 6 ounces
Total servings: 1

Nutritional information per serving:

Calories:	590
Protein:	28 g
Carbohydrates:	98 g
Sodium:	1,635 mg
Fiber:	11 g
Fat:	9 g
Cholesterol:	30 mg

Boot-Stomped Spuds

"I carry this as an emergency meal. It is very light, needs very little water, and doesn't have to stand to rehydrate. To take off the chill, we have eaten this on many a stormy day as soon as we got holed up in the tent."

MARION DAVISON
"LLAMALADY"
APPLE VALLEY, CALIFORNIA

Weight per serving: 4 ounces
Total servings: 1

Nutritional information per serving:

Calories:	314
Protein:	13 g
Carbohydrates:	56 g
Sodium:	1,278 mg
Fiber:	4 g
Fat:	5 g
Cholesterol:	7 mg

AT HOME:

2/3 cup mashed potato flakes
2 tablespoons nonfat powdered milk
1 teaspoon Butter Buds
1 teaspoon dried cilantro flakes
1 teaspoon onion flakes, finely minced
2 tablespoons powdered Alfredo sauce mix
2 tablespoons vegetarian imitation bacon bits
1 pinch pepper

Mix all dry ingredients together in a quart-size ziplock freezer bag.

ON THE TRAIL:

1 cup water

Add 1 cup of hot water to the single-serving bag of spud mix. Knead the contents thoroughly. Serve immediately from the bag.

Caution: See the "Using This Book" section regarding the use of ziplock bags with hot water.

Flyin' Brian's Garlic Potatoes

BRIAN ROBINSON
"FLYIN' BRIAN"
MOUNTAIN VIEW, CALIFORNIA

AT HOME:

1 cup instant mashed potato flakes
2 tablespoons granulated garlic
1/4 cup nonfat powdered milk
1 (0.75-ounce) package "chicken" flavored vegetarian gravy mix
1/4 cup Kraft Parmesan cheese
1/4 cup olive oil

Mix all dry ingredients together and carry in a ziplock bag. Package the olive oil separately.

ON THE TRAIL:

2 cups water

To make 1 serving, bring 2 cups of water to a boil. Stir in all ingredients and immediately remove from heat. Let stand until cool enough to serve.

Weight per serving: 8 ounces
Total servings: 1

Nutritional information per serving:

Calories:	1,067
Protein:	33 g
Carbohydrates:	99 g
Sodium:	1,522 mg
Fiber:	3 g
Fat:	66 g
Cholesterol:	26 mg

Instant potato flakes have a variety of uses: mashed potatoes, soup thickener, food breading, soup base, or as a crust poured over soup. Formed into patties, you can fry them into potato pancakes. In an emergency, they can be rolled into tiny balls and used as fish bait or as a soothing salve for bites and stings.

TRACI MARCROFT
ARCATA, CALIFORNIA

Lone Pine Lentils and Dumplings

SUZANNE ALLEN
SEATTLE, WASHINGTON

Weight per serving: 10 ounces
Total servings: 1

Nutritional information per serving:

Calories:	657
Protein:	29 g
Carbohydrates:	122 g
Sodium:	1,780 mg
Fiber:	20 g
Fat:	14 g
Cholesterol:	0 mg

AT HOME:

3/4 cup flour, either all-purpose bleached or whole wheat
1 teaspoon baking powder
1/4 teaspoon salt
1/4 teaspoon sugar
2 teaspoons soy milk powder
1/2 teaspoon garlic powder
1/2 cup brown lentils
1/2 teaspoon rosemary or sage
1 packet Hain Vegetarian Gravy Mix
Optional: dried vegetables

Mix the flour, baking powder, salt, sugar, soy milk powder, and garlic powder, and pack in a quart-size ziplock bag. In a separate bag, combine the lentils, rosemary or sage, gravy mix, and optional vegetables.

ON THE TRAIL:

2 1/4 cups water
1 tablespoon vegetable oil

In a pot, pour the lentil mix into 2 cups of water. Bring to a boil, stirring occasionally, then reduce to a simmer. Meanwhile, add 1 tablespoon oil and about 1/4 cup of water to the flour mixture. Thoroughly mix, then spoon the batter onto the simmering lentils in 5 or 6 globs. They will be touching but should stay distinct. Cover the pot and simmer for about 20 minutes until the lentils and dumplings are cooked through. Additional time may be required at very high altitudes. Hydrate the lentil mix with small additions of water if in danger of drying out and burning.

Note: The lentils will thoroughly cook in about 20 minutes at lower altitude; but, when I made some on a trip at about 10,000 feet, they were definitely still crunchy when I had dinner. However, if you add hot or boiling water to them in a bottle in the morning, the presoak will shorten the cooking time significantly in the evening. If you plan to use this method, you will need to package the lentils separately and add the rest of the ingredients at the time of cooking.

Tueeulala Thai Soup

"A delicious appetizer!"

HEATHER BURROR
MARTINEZ, CALIFORNIA

AT HOME:

1 (16-ounce) bag frozen Oriental-blend vegetables
¾ cup textured vegetable protein
3 (1.6-ounce) packages Thai Kitchen Garlic and Vegetable Instant Noodles

Thaw, chop, and dry the vegetables. Once thoroughly dehydrated, place ⅓ cup of vegetable mix into each of 3 ziplock quart-size freezer bags. To each bag also add ¼ cup textured vegetable protein. Package Thai noodles separately.

ON THE TRAIL:

2½ cups water per serving

To prepare 1 serving, bring 2½ cups of water to a boil. Add 1 package of vegetable mix and 1 package of Thai noodles along with the contents from its spice packet. Return to a boil for about 3 minutes. Remove from heat, cover, and let sit for an extra minute, giving time for the vegetables to rehydrate before serving.

TOTAL WEIGHT: 10 OUNCES
Weight per serving: about 3 ounces
Total servings: 3

Nutritional information per serving:

Calories:	300
Protein:	17 g
Carbohydrates:	50 g
Sodium:	422 mg
Fiber:	8 g
Fat:	2 g
Cholesterol:	0 mg

Blue Blazer's Soup

AT HOME:

1 (10-ounce) package frozen spinach
2 (2.4-ounce) packs Knorr Tomato with Basil Soup mix
1/4 cup nonfat powdered milk
1 (1.3-ounce) pack Knorr Creamy Cheddar mix
4 cups (16-ounce) vegetable alphabet pasta

Drain, chop, and dry spinach. In a large bowl, crumble dehydrated spinach and add the remainder of the dry ingredients. Mix well. Divide evenly into 4 ziplock quart-size freezer bags.

ON THE TRAIL:

2 1/2 cups water per serving

To make 1 serving, bring 2 1/2 cups of water to a boil. Add 1 bag of soup mix. Return to a boil for 3 to 5 minutes, stirring occasionally. Soup is ready to serve once noodles are soft.

HEATHER BURROR
MARTINEZ , CALIFORNIA

TOTAL WEIGHT: 1 POUND 9 OUNCES
Weight per serving: about 6 ounces
Total servings: 4

Nutritional information per serving:

Calories:	590
Protein:	22 g
Carbohydrates:	108 g
Sodium:	1,984 mg
Fiber:	5 g
Fat:	7 g
Cholesterol:	5 mg

Soup of Mount Inthanon

JASON RUMOHR
SEATTLE, WASHINGTON

Weight per serving: 4 ounces
Total servings: 1

Nutritional information per serving:

Calories:	411
Protein:	25 g
Carbohydrates:	70 g
Sodium:	412 mg
Fiber:	7 g
Fat:	3 g
Cholesterol:	0 mg

AT HOME:

1/4 cup dried beans
1 (1.6-ounce) package Thai Kitchen Spring Onion-Flavored Rice Noodles
1/4 cup unflavored textured vegetable protein

Cook and dehydrate your favorite beans. Combine dried beans, noodles, and textured vegetable protein in a quart-size ziplock freezer bag. Leave rice noodle spice packets intact.

ON THE TRAIL:

2 cups water

Bring 2 cups of water to a boil. Add seasonings and hot water to the 1-serving bag. Set aside for a few minutes, allowing the beans to rehydrate before serving.

Caution: See the "Using This Book" section regarding the use of ziplock bags with hot water.

Eastern Sun Miso Soup

"A great recipe to warm you up before your main course."

RACHEL JOLLY
BURLINGTON, VERMONT

Weight per serving: 2 ounces
Total servings: 1

AT HOME:

2 dried shiitake mushrooms, chopped

2 tablespoons dried carrot pieces

1 packet Kikkoman Instant Red Miso Soup mix

1/2 ounce dried tofu, broken into small pieces

1 sheet nori seaweed, torn into small pieces

Place all ingredients together in a quart-size ziplock freezer bag.

ON THE TRAIL:

1 1/2 cups water

Bring 1 1/2 cups of water to a boil and add to the mix in the single-serving ziplock bag. Let sit about 5 minutes. Can be eaten directly from the bag.

Caution: See the "Using This Book" section regarding the use of ziplock bags with hot water.

Nutritional information per serving:

Calories:	135
Protein:	9 g
Carbohydrates:	20 g
Sodium:	843 mg
Fiber:	6 g
Fat:	2 g
Cholesterol:	0 mg

Trail-Angel Cheese Soup

"This is one of the recipes I sent to my son, Mike, during his 20[illegible] hike. Because food can often sit in a mail drop-box for weeks waiting [illegible] would send one unopened 8-ounce box of Velveeta cheese along with two portions of soup mix in separate bags, providing him with two individual dinners. I used to put the dry ingredients in the quart bag along with the foil-wrapped cheese, but the powder would cling to the foil because of static electricity, making a mess when the cheese was removed from the bag.

"This recipe is dedicated to all of the trail angels who helped Mike on his trek and who continue to assist others who hike the long trails."

MIKE AND SUE REYNOLDS
"SPIDERMAN" AND "GROUND CONTROL"
COLUMBUS, INDIANA

AT HOME:

1/2 (8-ounce) package Velveeta cheese
1/4 cup mashed potato flakes
2 tablespoons all-purpose bleached wheat flour
1/2 teaspoon parsley flakes
1 teaspoon Butter Buds
1 cup oyster crackers

Remove Velveeta from the box, but keep the cheese in its original foil wrapper. Place potato mix, flour, parsley flakes, and Butter Buds into a ziplock bag. Package oyster crackers separately.

ON THE TRAIL:

2 cups water

To make 1 serving, cut half of the Velveeta log into small cubes. Add cheese to 2 cups of water and bring to a boil. Remove from heat. Add bag of potato contents a little at a time while stirring. Let stand for 5 minutes. Add crackers, then serve. The extra Velveeta can be used the next day to make a second pot of soup or served with crackers for lunch.

Weight per serving: 8 ounces
Total servings: 1

Nutritional information per serving:

Calories:	548
Protein:	27 g
Carbohydrates:	60 g
Sodium:	2,129 mg
Fiber:	1 g
Fat:	25 g
Cholesterol:	100 mg

unswick Stew

Brunswick Stew is a former first-place winner of the REI 'Back-Country One-Pot Cook-Off' competition held in College Park, Maryland."

AT HOME:

1 (16-ounce) bag frozen baby lima beans
1 (16-ounce) bag frozen corn
1 pound frozen southern-style hash-browned potatoes
1/2 cup finely chopped dried tomatoes
4 cubes vegetable bouillon
1/2 cup dried onion flakes
1 1/2 cups unflavored textured vegetable protein
4 teaspoons tomato powder
1/2 cup mashed potato flakes
4 pinches ground pepper

Thaw and dehydrate frozen vegetables, including hash-browned potatoes. In a large bowl combine the dried lima beans, corn, potatoes, and tomatoes. Place a heaping cup of mix into each of 4 separate quart-size ziplock freezer bags. Label each bag "Brunswick Stew A."

Next, into each of 4 separate quart-size ziplock freezer bags place 1 crushed bouillon cube, 2 tablespoons dried onion flakes, 6 tablespoons textured vegetable protein, 1 teaspoon tomato powder, 2 tablespoons potato flakes, and a pinch of pepper. Label each of these bags "Brunswick Stew B."

DAVE HICKS
"CHAINSAW"
DUBLIN, VIRGINIA

TOTAL WEIGHT: 1 POUND 12 OUNCES
Weight per serving: 7 ounces
Total servings: 4

Nutritional information per serving:

Calories:	835
Protein:	34 g
Carbohydrates:	108 g
Sodium:	1,139 mg
Fiber:	18 g
Fat:	30 g
Cholesterol:	0 mg

ON THE TRAIL:

2½ cups water per serving

1 tablespoon ghee (or your choice of butter, margarine, or light-flavored oil)

To make 1 serving, bring 2½ cups of water to a boil. Pour 1 bag of "Brunswick Stew A" into the boiling water and continue to cook until vegetables soften. Remove from heat and add 1 bag of "Brunswick Stew B" and ghee. Stir, cover, and allow to stand until the vegetables fully soften and the flavor develops. Note that if bag "B" is added prior to removing from heat, the mix may scorch.

Frozen vegetables (such as peas, corn, and carrots) or blanched and peeled potatoes (thinly sliced) can be dried to add the final touch to soups, stews, or pastas.

MATTHEW FARNELL
WOODLAND, WASHINGTON

North Mountain Okonomiyaki

"There was a definitive moment that converted us from eating prefabricated backpacker meals to creating our own. Once while hiking on Manitou Island in Lake Michigan, the enchilada-mush-in-a-bag that was our dinner was very unfulfilling, and I had to squeeze the bag like a tube of toothpaste to suck out the remaining drops. I knew then that I had to either find better food or stop backpacking. I'm still backpacking!"
— Rebecca

REBECCA AND JIM SPENCER
ALBANY, CALIFORNIA

TOTAL WEIGHT: 1 POUND 12 OUNCES
Weight per serving: 7 ounces
Total servings: 4

Nutritional information per serving:

Calories:	592
Protein:	18 g
Carbohydrates:	99 g
Sodium:	2,287 mg
Fiber:	2 g
Fat:	15 g
Cholesterol:	0 mg

AT HOME:

1 (8-ounce) bag precut deli-sliced coleslaw vegetable mix (green cabbage, red cabbage, and carrots)
2 cubes Rapunzel Vegan Vegetable Bouillon
4 cups all-purpose bleached wheat flour
8 teaspoons ginger powder
8 teaspoons Just Whites dried egg whites

Place coleslaw mix on parchment paper and dehydrate. Pour 1/4 cup of the dried coleslaw mix into each of 4 small ziplock bags. Add 1/2 bouillon cube to each bag. Into each of 4 separate ziplock quart-size bags, place 1 cup flour, 2 teaspoons ginger powder, and 2 teaspoons of Just Whites.

ON THE TRAIL:

Slightly more than 1 cup water per serving
1 tablespoon vegetable oil per serving
1 tablespoon soy sauce per serving

To make 1 serving, add 1/3 cup of water to 1 ziplock bag of coleslaw mix and allow to rehydrate for about an hour. Ensure that bouillon cube dissolves evenly. Add 3/4 cup of water to 1 bag of the flour mix and knead. Add rehydrated coleslaw mix to the bag and knead again. Place 1 tablespoon of oil in pan. Pour about 1/4 cup of dough at a time into a heated pan as you would for a pancake (exact amount depends upon your pan size). After the edges are cooked, flip. Remove patty from pan and repeat as required for the remainder of the mix. Sprinkle with 1 tablespoon of soy sauce and serve.

Secret Lake Garlic Lentils

AT HOME:

1/2 cup dried lentils
1 1/2 tablespoons dried garlic granules
2 tablespoons chopped dried tomatoes
1 teaspoon Italian herb seasoning
3/4 teaspoon salt

Combine all dry ingredients in a ziplock bag.

ON THE TRAIL:

1 1/4 cups water
2 tablespoons vegetable oil

To prepare 1 serving, heat 2 tablespoons of vegetable oil in a pan, then add lentil mixture. Stir to coat mixture with oil. Add 1 1/4 cups of water and bring to a boil for a few minutes. Cover and reduce heat. Simmer on low heat for about 30 minutes before serving.

TRACI MARCROFT
ARCATA, CALIFORNIA

Weight per serving: 5 ounces
Total servings: 1

Nutritional information per serving:

Calories:	618
Protein:	55 g
Carbohydrates:	71 g
Sodium:	611 mg
Fiber:	19 g
Fat:	28 g
Cholesterol:	0 mg

AUTHORS' NOTE:

Because of the long simmer time, this recipe works best if you are using a stove that can produce a low flame. Otherwise, fuel consumption and workload might make it impractical for the trail for some individuals or in certain situations. If you do have a low-flame cookstove, the recipe makes a good tasting, very nutritious, high-fiber meal.

Thanksgiving on the Hoof

"Much thanks to my good friend Spencer Newman, who provided the inspiration for this recipe. We've shared many good and not-so-good meals on the trail."

ALEX MESSINGER
BURLINGTON, VERMONT

AT HOME:

1 (8-ounce) package Worthington Prosage patties
2 cups dried peas and corn
1 1/3 cups dried mashed-potato flakes
2 cups Kellogg's-brand stuffing mix
2 cups dried cranberries

Cut each Prosage patty into 8 pieces as you would a pizza. Dry the pieces in a food dehydrator. When finished, divide evenly into 4 ziplock bags. Add 1/2 cup of the dried peas and corn to each bag. In each of 4 different ziplock bags, place 1/3 cup mashed-potato flakes, 1/2 cup stuffing mix, and 1/2 cup cranberries.

Note that Worthington Prosage patties can be found in the frozen-food section of the health-food store.

ON THE TRAIL:

1 tablespoon butter per serving
1 1/2 cups water per serving
Optional: salt to taste

To make 1 serving, add 1 bag of Prosage mix and 1 tablespoon of butter to 1 1/2 cups of water. Bring to a boil until the Prosage softens, typically a couple of minutes. Next add 1 bag of potatoes and stuffing mix. Stir well. Remove from the stove and allow to rehydrate for several more minutes. Add optional salt to taste.

TOTAL WEIGHT: 1 POUND 8 OUNCES
Weight per serving: 6 ounces
Total servings: 4

Nutritional information per serving:

Calories:	550
Protein:	21 g
Carbohydrates:	103 g
Sodium:	733 mg
Fiber:	9 g
Fat:	5 g
Cholesterol:	0 mg

Chiwaukum Quinoa

JASON RUMOHR
SEATTLE, WASHINGTON

TOTAL WEIGHT: 2 POUNDS 10 OUNCES
Weight per serving: about 11 ounces
Total servings: 4

Nutritional information per serving:

Calories:	923
Protein:	40 g
Carbohydrates:	125 g
Sodium:	1,840 mg
Fiber:	29 g
Fat:	36 g
Cholesterol:	0 mg

AT HOME:

1 (16-ounce) bag black beans
12 ounces quinoa grain
2 (26-ounce) jars spaghetti sauce (blend if chunky)
1 cup chopped pecans or nuts of your choice
4 cloves garlic (or 1/2 teaspoon powdered garlic)

Thoroughly cook the beans and quinoa. Dry the beans and quinoa in a dehydrator. Next, dry the spaghetti sauce on parchment-lined dehydrator trays, 1 jar of sauce per tray. Place the dried beans and quinoa in a large bowl. Add pecans and mix. Tear each sheet of dried spaghetti sauce evenly in half, 4 pieces total. Place each piece into a quart-size ziplock freezer bag. To each of these bags add 1 1/2 cups of the bean-quinoa mix and 1 clove of garlic (or 1/8 teaspoon powdered garlic).

ON THE TRAIL:

2 1/2 cups water per serving
2 tablespoons olive oil per serving

To prepare 1 serving, bring 2 1/2 cups of water to a boil. Tear the spaghetti leather into small pieces. Place sauce leather in boiling water along with 1 bag of mix and 2 tablespoons of oil. If using the garlic clove, chop and add to the pot as well. Cook, stirring occasionally, until the beans rehydrate.

Dirt Bagger's Pasta Parmesan

CRAIG TURNER
"NIGAL"
PIQUA, OHIO

Weight per serving: 6 ounces
Total servings: 1

AT HOME:

4 ounces thin pasta
3 tablespoons parsley flakes
1/4 cup Kraft Parmesan cheese

Carry each item separately. Otherwise, combining the parsley with the cheese will result in clumping when cooking.

ON THE TRAIL:

2 1/2 cups water
3 tablespoons olive oil
Optional: salt and pepper to taste

Cook the pasta in 2 1/2 cups of boiling water. Most of the water should be absorbed by the time the pasta is soft. Remove from heat. Stir in 3 tablespoons parsley flakes and 3 tablespoons olive oil. Top with 1/4 cup Parmesan cheese. Add optional seasonings, if desired.

Nutritional information per serving:

Calories:	879
Protein:	23 g
Carbohydrates:	84 g
Sodium:	289 mg
Fiber:	6 g
Fat:	51 g
Cholesterol:	18 mg

On Making Spaghetti Sauce Leather in the Oven: Take a large jar of your favorite spaghetti sauce and pour it onto a Teflon cookie sheet with high sides. Smack the sheet on the counter, tilt it to and fro, whatever it takes to distribute the sauce evenly on the sheet. Set it on a middle rack in your oven at 200°F or lower with the door slightly ajar. Warm the sauce until it loses all of its moisture. Cool, then remove from the cookie sheet with a spatula. Store in baggies in the fridge until you need it.

BARBARA HODGIN "MULE 2"
SACRAMENTO, CALIFORNIA

South Sister Stroganoff

BETH MURDOCK
PORTLAND, OREGON

TOTAL WEIGHT: 13 OUNCES
Weight per serving: about 7 ounces
Total servings: 2

Nutritional information per serving:

Calories:	782
Protein:	22 g
Carbohydrates:	108 g
Sodium:	934 mg
Fiber:	5 g
Fat:	24 g
Cholesterol:	86 mg

AT HOME:

2 tablespoons butter
1 small onion, minced
3 cloves garlic, minced
1 pound mushrooms, chopped
1/2 teaspoon salt
1/2 teaspoon pepper
2 tablespoons dry sherry
3/4 cup vegetable broth
2 tablespoons all-purpose wheat flour
1/2 cup sour cream
8 ounces angel-hair pasta

Sauté the onions, garlic, and mushrooms in the butter. Add the seasonings along with the sherry, then stir. In a separate bowl, mix the vegetable broth with the flour. Combine the broth mix with the vegetables and cook an additional 5 minutes or so. Finally, stir in the sour cream and let simmer momentarily. Remove from heat and spread the mixture thinly over 1 or 2 parchment-covered dehydrator trays. When dry, crumple the leather into small pieces or chop in a food processor, then divide evenly into 2 ziplock bags. Into 2 separate ziplock bags, evenly divide the noodles.

ON THE TRAIL:

2 cups water per serving

To prepare 1 serving, put a little water into 1 bag of dried sauce mix, enough to barely cover the contents, about 1 hour prior to dinner. Bring 2 cups of water to a boil and add the contents of 1 bag of noodles. Once the noodles are fully cooked, drain. Add the rehydrated sauce mix and stir. Let the pot sit, covered, for a few minutes before serving.

Golden Bear Gado-Gado

RACHEL JOLLY
BURLINGTON, VERMONT

Weight per serving: 11 ounces
Total servings: 1

Nutritional information per serving:

Calories:	1,209
Protein:	22 g
Carbohydrates:	136 g
Sodium:	1,187 mg
Fiber:	2 g
Fat:	39 g
Cholesterol:	0 mg

AT HOME:

2 tablespoons crushed peanuts
2 tablespoons dried onion
1/4 cup brown sugar
1/8 teaspoon ground cayenne pepper
1 teaspoon garlic powder
2 tablespoons low-sodium soy sauce
1/4 cup olive oil
1/4 cup rice vinegar
4 ounces orzo (a rice-shaped pasta)

Place all dry ingredients, except pasta, together in a ziplock bag. Combine all wet ingredients in a small plastic bottle. Package the pasta separately.

ON THE TRAIL:

1 pot water

Add the wet ingredients to the bag of dry ingredients, reseal, and knead bag to mix the contents. Bring a pot of water to a boil and add 4 ounces of pasta. Heat until tender, then drain excess water. Add sauce mix to the pasta and stir.

TrailDad's Spaghetti

"TrailDad is my father, Roy Robinson. He single-handedly packed fifty-seven resupply boxes for the Continental Divide and Pacific Crest legs of my Triple Crown hike. That required dehydrating gallons of sauce! TrailDad's Spaghetti is my favorite dish."

AT HOME:

1 (26-ounce) jar spaghetti sauce (your favorite brand)
4 ounces whole wheat angel-hair pasta
1/4 cup Kraft Parmesan cheese

Dehydrate your favorite spaghetti sauce until it is hard and brittle. Low-fat vegetarian sauce dries more readily. A chunky brand of sauce should be pureed in a blender prior to dehydration. Place dried spaghetti sauce in a ziplock bag. Carry pasta and cheese separately.

Note that thoroughly dried spaghetti leather will keep for a few weeks without refrigeration. If a longer period of time will elapse before it is used, it should be placed in a tightly sealed bag and stored in a freezer.

ON THE TRAIL:

2 1/2 cups water
2 tablespoons olive oil

For 1 serving, crumble dried spaghetti sauce into 2 1/2 cups of cold water and heat to boiling. Add 2 tablespoons of olive oil and 4 ounces of pasta. Stir quickly for a few minutes. Simmer if your stove will permit; otherwise, remove from heat to prevent burning, keeping the contents hot as long as possible. The pasta should soak up the liquid so that there is no need to drain the pot. Add 1/4 cup of Parmesan cheese, stir, and serve.

BRIAN ROBINSON
"FLYIN' BRIAN"
MOUNTAIN VIEW, CALIFORNIA

Weight per serving: 8 ounces
Total servings: 1

Nutritional information per serving:

Calories:	1,240
Protein:	34 g
Carbohydrates:	154 g
Sodium:	3,580 mg
Fiber:	24 g
Fat:	59 g
Cholesterol:	20 mg

Olancha Sweet Pepper Pasta

MARA NABER
MOUNTAIN RANCH, CALIFORNIA

TOTAL WEIGHT: 10 OUNCES
Weight per serving: 5 ounces
Total servings: 2

Nutritional information per serving:

Calories:	602
Protein:	15 g
Carbohydrates:	92 g
Sodium:	6 mg
Fiber:	3 g
Fat:	16 g
Cholesterol:	0 mg

AT HOME:

1 red onion, diced
2 sweet red peppers, diced
3 cloves garlic, pressed
1 tablespoon diced fresh basil
1 tablespoon diced fresh oregano
Optional: 1 teaspoon garlic salt per serving
8 ounces capellini noodles

In a bowl, combine all the vegetables and spices, except optional garlic salt. Place 1 cup of mix onto each of 2 parchment-lined dehydrator trays. Each tray will produce 1 serving of sauce mix. Once dry, place each serving of mix in a quart-size ziplock freezer bag. Add optional garlic salt to each bag if desired. Carry noodles and olive oil separately.

ON THE TRAIL:

1 pot of water
1 tablespoon olive oil per serving

To make 1 serving, bring a pot of water to a boil. Pour ½ cup of hot water into 1 bag of sauce mix and allow to rehydrate. Add 4 ounces of noodles to the remainder of the boiling water. Continue on high heat until the noodles are tender. Drain and add the sauce mix and 1 tablespoon of olive oil. Stir well and serve.

Caution: See the "Using This Book" section regarding the use of ziplock bags with hot water.

Wasatch Tomato Parmesan

BETH MURDOCK
PORTLAND, OREGON

TOTAL WEIGHT: 14 OUNCES
Weight per serving: 7 ounces
Total servings: 2

Nutritional information per serving:

Calories:	714
Protein:	24 g
Carbohydrates:	99 g
Sodium:	2,798 mg
Fiber:	<1 g
Fat:	22 g
Cholesterol:	60 mg

AT HOME:

2½ tablespoons butter
3 tablespoons all-purpose wheat flour
1 cup milk
1 cup tomato-based pasta sauce
¼ cup Kraft Parmesan cheese
2 tablespoons dry red wine
1 teaspoon salt
8 ounces angel-hair pasta

Melt the butter in a saucepan, stir in the flour, and cook for about 1 minute over medium heat. Add the milk and pasta sauce. Continue to cook, stirring often until the sauce is thick. Add cheese, wine, and salt. Simmer until the cheese melts and the alcohol evaporates. Spread the sauce thinly over 1 or 2 parchment-covered dehydrator trays. Dry. When finished, crumble the dried sauce leather into small pieces or chop finely in a food processor. Next, divide evenly into 2 ziplock bags. Into 2 separate ziplock bags, evenly divide the noodles.

ON THE TRAIL:

2 cups water per serving

To prepare 1 serving, put a little water into 1 bag of dried sauce mix, enough to barely cover the contents, about 1 hour before dinner. Bring 2 cups of water to a boil and add the contents of 1 bag of noodles. Once the noodles are fully cooked, drain. Add the rehydrated sauce mix and stir. Let the pot sit, covered, for a few minutes before serving.

Springer Mountain Pesto

"We'll never forget our three little ones huddled around the cook pot on Springer Mountain one quiet evening during our backpack trip at the AT's southern terminus. James was five years old at the time, Michael was almost four, and Maria had just turned two. While we watched the kids, I recalled how something seemed to have gone drastically wrong between the time when they were infants, eating virtually anything set before them, and now, when they typically frowned at everything. But not that evening. It had been a long day on the trail, and they simply could not shovel that pasta in fast enough! Christine and I enjoy the fact that food-related battles tend to be minor when we hike with the kids. Hard-won hunger has a way of doing that. This could be reason enough to drive any parent with small kids to backpacking."

—Tim

AT HOME:

1/4 teaspoon garlic powder
1/4 cup pine nuts
2 tablespoons chopped dried basil leaves
1/4 cup Kraft Parmesan cheese
4 ounces whole wheat angel-hair pasta

Combine garlic powder, pine nuts, basil, and Parmesan cheese in a ziplock freezer bag. Carry pasta separately.

ON THE TRAIL:

2 1/2 cups water
1/4 cup olive oil

For 1 serving, bring 2 1/2 cups of water to a boil. Cook pasta thoroughly. Most of the water should be absorbed, requiring little draining. Add 1/4 cup olive oil and pesto mix to the pasta, toss, and serve.

CHRISTINE AND TIM CONNERS
SAVANNAH, GEORGIA

Weight per serving: 8 ounces
Total servings: 1

Nutritional information per serving:

Calories:	842
Protein:	17 g
Carbohydrates:	15 g
Sodium:	604 mg
Fiber:	5 g
Fat:	80 g
Cholesterol:	30 mg

Pindos Mountain Pasta

AT HOME:

- 1/4 cup chopped dried tomatoes
- 1 tablespoon dried basil
- 1 tablespoon balsamic vinegar
- 1 tablespoon olive oil
- 4 ounces whole wheat angel-hair pasta
- 4 ounces feta cheese

Place dried tomatoes and basil together in a ziplock bag. Store vinegar and olive oil in a separate container. The pasta and cheese should be carried in separate bags.

ON THE TRAIL:

- 2 1/2 cups water

To prepare 1 serving, add a small amount of water to the tomato-basil mix to begin rehydration. Next, bring 2 1/2 cups of water to a boil. Cook pasta thoroughly. Most of the water should be absorbed, requiring little draining. Add the remainder of the ingredients to the pasta, then toss and serve.

KATARINA SENGSTAKEN
"KATGIRL"
HOLLIS, NEW HAMPSHIRE

Weight per serving: 10 ounces
Total servings: 1

Nutritional information per serving:

Calories:	961
Protein:	37 g
Carbohydrates:	116 g
Sodium:	1,707 mg
Fiber:	13 g
Fat:	43 g
Cholesterol:	60 mg

AUTHORS' NOTE:
Feta cheese does not keep long if it remains unrefrigerated, so use early in the trip or substitute with a more durable hard cheese.

If you have trouble chopping leather foods like dried spaghetti sauce or sun-dried tomatoes, try the following trick: Freeze the food first for at least 10 minutes, then chop with a blender or a knife.

KEN HARBISON
ROCHESTER, NEW YORK

Range Rovin' Ramen

"This was the first course that I ate every night while doing the Triple Crown. It's a really quick warm-up dish after a long, hard day."

AT HOME:

1 (3-ounce) package Maruchan Mushroom Flavored Ramen

1/2 cup mixed vegetables, dried

Keep ramen noodles in their package. Carry dried vegetables separately.

ON THE TRAIL:

2 1/2 cups water

To prepare 1 serving, crush the ramen noodles and pour them, along with the dried vegetables, into 2 1/2 cups of water. Bring to a boil, being careful to prevent the ramen from becoming mushy. Serve once the vegetables rehydrate.

BRIAN ROBINSON
"FLYIN' BRIAN"
MOUNTAIN VIEW, CALIFORNIA

Weight per serving: 5 ounces
Total servings: 1

Nutritional information per serving:

Calories:	505
Protein:	15 g
Carbohydrates:	77 g
Sodium:	1,920 mg
Fiber:	7 g
Fat:	16 g
Cholesterol:	0 mg

AUTHORS' NOTE:

We found it interesting that Brian referred to this as his first course every night on his long hike. What he calls an appetizer would probably be a full meal for those folks out on a weekend jaunt. The raging dietary furnace of the long-distance hiker is one of the wonders of the natural world. Brian states, "I consumed on average 6,000 calories each day and didn't gain or lose a pound all year."

Guitar Lake Melody

"Yes, it's true. I've camped at Guitar Lake below Mount Whitney numerous times. And I really do carry a backpack guitar and often play it while waiting for dinner!"

MARION DAVISON
"LLAMALADY"
APPLE VALLEY, CALIFORNIA

Weight per serving: 8 ounces
Total servings: 1

Nutritional information per serving:

Calories:	872
Protein:	24 g
Carbohydrates:	120 g
Sodium:	1,689 mg
Fiber:	10 g
Fat:	31 g
Cholesterol:	0 mg

AT HOME:

- **1 package Top Ramen Oriental-Flavored Ramen**
- **1 teaspoon curry powder**
- **1 teaspoon minced onion flakes**
- **1 teaspoon minced dried vegetable flakes**
- **1/3 cup beans, cooked and dried**
- **1/4 cup chopped unsalted cashews**
- **1/4 cup raisins**
- **1/2 teaspoon Mrs. Dash Garlic and Herb Seasoning**

Mix all dry ingredients together in a quart-size ziplock bag.

ON THE TRAIL:

- **2 1/2 cups water**

To prepare 1 serving, bring 2 1/2 cups of water to a boil, add contents from the ziplock bag, stir well, then cover. Remove from heat and let stand for 20 minutes before serving.

Rib-Stickin' Ramen

"This is a simple meal that I often ate while thru-hiking the Appalachian Trail in 1998. This was my so-called 'extra meal.' If I was five days out since my last resupply, this was my sixth dinner in case something happened or I was just extra hungry. It turned out to be my favorite meal on the trail. The recipe is lightweight, doesn't require much skill to prepare, and really sticks to the ribs. You can tailor this recipe to your tastes. I introduced it to others and we all had our own unique way of preparing it."

AT HOME:

2 tablespoons all-purpose wheat flour

1 tablespoon Mrs. Dash Salt-Free Garlic and Herb Seasoning

1/4 teaspoon garlic salt

1/8 teaspoon ground cayenne pepper

1 (3-ounce) packet ramen noodles, seasoning packet removed

2 ounces sharp cheddar cheese

In a small ziplock bag, combine flour with seasonings. Carry the remainder of the ingredients separately.

ON THE TRAIL:

2 cups water

1 tablespoon butter

Bring 2 cups of water to a boil and add noodles. Do not include the ramen seasoning packet, which often contains meat by-products. Once noodles are soft, remove from heat and add the flour-seasoning mix, 1 tablespoon butter, and 2 ounces of cheese. Stir until cheese melts.

WILL JAYNES
"HAYDUKE"
THREE RIVERS, CALIFORNIA

Weight per serving: 6 ounces
Total servings: 1

Nutritional information per serving:

Calories:	510
Protein:	18 g
Carbohydrates:	28 g
Sodium:	1,465 mg
Fiber:	1 g
Fat:	37 g
Cholesterol:	90 mg

Mexican Volcano

RAMONA HAMMERLY
ANACORTES, WASHINGTON

Weight per serving: 6 ounces
Total servings: 1

AT HOME:

1/2 cup Fantastic Foods Polenta
1/2 cup Fantastic Foods Refried Beans

Place each item into its own ziplock freezer bag.

ON THE TRAIL:

1 1/2 cups water

To prepare 1 serving, bring 1 1/2 cups of water to a boil. Pour 1/2 cup of the heated water into the bean mix and set aside to rehydrate. Add polenta to the remainder of the hot water. Once the polenta and beans are rehydrated, pour the bean mix directly onto the polenta and serve.

Caution: See the "Using This Book" section regarding the use of ziplock bags with hot water.

Nutritional information per serving:

Calories:	606
Protein:	25 g
Carbohydrates:	107 g
Sodium:	140 mg
Fiber:	21 g
Fat:	10 g
Cholesterol:	7 mg

Back Rock Bami Goreng

"I first witnessed the backpacking variety of bami goreng while accompanying Javanese friends on a night adventure in the jungles of South America. We were waiting for complete darkness and the moon to set, so we slung our hammocks in a clump of trees. Only trouble: I'd forgotten my hammock! So I scraped the leaves aside on the ground, made sort of a tube tent with some clear plastic, and padded the ground with dry cecropia leaves. In the meantime, Boefie, a close family friend and ex-combat medic, boiled Thai noodles, enough for the three of us. The method was very similar to that described in the recipe. Afterwards, I was off to a couple of hours of restless sleep. I *hate* sleeping on the jungle ground. Maybe it's just a basic fear of the scorpions, big hairy spiders, snakes . . ."

ANDREAS RAEHMI
"MARMOSET"
ZURICH, SWITZERLAND

TOTAL WEIGHT: 12 OUNCES
Weight per serving: 3 ounces
Total servings: 4

Nutritional information per serving (including hot drink):

Calories:	252
Protein:	6 g
Carbohydrates:	47 g
Sodium:	2,823 mg
Fiber:	3 g
Fat:	3 g
Cholesterol:	0 mg

AT HOME:

1 (8-ounce) bag precut deli-sliced coleslaw vegetable mix (green cabbage, red cabbage, and carrots)
1 onion, finely chopped
2 scallions, finely chopped
1 bell pepper, finely chopped
3 ounces fresh shiitake mushrooms, finely chopped
4 (1.6-ounce) packages Thai Kitchen Onion-Flavored Instant Rice Noodles
4 cubes vegan vegetable bouillon

Mix all finely chopped vegetables and mushrooms together and dry on parchment paper in a dehydrator. Once dry, divide the mix evenly between 4 small ziplock bags. Carry all other items separately. If you select another brand of noodles, one that does not come prepackaged with an oil packet, then you will need to separately pack 1 tablespoon of vegetable oil per serving.

ON THE TRAIL:

1⅓ cups water per serving

1 teaspoon soy sauce per serving

To make 1 serving, add ⅓ cup of filtered water to 1 bag of vegetable-mushroom mix and allow to rehydrate for approximately 1 hour. Once rehydrated, bring 1 cup of water to a boil along with 1 dissolved bouillon cube. Add the noodles, allowing them to cook for about 3 minutes. Drain off the broth from the noodles and pour into a cup as a hot drink on the side. Add the cooking oil from the Thai noodle package and stir-fry the cooked noodles for about 1 minute. Now open the seasoning packet from the Thai noodle package and pour over the noodles in the pot. Add the veggie-mushroom mix and stir-fry once again for an additional minute. Remove from heat and add the soy sauce before serving.

AUTHORS' NOTE:

To reduce the sodium content, boil the noodles without the bouillon cube.

If you need a serving plate, a Frisbee works nicely. You can wash it easily, pack it readily, play with it, use it as a fan, and eat out of it. It is a great, durable, multipurpose tool for eating well in the woods.

BEN HAHN "THE VEGAN SUPER HERO"
CORVALLIS, OREGON

Lost Cowboy Chili

"Legend has it that late one morning, after a long night of festivities, a cowboy awoke to find that his herd and buddies had hit the trail without him. Cattle and companions gone, Lost Cowboy was forced to invent the very first meatless chili recipe. He liked it so much that he abandoned his carnivorous ways and, despite intense ridicule from less-enlightened cowpokes, opened the first smoothie stand on the Chisholm Trail."

CHRISTINE AND TIM CONNERS
SAVANNAH, GEORGIA

TOTAL WEIGHT: 12 OUNCES
Weight per serving: 6 ounces
Total servings: 2

Nutritional information per serving:

Calories:	797
Protein:	32 g
Carbohydrates:	130 g
Sodium:	2,739 mg
Fiber:	33 g
Fat:	3 g
Cholesterol:	0 mg

AT HOME:

1 (15-ounce) can black beans
1 (15-ounce) can kidney beans
1 (14½-ounce) can stewed tomatoes
1 (10¾-ounce) can tomato soup
1 medium onion, diced
1 green pepper, diced
1 clove garlic, minced
1 cup frozen white corn
¼ teaspoon cayenne powder
¼ cup maple syrup

Drain and chop the beans, then place in a large pot. Drain the juice from the can of tomatoes into the pot, then chop tomatoes and add to the pot as well. Combine the rest of the ingredients in the pot and simmer over low heat until the diced onions are thoroughly cooked. Pour approximately 3 cups of mixture onto each of 2 parchment-lined dehydrator trays. Spread thinly. Each tray will produce 1 serving. Thoroughly dry the mixture in the dehydrator. Remove and place each sheet of dried bean-mix leather into its own quart-size ziplock freezer bag.

ON THE TRAIL:

2¼ cups water per serving

To make 1 serving, bring 2¼ cups of water to a boil. Tear the chili leather into small pieces and add to the boiling water. Stir occasionally until fully rehydrated.

AUTHORS' NOTE:

Each serving of this recipe contains enough methane-producing fiber to fuel a small suborbital launch vehicle. Please hike friendly, and warn your trail companions of their impending doom as you light the stove for this one!

Kilauea Chili

BRANDON STONE
"ULUHEMAN"
HONOLULU, HAWAII

Weight per serving: 5 ounces
Total servings: 1

Nutritional information per serving:

Calories:	472
Protein:	23 g
Carbohydrates:	89 g
Sodium:	630 mg
Fiber:	16 g
Fat:	4 g
Cholesterol:	0 mg

AT HOME:

1/2 cup Uncle Ben's Instant Brown Rice
1 (2.4-ounce) cup Fantastic Foods Cha-Cha Chili
1/4 cup corn, dried
1 teaspoon chili powder
1/4 teaspoon lemon powder
1 clove garlic or 1/8 teaspoon garlic powder

Place dry ingredients and the garlic clove or garlic powder into a quart-size ziplock freezer bag.

ON THE TRAIL:

1 3/4 cups water

For 1 serving, bring 1 3/4 cups of water to a boil. If using a garlic clove, cut into small pieces and toss back into the bag. Carefully pour the hot water into bag and allow to stand 8 to 10 minutes, kneading occasionally to help ensure that all ingredients are evenly hydrated. Serve straight from the bag.

Caution: See the "Using This Book" section regarding the use of ziplock bags with hot water.

Death Valley Chili

"Every summer, a motley group of NASA employees from the Dryden Flight Research Center in California's Mojave Desert would make a pilgrimage to Death Valley, typically in early August. Keeping with tradition, no air-conditioning was permitted on the drive through the pressing heat to the near-empty campground at Furnace Creek. We'd unpack under the sparse shade of some old mesquite bushes.

"In the meantime, as the sun climbed higher in the sky, the heat also intensified. At its peak, we'd meet for a foot race at Badwater, the lowest point in the United States at 280 feet below sea level. The group would line up at the BAD WATER sign that stood, true to its name, in front of a brackish pond of dead, foul-smelling water. With a wave of the starter's hand, we were off running across the desert along a vague race route, soon stringing out in a long line in the general direction of Telescope Peak, almost lost in the shimmering 120°F heat waves of the valley floor. Tourists, mostly Europeans, would gather to witness this strange ritual. As a runner or two eventually jogged to cross the 'finish line,' an etch marked in the salt, the rest walked or staggered slowly back from the jaws of Hell. As was our tradition, the winner received an ice-cold bottle of cheap champagne.

"Meanwhile, a round thermometer was placed flat on the hot asphalt of the parking lot. The large dial would quickly climb past 140°F. The gage was then placed prominently next to the BAD WATER sign, around which our group stood to have their picture taken. We avoided answering questions from curious onlookers about the truth of the biased temperature reading. Next, as was tradition, one of our vehicles parked in the burning sun was selected as a cooking surface for an egg. While partially successful, it would typically leave a mess along with some peeling auto paint. On one occasion, a recent hire with a new car wanted us to use his hood. He quit NASA soon after.

"Once, our group discovered a nearby motel, at which, by mingling with the guests, we eventually were able to sneak into the facility's large pool, continuously fed by a natural spring. The pool was not only very refreshing but also filled with scantily clad Europeans. This heightened our desire to linger a little longer and served as impetus to return in following years.

"As the sun went down behind the Panamint Range, the temperature would finally drop to a comfortable 100°F and we would prepare for the trip's crowning moment. A large, deep pan was cleaned of any sand and debris from last year's Death Valley Chili. Everyone gathered around and opened their favorite canned chili and added their unique contributions to the pot. The always eclectic mix was then brought to a boil, everyone grabbing a plate and heartily indulging.

"The chili, cheap wine, and cold beer helped deaden the senses ahead of an uncomfortably warm night of sleeping. After a poor night's sleep, we'd awake the next morning, usually not feeling well, before the sun's hot rays broke over the top of the Funeral Range. (I awoke once to find one individual kicking his car's tires and yelling that he would never come again in the summer.) After cleaning up camp, we'd roll away as the heat once again began to consume the Death Valley."

AT HOME:

- **5 (15-ounce) cans Hormel Vegetarian Chili**
- **1/3 cup raisins**
- **2/3 cup crushed pineapple, drained**
- **1 red onion, chopped**
- **1 white onion, chopped**
- **2–5 fresh jalapeños, chopped**
- **3 "bread-and-butter" pickle spears, chopped**
- **3 cloves fresh garlic, pressed**
- **1 tablespoon mustard**
- **1 teaspoon catsup**
- **1/4 cup honey**
- **2 Baker's semisweet chocolate squares**
- **8 ounces Monterey Jack cheese, cubed**
- **8 ounces longhorn cheddar cheese, cubed**
- **Optional: spaghetti noodles, antacid**

In a large pot, heat all ingredients except the chocolate and the cheese. Once the onions are soft, add the cheese and chocolate and stir until melted. Place chili in a blender and puree. Place parchment paper on each of 5 separate dehydrator trays. Pour 2 heaping cups of blended chili onto each tray. If any excess chili remains, divide the remainder among the trays. Ensure that the chili mixture is spread evenly and thinly before dehydrating. Dry. When finished, place the chili leather from each tray into its own quart-size ziplock bag.

ON THE TRAIL:

- **1 1/2 cups water per serving**

For each serving, tear chili leather into small pieces and return to the ziplock bag that it came from. Add 1 1/2 cups of water to the bag and let the chili mix rehydrate for a while. Kneading the bag occasionally will help accelerate the process. Pour mixture into a pan and bring to a low boil. Heat until the chili finishes rehydrating, stirring occasionally to prevent burning. Serve as is or use as a topping on optional cooked noodles.

DEAN WEBB
"DINUBA WOLF" AKA "EL LOBO"
LANCASTER, CALIFORNIA

TOTAL WEIGHT: 2 POUNDS 3 OUNCES
Weight per serving: 7 ounces
Total servings: 5

Nutritional information per serving:

Calories:	970
Protein:	45 g
Carbohydrates:	140 g
Sodium:	2,419 mg
Fiber:	17 g
Fat:	35 g
Cholesterol:	96 mg

AUTHORS' NOTE:

We've modified the base recipe by keeping it meatless and adapting it for use on the trail by creating a leather out of the ingredients. Next time you head for the mountains, take a little of Death Valley with you. And, in case you're wondering, Dean's story is absolutely true. We were firsthand participants!

Soul Food

MARION DAVISON
"LLAMALADY"
APPLE VALLEY, CALIFORNIA

Weight per serving: 5 ounces
Total servings: 1

Nutritional information per serving:

Calories:	623
Protein:	21 g
Carbohydrates:	123 g
Sodium:	1,869 mg
Fiber:	9 g
Fat:	4 g
Cholesterol:	0 mg

AT HOME:

1 cup Uncle Ben's Instant Brown Rice
1/3 cup beans, cooked and dried
2 tablespoons Lipton Onion Soup mix
1 teaspoon minced onion flakes
1 pinch black pepper
1/4 teaspoon garlic powder
1/2 teaspoon parsley flakes
2 tablespoons imitation bacon bits
1/4 teaspoon soul seasoning (Cajun or Creole seasoning will substitute)
Optional: 1/8 teaspoon cayenne

Mix all dry ingredients together in a quart-size ziplock bag.

ON THE TRAIL:

2 cups water

For 1 serving, bring 2 cups of water to a boil, add contents from the ziplock bag, stir well, then cover. Remove from heat and let stand for 20 minutes before serving.

Dinner in Denali

DAVE HICKS
"CHAINSAW"
DUBLIN, VIRGINIA

TOTAL WEIGHT: 13 OUNCES
Weight per serving: about 7 ounces
Total servings: 2

AT HOME:

1 (14-ounce) bag frozen baby lima beans
1 (10-ounce) box frozen spinach
1½ cups Uncle Ben's Instant Brown Rice
⅓ cup dried onion flakes
1 tablespoon dill weed
2 teaspoons whole milk powder
2 teaspoons whole egg powder
½ teaspoon salt
2 teaspoons lemon pepper

Dry the lima beans and spinach in a food dehydrator. Pulverize lima beans in a food grinder. Combine limas, spinach, rice, and onion flakes in a bowl. Divide mixture evenly into each of 2 individual quart-size ziplock freezer bags. To each bag add ½ tablespoon of dill weed, 1 teaspoon of dried milk, 1 teaspoon of egg powder, ¼ teaspoon of salt, and 1 teaspoon of lemon pepper.

ON THE TRAIL:

1½ cups water per serving

To prepare 1 serving, bring 1½ cups of water to a boil. Pour water into 1 bag of mixture. Seal, insulate to preserve heat, and allow to sit for about 10 minutes. Can be eaten straight out of the bag.

Caution: See the "Using This Book" section regarding the use of ziplock bags with hot water.

Nutritional information per serving:

Calories:	661
Protein:	27 g
Carbohydrates:	134 g
Sodium:	2,098 mg
Fiber:	21 g
Fat:	5 g
Cholesterol:	34 mg

Taconic Mountain Cheesy Rice

RACHEL JOLLY /
CHEWONKI FOUNDATION
BURLINGTON, VERMONT

Weight per serving: 7 ounces
Total servings: 1

Nutritional information per serving:

Calories:	760
Protein:	22 g
Carbohydrates:	84 g
Sodium:	1,820 mg
Fiber:	4 g
Fat:	23 g
Cholesterol:	60 mg

AT HOME:

1⁄2 cup Uncle Ben's Instant Brown Rice
1 tablespoon dried onion
1 teaspoon garlic salt
1⁄4 teaspoon pepper
1 teaspoon oregano
2 (1-ounce) sticks string cheese

Place rice and seasonings in a ziplock bag. Carry cheese separately.

ON THE TRAIL:

1 1⁄4 cups water
1 tablespoon butter or margarine

Bring 1 1⁄4 cups of water to a boil. Add all the ingredients including 1 tablespoon of butter and 2 ounces of string cheese. Stir until rice is rehydrated and cheese is melted.

Chainsaw's Pumpkin Pleaser

DAVE HICKS
"CHAINSAW"
DUBLIN, VIRGINIA

TOTAL WEIGHT: 15 OUNCES
Weight per serving: 5 ounces
Total servings: 3

Nutritional information per serving:

Calories:	414
Protein:	12 g
Carbohydrates:	70 g
Sodium:	315 mg
Fiber:	17 g
Fat:	10 g
Cholesterol:	0 mg

AT HOME:

1 (29-ounce) can pure pumpkin
1/2 cup dry sherry
3/4 teaspoon ground black pepper
1 red bell pepper, chopped
2 tablespoons dried onion
1 tablespoon brown sugar
2 teaspoons ground coriander seed
2 teaspoons dried mustard powder
1 teaspoon dried lemon peel
1 teaspoon dried garlic powder
1/4 teaspoon cayenne pepper
1/4 teaspoon turmeric
2 tablespoons dry-roasted peanuts
1/2 cup dried coconut flakes
11/2 cups Uncle Ben's Instant Brown Rice

Mix together pumpkin, sherry, and black pepper. Spread thinly on a parchment-lined dehydrator tray. Cut bell pepper into small pieces and place on a separate dehydrator tray. Dry both. When ready, tear the pumpkin leather into small pieces and place in a large bowl with the dried bell pepper and all the seasonings, including the peanuts and coconut flakes. Mix well.

Into each of 3 ziplock quart-size freezer bags place 1/2 cup of rice. To each bag also add 1 cup of the pumpkin mix.

ON THE TRAIL:

2 cups water per serving
Optional: generous dollop of ghee or olive oil

To make 1 serving, bring 2 cups of water to a boil and add the contents from 1 bag of pumpkin-rice mix. As an option, olive oil or ghee can also be added at this time. Serve once ingredients have fully rehydrated.

Procrastinator's Deliverance

AT HOME:

1 cup Uncle Ben's Instant Brown Rice
1 envelope Lipton Recipe Secrets Vegetable Soup mix
1/4 teaspoon dried basil
1/4 teaspoon dried oregano
1/4 teaspoon ground cumin

Combine all dry ingredients in a quart-size ziplock freezer bag.

ON THE TRAIL:

1 1/2 cups water

To prepare 1 serving, bring 1 1/2 cups of water to a boil. Add hot water to the ziplock bag and allow to rehydrate for about 5 minutes. Can be eaten directly from the bag.

Caution: See the "Using This Book" section regarding the use of ziplock bags with hot water.

MARA NABER
MOUNTAIN RANCH, CALIFORNIA

Weight per serving: 5 ounces
Total servings: 1

Nutritional information per serving:

Calories:	460
Protein:	12 g
Carbohydrates:	100 g
Sodium:	1,541 mg
Fiber:	7 g
Fat:	3 g
Cholesterol:	0 mg

AUTHORS' NOTE:

If you've procrastinated on your food preparation for your next backpacking trip, consider this recipe. It's simple and takes less than 5 minutes to prepare. We'd also like to point out that there is no implied relationship between this recipe's title and banjos, bows and arrows, and canoes!

Kincora Rice

AT HOME:

1 (10-ounce) package frozen spinach
3 cups Uncle Ben's Instant Brown Rice
2/3 cup raisins
2/3 cup pine nuts
1 teaspoon nutmeg
1 teaspoon salt
2 teaspoons ground ginger

Thaw, drain, and dehydrate spinach. Once ready, mix all dry ingredients together in a large bowl. Place 1 heaping cup of mixture into each of 4 ziplock quart-size freezer bags.

ON THE TRAIL:

1 1/4 cups water per serving

To make 1 serving, bring 1 1/4 cups of water to a boil. Add water to the ziplock bag, reseal, and allow to sit until rice is fully rehydrated. Can be eaten directly out of the bag.

Caution: See the "Using This Book" section regarding the use of ziplock bags with hot water.

DAVE HICKS
"CHAINSAW"
DUBLIN, VIRGINIA

TOTAL WEIGHT: 1 POUND 4 OUNCES
Weight per serving: 5 ounces
Total servings: 4

Nutritional information per serving:

Calories:	521
Protein:	19 g
Carbohydrates:	93 g
Sodium:	680 mg
Fiber:	9 g
Fat:	13 g
Cholesterol:	0 mg

Peaks of Dolomiti Rice and Beans

"I often crave spaghetti on the trail, and the Italian flavor of this recipe helps satisfy that desire! We prepare our own dried beans by cooking them, rinsing them with cool water, and spreading them onto dehydrator trays. I dry the beans on low heat (115°F) for 8 to 12 hours. They split and curl as they dry. I store them in large Tupperware bins until I am ready to prepare recipes. They rehydrate very readily in boiling water. Onion flakes and dried vegetable flakes can be run through a food processor before packing to make the pieces smaller. They will rehydrate more rapidly and thoroughly as a result."

AT HOME:

1/3 cup beans, cooked and dried
1/2 cup Uncle Ben's Instant Brown Rice
1/4 cup minced textured vegetable protein
2 tablespoons minced dried vegetable flakes
1 teaspoon Italian seasoning
1 teaspoon minced onion flakes
1 teaspoon Mrs. Dash Garlic and Herb Seasoning
3 tablespoons Knorr Tomato with Basil Soup Mix

Mix all dry ingredients together in a quart-size ziplock bag.

ON THE TRAIL:

2 cups water

To make 1 serving, bring 2 cups of water to a boil, add contents from the ziplock bag, stir well, then cover. Remove from heat and let stand for 20 minutes before serving.

MARION DAVISON
"LLAMALADY"
APPLE VALLEY, CALIFORNIA

Weight per serving: 5 ounces
Total servings: 1

Nutritional information per serving:

Calories:	596
Protein:	31 g
Carbohydrates:	85 g
Sodium:	990 mg
Fiber:	11 g
Fat:	5 g
Cholesterol:	0 mg

Leahi Trail Rice

AT HOME:

3/4 cup Uncle Ben's Instant Brown Rice
1/4 cup chopped walnuts
1/4 cup dried cranberries
1/2 Rapunzel Vegan Vegetable Bouillon Cube with Sea Salt
1/4 teaspoon lemon pepper
1 clove garlic or 1/8 teaspoon garlic powder

Place dry ingredients and the garlic clove or garlic powder into a quart-size ziplock freezer bag.

ON THE TRAIL:

3/4 cups water

To prepare 1 serving, bring 3/4 cup of water to a boil. If using a garlic clove, cut into small pieces and toss back into the bag. Carefully pour the hot water into the bag and allow to stand 8 to 10 minutes, kneading occasionally to help ensure that all ingredients are evenly hydrated. Serve straight from the bag.

Caution: See the "Using This Book" section regarding the use of ziplock bags with hot water.

BRANDON STONE
"ULUHEMAN"
HONOLULU, HAWAII

Weight per serving: 6 ounces
Total servings: 1

Nutritional information per serving:

Calories:	562
Protein:	12 g
Carbohydrates:	77 g
Sodium:	1,096 mg
Fiber:	7 g
Fat:	5 g
Cholesterol:	0 mg

AUTHORS' NOTE:
Leahi is the Hawaiian name for Diamond Head, an extinct volcano on the island of Oahu.

Breads

Kentuckiana Logan Bread

"This recipe was given to me by the Kentuckiana Girl Scout Council."

PEGGY KINNETZ
"MAMA LLAMA"
LOUISVILLE, KENTUCKY

AT HOME:

- **6 cups whole wheat flour**
- **2/3 cup granulated sugar**
- **1/4 cup nonfat powdered milk**
- **1/2 teaspoon salt**
- **1 teaspoon baking powder**
- **1 cup chopped nuts**
- **2 cups water**
- **2/3 cup shortening, melted**
- **3/4 cup honey**
- **3/4 cup dark molasses**

Preheat oven to 300°F. Mix dry ingredients together. Add water, shortening, honey, and molasses. Divide mix evenly between 4 small loaf pans (5 5/8 x 3 x 2 inches) and bake for 1 hour. Cool the loaves before removing them from the pans. Next, dry the loaves in the oven for approximately 5 hours at very low heat with the oven door slightly ajar. Once the bread is very hard, it's ready for removal. Cool and cut each loaf into 4 slices.

MAKES 4 SMALL LOAVES (4 SLICES PER LOAF)
WEIGHT PER LOAF: 1 POUND
Weight per serving: 4 ounces
Total servings: 16 (1 slice per serving)

Nutritional information per serving:

Calories:	391
Protein:	7 g
Carbohydrates:	64 g
Sodium:	75 mg
Fiber:	5 g
Fat:	14 g
Cholesterol:	1 mg

AUTHORS' NOTE:

None of the bread recipes in our book produce a fluffy, yeast-raised loaf. Traditional breads can certainly be baked on the trail using a backpacking oven or wrapped in foil over coals. With care, slices of light and airy breads can even be dehydrated at home and then successfully resurrected on the trail with a light sprinkling of water. However, for the rigors of the trail, this book places a higher value on durability and storage life, and so you'll find breads that, once prepared, don't closely resemble bakery-bought loaves. Instead, these tend to be more dense and chewy. And, although there might at times seem to be a strong overlap between the backpacking bread and snack-bar categories, the bread recipes in our book typically have less added sugar and often more readily lend themselves to the use of condiments such as jellies and butter.

Hardtack

"Hardtack was used as a basic means of survival for many people during the early days of the United States. Hunters, explorers, and miners were all known to carry hardtack. During the Civil War, it was a basic ration issued by the U.S. government. Many Civil War soldiers disliked hardtack because it was, in fact, very hard. Sometimes referred to as "teeth-dullers," it often had to be broken with a rifle butt, rock, or blow of the fist. As a parody, a popular song of the 1850s, *Hard Times, Come Again No More,* was adapted and renamed by the soldiers as *Hard Crackers, Come Again No More.* Lines of the revamped song included: 'Many days have you lingered upon our stomachs sore, oh hard crackers come again no more.' Only when forced to eat horse feed because of lack of better rations did the troops later change their negative opinion toward hardtack, and they ended their parody with *Hard Crackers, Come Again Once More!* Soldiers sometimes softened their hardtack by soaking it in a wet cloth or coffee, frying it in grease, or adding it to their soup. They even discovered a way to make a nice pudding by pouring boiling water on it and adding a little molasses or honey."

AT HOME:

2 cups all-purpose bleached wheat flour

2 cups white whole wheat flour

1 teaspoon salt

2 tablespoons sugar

1 cup and 1 tablespoon water

Preheat oven to 300°F. Mix flour, salt, and sugar. Add water and knead mixture with your hands. Dough should be firm and pliable. Cut a sheet of parchment paper to fit your cookie sheet. Using a rolling pin, flatten dough on paper, making sure to leave adequate space on the sides so that it will fit on the cookie sheet. Dough should be about 1/4-inch thick. Cut into squares of about 3 inches by 3 inches. Score each square numerous times. Bake 1 1/2 to 2 hours. Once finished, the dough should be hard and the moisture completely gone.

AUTHORS' NOTE:

Despite its seemingly endless line of critics, hardtack remains one of the most pack-friendly trail breads you can prepare.

DAVE HICKS
"CHAINSAW"
DUBLIN, VIRGINIA

TOTAL WEIGHT: 1 POUND 8 OUNCES

Weight per serving: less than 1 ounce

Total servings: approximately 30 (1 square per serving)

Nutritional information per serving:

Calories:	56
Protein:	2 g
Carbohydrates:	12 g
Sodium:	79 mg
Fiber:	1 g
Fat:	1 g
Cholesterol:	0 mg

Oasis Fruit Bars

BARBARA HODGIN
"MULE 2"
SACRAMENTO, CALIFORNIA

TOTAL WEIGHT: 2 POUNDS
Weight per serving: 2 ounces
Total servings: 16 (1 bar per serving)

Nutritional information per serving:

Calories:	290
Protein:	4 g
Carbohydrates:	38 g
Sodium:	33 mg
Fiber:	8 g
Fat:	15 g
Cholesterol:	31 mg

AT HOME:

1 cup chopped dates
1 cup chopped figs, stems removed
1 cup raisins
1 1/3 cups walnuts
1 1/3 cups pecans
1 tablespoon all-purpose bleached wheat flour
1/2 cup brown sugar
2 tablespoons butter
2 eggs
2 teaspoons vanilla extract
1 teaspoon ground cardamom (an Indian spice)
1/2 cup all-purpose bleached wheat flour, sifted
1/2 teaspoon baking powder

Preheat oven to 325°F. In a bowl, mix together the dried fruit, nuts, and the tablespoon of flour. In a second bowl, cream the brown sugar with the butter. Add eggs, vanilla, and cardamom. Sift the 1/2 cup of flour along with the baking powder and add to the mixture in the second bowl. Combine fruit and nut mix from the first bowl with batter in the second. Line a 13 x 9-inch tray with parchment paper. Add mixture, making sure it's pressed firmly against the sides of the pan. Bake for 35 minutes. Cool, then cut into 16 bars.

Brooks Range Bannock

"Also referred to as trail bread, bush bread, or grease bread, the outdoor use of this basic biscuit dates back hundreds of years. The beauty of the recipe is its flexibility: It can be served as a bread, dumpling, or, with a little additional water, even as a pancake. The recipe can be varied by adding fruit, nuts, sugar, or powdered buttermilk; using different flours; or topping with honey."

AT HOME:

1/2 cup all-purpose bleached wheat flour
1 teaspoon baking powder
1/8 teaspoon salt
4 teaspoons vegetable shortening

Mix dry ingredients. Blend in shortening using a pastry cutter or fork. Mixture should have the consistency of coarse cornmeal. When finished, place into ziplock bag.

ON THE TRAIL:

1 tablespoon vegetable oil
1/4 cup water

Being careful not to use too much, add 1/4 cup water to mixture, adjusting the amount as required to make a soft dough. First cooking method: Flatten dough with the palm of your hand and fry in 1 tablespoon of vegetable oil, turning once. Second cooking method: Forgoing the oil, wrap dough around a stick and bake over a campfire.

Caution! If using the second cooking method, ensure that the branch you've selected does not come from a poisonous tree or shrub.

DAVE HICKS
"CHAINSAW"
DUBLIN, VIRGINIA

Weight per serving: 4 ounces
Total servings: 1

Nutritional information per serving:

Calories:	467
Protein:	6 g
Carbohydrates:	44 g
Sodium:	775 mg
Fiber:	1 g
Fat:	30 g
Cholesterol:	0 mg

Hopi Fry Bread

"Many years ago, I was a teacher on the Hopi Indian Reservation. The people taught me the art of cooking Indian fry bread as a staple food and a means of sustenance on a low budget. During those days, fry bread and pinto beans became my primary means of survival."

THERÉSE AND MICHAELA POLACCA
MOJAVE, CALIFORNIA

TOTAL WEIGHT: 8 OUNCES
Total servings: 1

Nutritional information per serving:

Calories:	648
Protein:	14 g
Carbohydrates:	90 g
Sodium:	902 mg
Fiber:	6 g
Fat:	29 g
Cholesterol:	0 mg

AT HOME:

1/2 cup all-purpose bleached wheat flour
1/2 cup white whole wheat flour
2 teaspoons baking powder
1/4 teaspoon garlic salt
2 teaspoons dried parsley

Place flours and baking powder into a quart-size ziplock bag. Seal and shake until mixed. Bread-topping options include chopped nuts, Parmesan cheese, or your favorite herbs and spices. Combine garlic salt, parsley, and any optional ingredients in a separate bag.

ON THE TRAIL:

1/2 cup water
2 tablespoons vegetable oil

To make 1 serving, slowly add 1/2 cup of warm water to the bag. Seal the bag, then knead the mixture. Remove the dough from the bag once the consistency thickens, then continue kneading until the mixture forms an elastic ball of dough. Elasticity will improve further if the dough is left in the open air for a brief period of time. Meanwhile, heat half of the oil (1 tablespoon) until sizzling hot. Split the ball of dough in two, take half, roll it and then knead it into a flat, waferlike tortilla approximately 1/2-inch thick. This can be done by repeatedly pinching the dough in circles in your hand or using a water bottle as a rolling pin. Once the dough has been thoroughly stretched, pinch a hole in the middle—like a flat doughnut. Place it carefully in the hot oil. Flip over once the sides begin to brown. Pour half of the contents of the bag of seasoning mix onto the fry bread. Repeat with the remainder of the dough.

Sacagawea Corn Bread

SUZANNE ALLEN
SEATTLE, WASHINGTON

TOTAL WEIGHT: 8 OUNCES
Total servings: 1

Nutritional information per serving:

Calories:	818
Protein:	19 g
Carbohydrates:	101 g
Sodium:	846 mg
Fiber:	4 g
Fat:	45 g
Cholesterol:	30 mg

AT HOME:

2/3 cup cornmeal
1/3 cup all-purpose bleached wheat flour
1/2 teaspoon baking powder
1/4 teaspoon baking soda
1 teaspoon sugar
1/8 teaspoon ground cumin
1 pinch red pepper powder
1/4 teaspoon chili powder
1 ounce cheddar cheese

Mix all dry ingredients well and store in a ziplock bag. Carry cheese separately.

ON THE TRAIL:

2 tablespoons vegetable oil
1/3 cup water

Cube 1 ounce of cheese into small pieces. Add 1 tablespoon of oil and 1/3 cup of water along with the cubed cheese to the mix in the ziplock bag and thoroughly knead until a very stiff dough forms. Note that if too much water is added, the corn bread will fall apart while cooking. Heat 1 tablespoon of vegetable oil on low flame in a nonstick pan and spread 1/2-inch-thick rounds of batter onto the cooking surface. Rounds can be of any manageable diameter. Continue to cook on low heat until the bottom of the bread is browned and the top begins to lose its shine. It is very important that the stove heat remains low; otherwise, the bread will burn. Flip the bread, flatten slightly, and continue cooking until the remaining side is browned.

AUTHORS' NOTE:

Sacagawea was the Shoshone Indian who helped guide the Lewis and Clark expedition from the northern Great Plains to the Pacific Ocean. Sacagawea not only led the way through her own country, but she also taught the men how to gather edible plants in addition to serving as a translator with other native tribes. No other woman in American history has had as many streams, lakes, landmarks, parks, songs, poems, or monuments named in her honor.

Poppy Field Bread

"When backpacking, I generally eat four pieces of bread each day, two in the late morning and the other two in the early afternoon. Using different bread recipes, I am able to bring variety to my camping meals."

FRED FIRMAN
"GREYBEARD"
COLUMBIA, MARYLAND

AT HOME:

2 cups whole wheat flour
2 cups all-purpose bleached flour
1 cup soy flour
1 tablespoon orange peel
1/2 teaspoon salt
1/2 teaspoon Nu-Salt
2 large eggs
2 (12.5-ounce) cans poppy seed filling
6 ounces frozen orange juice concentrate
1/2 cup honey
2 cups 1-percent milk

Preheat oven to 250°F. In a large bowl, mix all dry ingredients. In a separate bowl, beat eggs, then add the remainder of the wet ingredients and continue mixing. Now merge all ingredients and thoroughly combine. Pour batter into a greased 11x17x1-inch (jelly roll) pan and smooth to an even depth. Bake for 90 minutes, then remove from oven and poke with a fork to form vents. If the batter sticks to the fork, return the bread to the oven for an additional 30 minutes. When the fork comes out of the bread clean, it is ready. Cut the bread into 24 squares.

Separate the pieces and dry them in an oven or dehydrator for approximately 6 hours. The more moisture removed from the bread, the longer it will keep and the more durable it will become. During the drying process, occasionally sample the bread and stop before it becomes too tough to bite into.

Package the bread into 1-pint freezer bags, 4 pieces to a bag. Freeze until ready to use.

TOTAL WEIGHT: 2 POUNDS 12 OUNCES
Weight per serving: about 2 ounces
Total servings: 24 (1 square per serving)

Nutritional information per serving:

Calories:	340
Protein:	7 g
Carbohydrates:	50 g
Sodium:	88 mg
Fiber:	4 g
Fat:	6 g
Cholesterol:	19 mg

AUTHORS' NOTE:

Greybeard has developed a series of bread recipes that, in our experience, are exceptional. You'll find them all to be easy to prepare, very durable, full of flavor, and well balanced nutritionally. We've included six of them in our book because each represents a unique taste experience. For long trips, consider Greybeard's advice and bring along a varied selection.

Ginger Kick Bread

FRED FIRMAN
"GREYBEARD"
COLUMBIA, MARYLAND

TOTAL WEIGHT: 3 POUNDS 2 OUNCES
Weight per serving: about 2 ounces
Total servings: 24 (1 square per serving)

Nutritional information per serving:

Calories:	233
Protein:	7 g
Carbohydrates:	28 g
Sodium:	78 mg
Fiber:	4 g
Fat:	9 g
Cholesterol:	19 mg

AT HOME:

2 cups whole wheat flour
1 cup cornmeal
1 cup soy flour
1 cup rye flour
2/3 cup raisins
2/3 cup chopped walnuts
1/2 cup brown sugar
2 teaspoons ginger
2 teaspoons ground cinnamon
1/2 teaspoon ground nutmeg
1/2 teaspoon salt
1/2 teaspoon Nu-Salt
2 large eggs
1/2 cup canola oil
1 cup dark molasses
2 cups 1-percent milk

Preheat oven to 250°F. In a large bowl, mix all dry ingredients. In a separate bowl, beat eggs, then add the remainder of the wet ingredients and continue mixing. Now merge all ingredients and thoroughly combine. Pour batter into a greased 11x17x1-inch (jelly roll) pan and smooth to an even depth. Bake for 90 minutes, then remove from oven and poke with a fork to form vents. If the batter sticks to the fork, return the bread to the oven for an additional 30 minutes. When the fork comes out of the bread clean, it is ready. Cut the bread into 24 squares.

Separate the pieces and dry them in an oven or dehydrator for approximately 6 hours. The more moisture removed from the bread, the longer it will keep and the more durable it will become. During the drying process, occasionally sample the bread and stop before it becomes too tough to bite into.

Package the bread into 1-pint freezer bags, 4 pieces to a bag. Freeze until ready to use.

Altitude Bread

AT HOME:

- **3 cups whole wheat flour**
- **2 cups all-purpose bleached wheat flour**
- **1½ cups soy flour**
- **1 (8-ounce) can almond paste**
- **2 cups chopped dried apricots (about 20 pieces)**
- **1 cup chopped almonds**
- **¾ teaspoon salt**
- **¾ teaspoon Nu-Salt**
- **2 large eggs**
- **⅔ cup canola oil**
- **⅔ cup honey**
- **2½ cups 1-percent milk**
- **1 teaspoon vanilla extract**

Preheat oven to 250°F. In a large bowl, mix all dry ingredients. In a separate bowl, beat eggs, then add the remainder of the wet ingredients and continue mixing. Now merge all ingredients and thoroughly combine. Pour batter into a greased 11x17x1-inch (jelly roll) pan and smooth to an even depth. Bake for 90 minutes, then remove from oven and poke with a fork to form vents. If the batter sticks to the fork, return the bread to the oven for an additional 30 minutes. When the fork comes out of the bread clean, it is ready. Cut the bread into 24 squares.

Separate the pieces and dry them in an oven or dehydrator for approximately 6 hours. The more moisture removed from the bread, the longer it will keep and the more durable it will become. During the drying process, occasionally sample the bread and stop before it becomes too tough to bite into.

Package the bread into 1-pint freezer bags, 4 pieces to a bag. Freeze until ready to use.

FRED FIRMAN
"GREYBEARD"
COLUMBIA, MARYLAND

TOTAL WEIGHT: 4 POUNDS 9 OUNCES
Weight per serving: about 3 ounces
Total servings: 24 (1 square per serving)

Nutritional information per serving:

Calories:	329
Protein:	10 g
Carbohydrates:	47 g
Sodium:	133 mg
Fiber:	6 g
Fat:	13 g
Cholesterol:	19 mg

Greybeard's Apricot-Almond Bread

FRED FIRMAN
"GREYBEARD"
COLUMBIA, MARYLAND

TOTAL WEIGHT: 3 POUNDS 4 OUNCES
Weight per serving: about 2 ounces
Total servings: 24 (1 square per serving)

AT HOME:

2 cups whole wheat flour
2 cups all-purpose bleached wheat flour
1 cup soy flour
1 1/2 cups chopped dried apricots (about 15 pieces)
1 cup sliced almonds
1/2 teaspoon salt
1/2 teaspoon Nu-Salt
2 large eggs
1/2 cup canola oil
1/2 cup honey
2 cups 1-percent milk
1 teaspoon vanilla extract

Preheat oven to 250°F. In a large bowl, mix all dry ingredients. In a separate bowl, beat eggs, then add the remainder of the wet ingredients and continue mixing. Now merge all ingredients and thoroughly combine. Pour batter into a greased 11x17x1-inch (jelly roll) pan and smooth to an even depth. Bake for 90 minutes, then remove from oven and poke with a fork to form vents. If the batter sticks to the fork, return the bread to the oven for an additional 30 minutes. When the fork comes out of the bread clean, it is ready. Cut the bread into 24 squares.

Separate the pieces and dry them in an oven or dehydrator for approximately 6 hours. The more moisture removed from the bread, the longer it will keep and the more durable it will become. During the drying process, occasionally sample the bread and stop before it becomes too tough to bite into.

Package the bread into 1-pint freezer bags, 4 pieces to a bag. Freeze until ready to use.

Nutritional information per serving:

Calories:	219
Protein:	7 g
Carbohydrates:	29 g
Sodium:	64 mg
Fiber:	3 g
Fat:	9 g
Cholesterol:	19 mg

Dusty Roads Date-n-Walnut Bread

AT HOME:

- 2 cups whole wheat flour
- 2 cups oatmeal
- 1 cup soy flour
- 8 ounces chopped dates
- 1 1/2 cups chopped walnuts
- 1 cup brown sugar
- 2 teaspoons ground cinnamon
- 1/2 teaspoon salt
- 1/2 teaspoon Nu-Salt
- 2 large eggs
- 1/2 cup canola oil
- 2 cups 1-percent milk
- 2 teaspoons vanilla extract

Preheat oven to 250°F. In a large bowl, mix all dry ingredients. In a separate bowl, beat eggs, then add the remainder of the wet ingredients and continue mixing. Now merge all ingredients and thoroughly combine. Pour batter into a greased 11x17x1-inch (jelly roll) pan and smooth to an even depth. Bake for 90 minutes, then remove from oven and poke with a fork to form vents. If the batter sticks to the fork, return the bread to the oven for an additional 30 minutes. When the fork comes out of the bread clean, it is ready. Cut the bread into 24 squares.

Separate the pieces and dry them in an oven or dehydrator for approximately 6 hours. The more moisture removed from the bread, the longer it will keep and the more durable it will become. During the drying process, occasionally sample the bread and stop before it becomes too tough to bite into.

Package the bread into 1-pint freezer bags, 4 pieces to a bag. Freeze until ready to use.

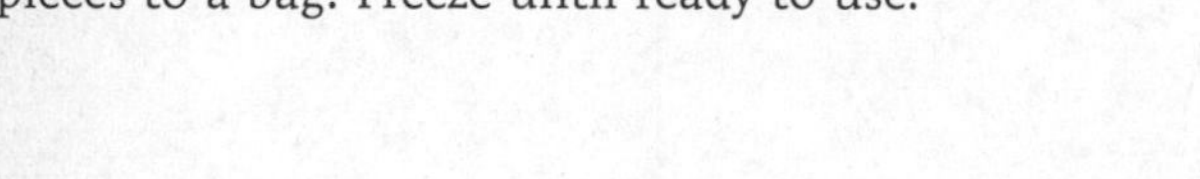

FRED FIRMAN
"GREYBEARD"
COLUMBIA, MARYLAND

TOTAL WEIGHT: 3 POUNDS 2 OUNCES

Weight per serving: about 2 ounces

Total servings: 24 (1 square per serving)

Nutritional information per serving:

Calories:	220
Protein:	7 g
Carbohydrates:	26 g
Sodium:	70 mg
Fiber:	3 g
Fat:	10 g
Cholesterol:	19 mg

Traveler's Tahini-Lemon Bread

AT HOME:

- 2 cups whole wheat flour
- 2 cups all-purpose bleached wheat flour
- 1 cup soy flour
- 1/2 teaspoon salt
- 1/2 teaspoon Nu-Salt
- 3 large eggs
- 1 large lemon, zest and juice
- 1 (8-ounce) can tahini
- 1/2 cup canola oil
- 1 1/2 cups honey
- 1 1/2 cups 1-percent milk
- 1 teaspoon vanilla extract

Preheat oven to 250°F. In a large bowl, mix all dry ingredients. In a separate bowl, beat eggs, then add the remainder of the wet ingredients and continue mixing. Now merge all ingredients and thoroughly combine. Pour batter into a greased 11x17x1-inch (jelly roll) pan and smooth to an even depth. Bake for 90 minutes, then remove from oven and poke with a fork to form vents. If the batter sticks to the fork, return the bread to the oven for an additional 30 minutes. When the fork comes out of the bread clean, it is ready. Cut the bread into 24 squares.

Separate the pieces and dry them in an oven or dehydrator for approximately 6 hours. The more moisture removed from the bread, the longer it will keep and the more durable it will become. During the drying process, occasionally sample the bread and stop before it becomes too tough to bite into.

Package the bread into 1-pint freezer bags, 4 pieces to a bag. Freeze until ready to use.

FRED FIRMAN
"GREYBEARD"
COLUMBIA, MARYLAND

TOTAL WEIGHT: 3 POUNDS 7 OUNCES
Weight per serving: about 2 ounces
Total servings: 24 (1 square per serving)

Nutritional information per serving:

Calories:	264
Protein:	7 g
Carbohydrates:	36 g
Sodium:	71 mg
Fiber:	3 g
Fat:	11 g
Cholesterol:	27 mg

Mama Llama's Fruit Bread

PEGGY KINNETZ
"MAMA LLAMA"
LOUISVILLE, KENTUCKY

MAKES 3 LOAVES (4 SLICES PER LOAF)
WEIGHT PER LOAF: 1 POUND
Weight per serving: 4 ounces
Total servings: 12 (1 slice per serving)

AT HOME:

1 cup granulated sugar
1 1/2 cups all-purpose bleached wheat flour
1 cup whole wheat flour
1 teaspoon baking soda
1 1/2 teaspoons cinnamon
1/4 teaspoon nutmeg
1 cup chopped walnuts
3/4 cup chopped dried apricots
3/4 cup raisins
1/2 cup date pieces
1/2 cup coconut
3/4 cup honey
1 cup boiling water

Preheat oven to 325°F. Excluding fruit, mix dry ingredients. Next add fruit and mix again. Stir in honey and boiling water, mixing well. Line 3 small (5 5/8 x 3 x 2 inches) loaf pans with parchment paper. Fill each two-thirds full with batter and bake for 45 minutes. Reduce temperature to 300°F, cover loosely with foil, then bake for an additional 30 minutes. Cool and cut each loaf into 4 slices. Store in refrigerator or freezer.

Nutritional information per serving:

Calories:	375
Protein:	6 g
Carbohydrates:	77 g
Sodium:	122 mg
Fiber:	3 g
Fat:	7 g
Cholesterol:	0 mg

Snacks and Desserts

Fabulous Fry Brownies

SUZANNE ALLEN
SEATTLE, WASHINGTON

TOTAL WEIGHT: 1 POUND 2 OUNCES
Weight per serving: 3 ounces
Total servings: 6

Nutritional information per serving:

Calories:	336
Protein:	5 g
Carbohydrates:	49 g
Sodium:	173 mg
Fiber:	2 g
Fat:	19 g
Cholesterol:	0 mg

AT HOME:

- **1 cup all-purpose bleached wheat flour**
- **1/4 cup unsweetened baking cocoa**
- **3/4 cup sugar**
- **1 teaspoon baking powder**
- **1/4 teaspoon salt**
- **2 tablespoons nonfat powdered milk**
- **1/2 cup mini chocolate chips**
- **1/4 cup walnuts**

In a bowl, combine flour, cocoa, sugar, baking powder, salt, and powdered milk. Thoroughly mix, then add chocolate chips and nuts and mix again. Place 1/2 cup of mixture into each of 6 ziplock quart-size freezer bags.

ON THE TRAIL:

- **2 teaspoons vegetable oil per serving**
- **2 tablespoons water per serving**

To make 1 serving, heat 1 teaspoon of oil in a pan at low heat. Add a second teaspoon of oil and 2 tablespoons of water to 1 bag of brownie mix. Knead the mixture in the bag. Once the pan is hot, scoop small, spoon-size mounds into the pan or cut a corner from the bag and squeeze out small brownie batter blobs. Cook until the bottoms are browned and the tops are no longer shiny. Flip, flatten, and brown the other sides.

Carob chips can be substituted for the chocolate chips.

Chocolate Chip Fry Cookies

SUZANNE ALLEN
SEATTLE, WASHINGTON

TOTAL WEIGHT: 12 OUNCES
Weight per serving: 3 ounces
Total servings: 4

Nutritional information per serving:

Calories:	380
Protein:	6 g
Carbohydrates:	53 g
Sodium:	248 mg
Fiber:	2 g
Fat:	18 g
Cholesterol:	0 mg

AT HOME:

1 cup all-purpose bleached wheat flour
1/4 cup sugar
1 teaspoon baking powder
1/4 teaspoon salt
1/2 cup mini chocolate chips
1/4 cup walnuts
Optional: 1/4 teaspoon cinnamon, cloves, or nutmeg

In a bowl, combine flour, sugar, baking powder, salt, and any optional spices. Thoroughly mix, then add chocolate chips and nuts and mix again. Place 1/2 cup of mix into each of 4 ziplock quart-size freezer bags.

ON THE TRAIL:

1 teaspoon vegetable oil per serving
2 tablespoons water per serving

To make 1 serving, heat 1 teaspoon of oil in a pan at low heat. Add 2 tablespoons of water to 1 bag of cookie mix. Knead the mixture in the bag. Once the pan is hot, scoop small, spoon-size mounds into the pan or cut a corner from the bag and squeeze out small cookie batter blobs. Cook until the bottoms are browned and the tops are no longer shiny. Flip, flatten, and brown the other sides.

Whole wheat flour substitutes well for all-purpose flour in this recipe.

Firehouse Apples

"I obtained this recipe from a fire victim at an annual gathering of burn survivors. Our meeting was at the Firefighter's Museum in Oklahoma City, where I was employed as a social worker for the group."

PHIL HEFFINGTON
"SCODWOD"
EDMOND, OKLAHOMA

AT HOME:

2⁄3 cup cinnamon imperials ("red hots")
6 medium apples
3 cups hot water

Dissolve cinnamon imperials in hot water. Peel, core, and thinly slice the apples. Soak the apples in the cinnamon solution for 5 to 10 minutes. Dehydrate the apples. Hide them from the kids or you won't have any for the trail!

TOTAL WEIGHT: 4 OUNCES
Weight per serving: 2 ounces
Total servings: 2

Nutritional information per serving:

Calories:	219
Protein:	1 g
Carbohydrates:	57 g
Sodium:	0 mg
Fiber:	7 g
Fat:	1 g
Cholesterol:	0 mg

Algonquin Apple Leather

AT HOME:

1 pound apples
1 lemon, juiced
2 tablespoons sugar
1/4 teaspoon cinnamon

Remove apple cores. Puree the lemon juice together with the apples. (The lemon juice is added to delay browning of the leather.) Blend in the sugar and cinnamon. Spread mixture evenly on one parchment-lined dryer tray. The mixture should be about 1/8-inch thick. Try to make the center of the puree "pool" a little thinner so that it will dry more evenly. Dehydrate. The leather is ready when the edges are no longer sticky to the touch.

LAURIE ANN MARCH
GUELPH, ONTARIO, CANADA

Weight per serving: 2 ounces
Total servings: 1

Nutritional information per serving:

Calories:	340
Protein:	1 g
Carbohydrates:	89 g
Sodium:	3 mg
Fiber:	11 g
Fat:	2 g
Cholesterol:	0 mg

Point Pelee Peach Leather

LAURIE ANN MARCH
GUELPH, ONTARIO, CANADA

Weight per serving: 1 ounce
Total servings: 1

Nutritional information per serving:

Calories:	185
Protein:	3 g
Carbohydrates:	49 g
Sodium:	0 mg
Fiber:	7 g
Fat:	1 g
Cholesterol:	0 mg

AT HOME:

5 fresh peaches

Peel fruit and cut into small pieces. Place into a pot of water. Bring the water to a brief boil. Remove the fruit, making sure that it is well drained. Puree, then spread the mixture evenly onto a parchment-lined dehydrator tray. The mixture should be about 1/8-inch thick. Try to make the center of the puree "pool" a little thinner so that it will dry more evenly. Dehydrate. The leather is ready when the edges are no longer sticky to the touch.

Nectarine, plum, or pear leather can be made using the same method.

Wild Berry Fruit Leather

AT HOME:

2 pounds fresh strawberries

Puree the berries in a blender. If you would like to remove the seeds, strain the puree through a cheesecloth. Spread mixture evenly onto 2 sheets of parchment-lined dehydrator trays. The mixture should be about 1/8-inch thick. Try to make the center of each puree "pool" a little thinner so that it will dry more evenly. Dehydrate. The leather is ready when the edges are no longer sticky to the touch. Each tray will make 1 serving.

You can also make leather from your favorite combination of blueberries, loganberries, boysenberries, and pitted cherries using the same method.

LAURIE ANN MARCH
GUELPH, ONTARIO, CANADA

TOTAL WEIGHT: 4 OUNCES
Weight per serving: 2 ounces
Total servings: 2

Nutritional information per serving:

Calories:	130
Protein:	3 g
Carbohydrates:	30 g
Sodium:	5 mg
Fiber:	11 g
Fat:	2 g
Cholesterol:	0 mg

Applesauce Leather

LAURIE ANN MARCH
GUELPH, ONTARIO, CANADA

AT HOME:

1 (24-ounce) jar applesauce

Spread mixture evenly onto 2 sheets of parchment-lined dehydrator trays. The mixture should be about 1/8-inch thick. Try to make the center of each puree "pool" a little thinner so that it will dry more evenly. Dehydrate. The leather is ready when the edges are no longer sticky to the touch. Each tray will make 1 serving.

TOTAL WEIGHT: 4 OUNCES
Weight per serving: 2 ounces
Total servings: 2

Nutritional information per serving:

Calories:	288
Protein:	0 g
Carbohydrates:	66 g
Sodium:	0 mg
Fiber:	3 g
Fat:	0 g
Cholesterol:	0 mg

Mountain Mango Leather

LAURIE ANN MARCH
GUELPH, ONTARIO, CANADA

AT HOME:

5 large mangos, very ripe
1 lime

Peel and core the mangos then puree along with the juice of 1 lime. Spread mixture evenly onto 2 parchment-lined dehydrator trays. The mixture should be about 1/8-inch thick. Try to make the center of the puree "pool" a little thinner so that it will dry more evenly. Dehydrate. The leather is ready when the edges are no longer sticky to the touch. Divide the leather from each tray into 2 separate servings each.

TOTAL WEIGHT: 4 OUNCES
Weight per serving: 1 ounce
Total servings: 4

Nutritional information per serving:

Calories:	174
Protein:	2 g
Carbohydrates:	46 g
Sodium:	5 mg
Fiber:	5 g
Fat:	<1 g
Cholesterol:	0 mg

Green Mountain Grasshopper

"Adapted from a recipe that I presented in the *Geneseean,* the newsletter of the Genesee Valley Chapter of the Adirondack Mountain Club."

KEN HARBISON
ROCHESTER, NEW YORK

AT HOME:

1 (3.4-ounce) package pistachio-flavored instant pudding mix
3/4 cup nonfat powdered dry milk
9 Oreo cookies, broken in pieces (or 1 cup of Mini Oreo cookies)
6 teaspoons crème de menthe liquor

Into each of 3 separate quart-size freezer bags place 3 tablespoons of pudding and 1/4 cup milk. Carry cookies and crème de menthe separately. (The small "personal-size" plastic bottles, as used on airplanes, are ideal for carrying liquor on the trail.)

ON THE TRAIL:

1/2 cup cold water per serving

To make 1 serving, add 1/2 cup cold water to 1 bag of pudding mixture. Shake vigorously for 1 to 2 minutes. Allow to set for at least 5 minutes. Impress your friends by artistically topping your pudding with 3 broken Oreo cookies and 2 teaspoons of crème de menthe. (If you are feeling generous, let them lick the bag.)

For a nonalcoholic version, use crushed mint candies or substitute Mint 'n Creme Oreo cookies.

TOTAL WEIGHT: 11 OUNCES
Weight per serving: about 4 ounces
Total servings: 3

Nutritional information per serving:

Calories:	450
Protein:	8 g
Carbohydrates:	70 g
Sodium:	760 mg
Fiber:	2 g
Fat:	11 g
Cholesterol:	6 mg

AUTHORS' NOTE:
It is important to use cool water with recipes requiring thickened instant pudding mix. If the water is warm, the mix may not congeal properly.

Whitewater Moon Pie

"Miami-Whitewater Park is a beautiful hardwood forest enclave west of Cincinnati. There are several excellent day-use trails in Miami-Whitewater that make up for in geographical and flora quality what they lack in length. During our time in Ohio, when the kids were very young, we repeatedly hoofed those trails near our home. It was here that James, Michael, and Maria gained their walking legs as toddlers and learned to click off distances measured in miles, not yards. No, it isn't the John Muir Wilderness, but because of the foresight of those who set aside this wonderful parcel of land in order to protect it from urban sprawl, our kids were able to learn at a very young age to love the outdoors too."

CHRISTINE AND TIM CONNERS
SAVANNAH, GEORGIA

TOTAL WEIGHT: 13 OUNCES
Weight per serving: about 7 ounces
Total servings: 2

AT HOME:

2⁄3 cup nonfat powdered milk
1 (3.5-ounce) package Jell-O Instant Vanilla Pudding
1 cup shredded sweetened coconut
20 vanilla wafers

In a bowl, mix powdered milk, pudding mix, and coconut together. Divide the mixture evenly between 2 ziplock quart-size freezer bags. Next, place 10 vanilla wafers into each of 2 separate plastic bags and crush. At this point you should have a total of 4 bags equaling 2 servings.

ON THE TRAIL:

1 cup water per serving

To make 1 serving, add 1 cup of cold water to 1 bag of the pudding mix and shake vigorously until the mixture thickens. This may take a couple of minutes. Next add 1 serving of wafer mix to the bag and knead. Serve straight from the bag.

Nutritional information per serving:

Calories:	740
Protein:	13 g
Carbohydrates:	113 g
Sodium:	1,290 mg
Fiber:	4 g
Fat:	27 g
Cholesterol:	0 mg

Chocolate Raspberry Indulgence

"This recipe recommends the use of a 'heat disperser' on those stoves that tend to scorch foods while cooking. We made our own lightweight version from the top of a large (3-pound) can of coffee. We removed the top using a smooth-edge can opener, one that cut just below the rim, leaving a safe, nonjagged edge."

KEN HARBISON
ROCHESTER, NEW YORK

AT HOME:

1 (3.5-ounce) package of Jell-O cook-and-serve chocolate pudding mix
2/3 cup nonfat powdered milk
1 ounce Just Raspberries–brand dried raspberries

Each item can be carried separately, or the pudding mix and the powdered milk can be combined in a quart-size ziplock freezer bag and the dried raspberries carried separately.

ON THE TRAIL:

2 cups water

To make 2 servings, combine 2 cups of water with the powdered milk and pudding mix in a pot. Heat until the mixture comes to a full boil, stirring constantly. It is helpful to use a heat disperser between the pot and some stoves to minimize scorching.

Divide the raspberries between 2 bowls, cups, or ziplock bags. Pour the cooked chocolate pudding over the raspberries. Serve warm or cold. If not eaten immediately, cover or close the bag to prevent a crust from forming.

TOTAL WEIGHT: 14 OUNCES
Weight per serving: about 7 ounces
Total servings: 2

Nutritional information per serving:

Calories:	310
Protein:	11 g
Carbohydrates:	68 g
Sodium:	405 mg
Fiber:	5 g
Fat:	2 g
Cholesterol:	4 mg

Dirty Socks Peach Cobbler

"Okay, so it may look a little like dirty hiking socks once it's finished cooking, but it sure tastes great!"

CHRISTINE AND TIM CONNERS
SAVANNAH, GEORGIA

TOTAL WEIGHT: 9 OUNCES
Weight per serving: about 4 ounces
Total servings: 2

Nutritional information per serving:

Calories:	496
Protein:	3 g
Carbohydrates:	113 g
Sodium:	396 mg
Fiber:	2 g
Fat:	5 g
Cholesterol:	0 mg

AT HOME:

1 (15-ounce) can sliced peaches in heavy syrup (or 2 ounces dried peaches)
1/2 cup Bisquick
1/4 cup white granulated sugar
1/4 cup brown sugar
1/4 teaspoon cinnamon

Drain peaches and cut into thin slices. Dry on a parchment-lined dehydrator tray, then place in a sandwich-size ziplock bag. In a quart-size ziplock bag, place the remainder of the dried ingredients and shake until mixed.

ON THE TRAIL:

1/2 cup water

To prepare 2 servings, pour 1/4 cup of water and the peaches into a nonstick cook pan. If not using a nonstick pan, spread a little butter or oil within the pan to prevent sticking. Bring to a boil, then reduce heat. Add 1/4 cup of water to the bag containing the Bisquick mix and knead. Cut a corner from the bottom of the bag and squeeze the mixture onto the peaches. Continue to scramble the mixture in the pan until the batter is fully cooked.

Skidaway Banana Puddin'

"The Skidaway is a beautiful intracoastal estuary river near our home in Savannah. It isn't uncommon to see dolphins maneuvering the waterway in the mornings and evenings alongside the sailboats. Lined by marshy wire grass and huge Spanish moss–covered live oak, the Skidaway has been suggesting rather strongly lately that we consider canoeing as a family sport. It's becoming increasingly obvious that we should probably pay attention to what it's saying."

AT HOME:

2/3 cup nonfat powdered milk
1 (3.5-ounce) package banana cream instant pudding
20 vanilla wafers
1 cup banana chips

In a bowl, combine powdered milk with banana cream pudding mix. Divide the mixture evenly into each of 2 ziplock quart-size bags. Next, crush the vanilla wafers and banana chips into pieces, combine, and again divide evenly into each of 2 separate ziplock bags. At this point, you should have a total of 4 bags equivalent to 2 servings.

ON THE TRAIL:

1 cup water per serving

To produce 1 serving, add 1 cup of cold filtered water to 1 bag of the pudding-milk mix. Shake vigorously for about 1 minute. The pudding will thicken within a couple of minutes. At this point, add the wafer-banana mix to the pudding bag and knead. Can be served straight from the bag.

CHRISTINE AND TIM CONNERS
SAVANNAH, GEORGIA

TOTAL WEIGHT: 12 OUNCES
Weight per serving: 6 ounces
Total servings: 2

Nutritional information per serving:

Calories:	708
Protein:	17 g
Carbohydrates:	105 g
Sodium:	1,051 mg
Fiber:	0 g
Fat:	15 g
Cholesterol:	6 mg

Wendjidu Zinzibahkwud

"Maple sugar was the basic seasoning for the Anishnabeg people and used with grains, breads, berries, stews, teas, and vegetables. So important was the making of this sugar that the several weeks of spring, during which the maple syrup was boiled down, were referred to as the 'moon month of boiling.' In summer they dissolved the syrup in water to make a cooling drink. In the winter it was added to various leaf, root, and bark teas. This recipe can be used as a seasoning or eaten like a candy. At room temperature, it has the consistency of a Sugar Daddy candy bar."

AT HOME:

2 cups 100 percent pure maple syrup

Place a muffin pan into the freezer and allow to chill. Bring syrup to a boil. Stir constantly and watch to make sure that it doesn't boil over. The syrup will eventually take on a milky appearance, indicating that it is almost ready to set.

Continue to boil until the syrup reaches 236°F, measured using a candy thermometer, or, alternately, until the syrup reaches the "hardball" stage. The "hardball" method requires placing a tiny drop of syrup into a glass of cold water. If the syrup solidifies into a little hard ball, it is ready to remove from the heat. If it dissipates into the water, continue stirring until it eventually makes a solid ball. Once ready, pour into 6 individual muffin pan cups. (For smaller pieces, use a mini muffin pan or pour smaller amounts into more cups.) Return pan to the freezer and allow to chill for about 30 minutes. Remove candy and wrap in parchment paper for the trail.

:: A double boiler is useful for helping to prevent the syrup from overheating.

LAURIE ANN MARCH
GUELPH, ONTARIO, CANADA

TOTAL WEIGHT: 12 OUNCES
Weight per serving: 2 ounces
Total servings: 6

Nutritional information per serving:

Calories:	267
Protein:	0 g
Carbohydrates:	71 g
Sodium:	1 mg
Fiber:	0 g
Fat:	0 g
Cholesterol:	0 mg

Blueberry Nian-Gao Rice Cake

"This recipe produces rice cakes, but don't expect them to resemble the bland, very-low-calorie versions found at the grocery store. The cakes from this recipe are a dense, durable, sweet-tasting treat!"

CHRISTINE AND TIM CONNERS
SAVANNAH, GEORGIA

AT HOME:

3 cups sweet rice flour
1 1/4 cups sugar
1 1/3 cups dried blueberries
3 eggs
3/4 cup canola oil
1 1/2 cups water

Preheat oven to 375°F. In a large bowl, combine all the dry ingredients. In a separate bowl, beat the eggs, then add the canola oil and water. Next, combine the dry ingredients with the wet and mix again. Pour into 24 greased muffin holes. Bake for 30 minutes or until golden brown. A knife poked into the middle should come out clean.

TOTAL WEIGHT: 3 POUNDS
Weight per serving: 2 ounces
Total servings: 24 (1 cake per serving)

Nutritional information per serving:

Calories:	214
Protein:	2 g
Carbohydrates:	34 g
Sodium:	12 mg
Fiber:	1 g
Fat:	8 g
Cholesterol:	27 mg

:: Sweet rice flour can be found in Oriental food stores.

hi sugar

Half Domes

"I was given this recipe long ago by a nurse named Claire. I've made some changes to it over the years. I like it with chocolate chips and dried cranberries. I put these in care packages to my hiking friends when they are on a long-distance trip."

AT HOME:

1 cup butter

1 cup brown sugar

1 cup white granulated sugar

1 teaspoon vanilla

2 eggs

2 cups all-purpose bleached wheat flour, sifted

2¼ cups Quaker Old Fashioned Oats

1 teaspoon baking powder

1 teaspoon salt

1 cup semisweet chocolate chips

½ cup chopped walnuts

½ cup dried cranberries

Preheat oven to 375°F. Beat the butter and sugars together until light and fluffy. Add the vanilla and eggs and beat further until completely combined. Mix the dry ingredients together, then add to the butter mixture. Stir in the chips, nuts, and fruit. Drop on baking sheets by the large teaspoonful. Bake for 10 to 12 minutes. The cookies should be thoroughly cooked, but slightly chewy when cooled.

BETH MURDOCK
PORTLAND, OREGON

TOTAL WEIGHT: 2 POUNDS 12 OUNCES
Weight per serving: less than 1 ounce
Total servings: 72 (1 dome per serving)

Nutritional information per serving:

Calories:	82
Protein:	1 g
Carbohydrates:	10 g
Sodium:	60 mg
Fiber:	1 g
Fat:	4 g
Cholesterol:	13 mg

Drinks

Switchback Smoothie

"Over the years, we have recommended fruit shakes and smoothies to friends and relatives who were suffering from serious health problems. We found that a cold fruit smoothie typically appealed to the appetite when nothing else would, and regular servings were instrumental in helping these folks regain their weight and health. They are obviously packed with good things for your body, and they really do taste fantastic. If you are new to smoothies, be advised that they are addicting! If you are already a fan, you may have thought that this was one category of food that you had to leave at home when you hit the trail. Well, there is good news. We discovered that with a blender and a dehydrator, you already have all the kitchen tools you need to make a durable, portable, and great-tasting version of this wonderful drink. Carry extra to help you up those final switchbacks!"

CHRISTINE AND TIM CONNERS
SAVANNAH, GEORGIA

AT HOME:

1 (16-ounce) bag frozen blueberries
1 (16-ounce) bag frozen fruit blend (such as strawberries, mango, pineapple)
2 bananas
2 cups almond milk
1/2 cup honey
2 tablespoons lemon juice

Allow frozen fruit to thaw slightly to take some of the burden off your blender. Add all ingredients together in the blender container. Puree, then spread 1 cup of mixture evenly over each of 7 parchment-lined dehydrator trays. Dry, rotating the trays periodically to improve evenness of drying. The mixture is ready once it becomes leathery. Remove the leather from the parchment paper. There is enough fruit mixture to make 7 servings. Store each serving in a separate ziplock bag.

ON THE TRAIL:

1 cup water per serving

Tear 1 serving of leather into very small pieces and place in a widemouthed bottle containing 1 cup of cold water. Allow mixture to dissolve for about 30 minutes, periodically shaking vigorously to help speed the process.

TOTAL WEIGHT: 14 OUNCES
Weight per serving: 2 ounces
Total servings: 7

Nutritional information per serving:

Calories:	231
Protein:	2 g
Carbohydrates:	59 g
Sodium:	33 mg
Fiber:	3 g
Fat:	1 g
Cholesterol:	0 mg

AUTHORS' NOTE:
The fruit leather itself is also very tasty and can be eaten as is.

Grooovy Smoothie

AT HOME:

1 (3.4-ounce) package Jell-O Vanilla Instant Pudding

1/2 cup orange drink powder

1/2 cup Better Than Milk Soy Drink powder

Combine all the ingredients in a quart-size ziplock bag.

ON THE TRAIL:

1 cup cold water per serving

Add 3 tablespoons of drink mix to 1 cup cold water. Stir or shake.

RICHARD HALBERT
"RANGER RICK"
TRAVERSE CITY, MICHIGAN

TOTAL WEIGHT: 9 OUNCES
Weight per serving: about 1 ounce
Total servings: 8

Nutritional information per serving:

Calories:	133
Protein:	1 g
Carbohydrates:	30 g
Sodium:	300 mg
Fiber:	0 g
Fat:	1 g
Cholesterol:	0 mg

Earth Smoothie

"I fell asleep after dinner on the beach while backpacking in Hawaii. When I woke up, I saw a huge comet, with its tail filling nearly the whole sky."

JASON RUMOHR
SEATTLE, WASHINGTON

AT HOME:

1 1/2 ounces dried raspberries

4 tablespoons Dr. Schulze's SuperFood drink mix

2 tablespoons rice protein powder

2 tablespoons ground flaxseed

Crush dried raspberries in a plastic bag. Into each of 2 small ziplock bags place 2 heaping tablespoons of crushed raspberries, 2 heaping tablespoons of Super-Food, 1 heaping tablespoon of rice protein powder, and 1 heaping tablespoon of flaxseed. Seal bags for trail use.

ON THE TRAIL:

2 cups water per serving

To make a single serving, add mixture from a single bag to a widemouthed water bottle. Add 2 cups of water and shake vigorously until well mixed.

TOTAL WEIGHT: 6 OUNCES
Weight per serving: 3 ounces
Total servings: 2

Nutritional information per serving:

Calories:	169
Protein:	20 g
Carbohydrates:	17 g
Sodium:	39 mg
Fiber:	6 g
Fat:	5 g
Cholesterol:	0 mg

AUTHORS' NOTE:

SuperFood is a very nutritious natural drink mix that includes, in its long list of ingredients, spirulina, algae, seaweed, chlorella, barley, wheat grass, alfalfa, and spinach leaf. SuperFood can be ordered by calling (800) 437-2362. It has a pronounced seaweed flavor, which for some can be an acquired taste. If this is true for you, any type of drink mix made from greens, such as barley grass, may be substituted. Also, any vegetable-based protein powder can be substituted for the rice powder as well.

Hurricane Hill Hot Chocolate

AT HOME:

1 cup pure unsweetened cocoa powder

1 cup granulated sugar

3 cups nonfat powdered milk

Optional: pinch of salt

Combine all ingredients together. Partition into individual servings at home, or bring in bulk to divide on the trail. Note that health-food stores typically carry pure, unsweetened cocoa powder.

ON THE TRAIL:

1 cup water per serving

For 1 serving, bring 1 cup of water to a boil. Place 1/3 cup of mixture into your mug. Add boiling water and stir well.

RAMONA HAMMERLY
ANACORTES, WASHINGTON

TOTAL WEIGHT: 12 OUNCES
Weight per serving: less than 1 ounce
Total servings: 15

Nutritional information per serving:

Calories:	115
Protein:	6 g
Carbohydrates:	25 g
Sodium:	82 mg
Fiber:	0 g
Fat:	1 g
Cholesterol:	3 mg

AUTHORS' NOTE:
Here's a recipe for "homemade" hot chocolate at its best.

Inka and Pero are instant grain beverages that contain roasted barley, rye, chicory, and beet root. They make for a nice drink in cold weather. There are many sorts of tea, both traditional and herbal. The most interesting I've had is red mellow bush, or rooibus, from southern Africa. It has a powerful taste, and one bag makes several cups.

RAMONA HAMMERLY
ANACORTES, WASHINGTON

Moo-Less Hot Chocolate

AT HOME:

1 cup pure unsweetened cocoa powder
1 cup granulated sugar
1½ cups Better Than Milk Soy Drink powder

Combine all ingredients together. Partition into individual servings at home, or bring in bulk to divide on the trail. Note that health-food stores typically carry pure, unsweetened cocoa powder.

ON THE TRAIL:

1 cup water per serving

For 1 serving, bring 1 cup of water to a boil. Place ¼ cup of mixture into your mug. Add boiling water and stir well.

RAMONA HAMMERLY
ANACORTES, WASHINGTON

TOTAL WEIGHT: 8 OUNCES
Weight per serving: less than 1 ounce
Total servings: 14

Nutritional information per serving:

Calories:	101
Protein:	1 g
Carbohydrates:	23 g
Sodium:	36 mg
Fiber:	0 g
Fat:	1 g
Cholesterol:	0 mg

AUTHORS' NOTE:

This is a vegan version of Ramona's dairy-based hot chocolate milk recipe. By substituting the powdered dairy milk with the soy-based drink mix, you'll end up with an excellent-tasting alternative. Note that the amount of dry powder mix used per serving in this recipe is less than in the dairy-based version.

White Bear Mocha

"The Tsimshian Native Americans believed the raven descended from the heavens to an earthly world of white. He used his spiritual powers to turn the land green. As a reminder of the precious gift from the spirits and the harsh climate that once was, the raven made some of the bears white. First Nations people believe that this bear is very sacred and the Tsimshian call him *moskgm'ol,* meaning 'white bear.' This drink is named for this special albino bear."

LAURIE ANN MARCH
GUELPH, ONTARIO, CANADA

AT HOME:

1/3 cup instant hot cocoa mix
3/4 cup Nestlé Nido or whole powdered milk
1/2 cup granulated sugar
1/2 cup instant coffee crystals

Place ingredients into a quart-size ziplock bag and shake.

ON THE TRAIL:

1 cup water per serving

Boil 1 cup of water and pour into your mug. Add 2 tablespoons of White Bear Mocha mixture and stir.

TOTAL WEIGHT: 10 OUNCES
Weight per serving: less than 1 ounce
Total servings: 16

Nutritional information per serving:

Calories:	55
Protein:	1 g
Carbohydrates:	9 g
Sodium:	26 mg
Fiber:	0 g
Fat:	2 g
Cholesterol:	4 mg

AUTHORS' NOTE:
Due to its lower acid content, Kava is less bitter than many other instant coffees and makes for a smoother tasting drink. We recommend it for recipes calling for instant coffee.

Lightning Coffee

"This recipe is sure to zap the ice off your tent in the morning!"

AT HOME:

- **20 hard peppermint candies**
- **1/2 cup Kava instant coffee**
- **1/2 cup Carnation Malted Milk powder**

Place the 20 candies in a ziplock bag. After sealing the bag, gently hammer the candies into small chips. Add the candy chips, coffee powder, and malted milk powder to a new quart-size ziplock freezer bag for the trail.

ON THE TRAIL:

- **1 cup water per serving**

Boil 1 cup of water and pour into your mug. Add 3 tablespoons of Lightning Coffee mixture and stir.

CHRISTINE AND TIM CONNERS
SAVANNAH, GEORGIA

TOTAL WEIGHT: 6 OUNCES
Weight per serving: 1 ounce
Total servings: 6

Nutritional information per serving:

Calories:	213
Protein:	3 g
Carbohydrates:	47 g
Sodium:	49 mg
Fiber:	0 g
Fat:	1 g
Cholesterol:	2 mg

Alaskan Winter Coffee

AT HOME:

1/2 cup pure unsweetened cocoa powder
1/2 cup Coffee Mate, powdered original flavor
1/2 cup Kava instant coffee
1/2 cup granulated sugar
1/4 teaspoon nutmeg
1 teaspoon cinnamon

Place all dry ingredients into a quart-size ziplock bag and shake well.

ON THE TRAIL:

1 cup water per serving

Boil 1 cup of water and pour into your mug. Add 3 tablespoons of Alaskan Winter Coffee mixture and stir.

CHRISTINE AND TIM CONNERS
SAVANNAH, GEORGIA

TOTAL WEIGHT: 10 OUNCES
Weight per serving: 1 ounce
Total servings: 10

Nutritional information per serving:

Calories:	91
Protein:	1 g
Carbohydrates:	17 g
Sodium:	25 mg
Fiber:	0 g
Fat:	2 g
Cholesterol:	0 mg

To make vanilla coffee, split open 1 or more vanilla beans. Place them in an airtight container along with your coffee. After a few days, your coffee will pick up the slight hint of vanilla flavor. Throw out the beans before you make the coffee.

LAURIE ANN MARCH
GUELPH, ONTARIO, CANADA

Cloudy Mountain Latte

"This recipe was born from my love of decent trail coffee as well as an aversion to cooking when I solo-hike. It's a quick way to get a lot of calories, calcium, and a morning caffeine fix without a stove. Nestlé Nido, at almost 150 calories per ounce, is a great energy-dense trail food."

AT HOME:

2/3 cup Nestlé Nido or whole powdered milk

3 1/2 teaspoons instant coffee crystals (adjust to taste)

Optional: sugar to taste

Premix and seal dry ingredients in a single-serving ziplock bag.

ON THE TRAIL:

2 cups water

Pour 1 cup of water into a rigid widemouthed bottle. The bottle should be large enough to accommodate at least 20 fluid ounces to provide adequate additional volume for shaking. Add mix. Shake vigorously for about 10 seconds once per minute for 3 to 5 minutes, at which point the coffee and milk will have dissolved. Add remaining cup of water and shake again.

ALAN DIXON
"ADVENTURE ALAN"
ARLINGTON, VIRGINIA

Weight per serving: 3 ounce
Total servings: 1

Nutritional information per serving:

Calories:	300
Protein:	16 g
Carbohydrates:	24 g
Sodium:	230 mg
Fiber:	0 g
Fat:	18 g
Cholesterol:	60 mg

Nestlé Nido is a whole-fat powdered milk product. It has almost twice the calories of nonfat or low-fat powdered milk. It's creamy and delicious and a tasty alternative to regular powdered milk for cereals and drinks. It also mixes more easily than most brands of powdered milk. Nido can be found in Latino markets as well as in the international food sections of larger grocery stores.

ALAN DIXON
"ADVENTURE ALAN"
ARLINGTON, VIRGINIA

Electro-Tea

AT HOME:

1/4 cup lemon-flavored Nutribiotic Electro-C mix

3/4 cup powdered ginger tea

Combine all ingredients together. Partition and package as desired for the trail. Note that powdered ginger tea can often be found in Oriental food stores.

ON THE TRAIL:

1 cup water per serving

Heat 1 cup of water and add 1 teaspoon of tea mix. Stir well.

JACK YOUNG AND JO CRESCENT
WINTERS, CALIFORNIA

TOTAL WEIGHT: 7 OUNCES
Weight per serving: less than 1 ounce
Total servings: 24

Nutritional information per serving:

Calories:	0
Protein:	0 g
Carbohydrates:	0 g
Sodium:	0 mg
Fiber:	0 g
Fat:	0 g
Cholesterol:	0 mg

AUTHORS' NOTE:

Electro-C is a supplement formula in a drink-mix form that contains high concentrations of natural vitamin C and mineral electrolytes and is sweetened with stevia. Because it is a dietary supplement, it should be used cautiously. Electro-C can be found in many health-food stores or purchased directly from the company by calling (800) 225-4345.

Moonlight Mint Tea

"Thanks to our friend Sana Al-Arashi for providing our delicious Mediterranean tea recipes: Moonlight Mint and Shawnee Sage."

CHRISTINE AND TIM CONNERS
SAVANNAH, GEORGIA

AT HOME:

2 standard-size bags black tea
1/4 cup granulated sugar
2 heaping tablespoons dried whole mint or peppermint leaves

Package ingredients separately for the trail. If the mint or peppermint leaves are grown fresh, do not water the plant for at least two days prior to picking the leaves.

ON THE TRAIL:

4 cups water

Bring 4 cups of water to a boil, then add 1/4 cup of sugar. (Doing so in this order helps to keep the tea clear.) Remove from heat. Add tea bags and mint or peppermint leaves. Let simmer for several minutes. Makes 2 servings.

TOTAL WEIGHT: 2 OUNCES
Weight per serving: 1 ounce
Total servings: 2 (2 cups per serving)

Nutritional information per serving:

Calories:	110
Protein:	0 g
Carbohydrates:	18 g
Sodium:	8 mg
Fiber:	0 g
Fat:	0 g
Cholesterol:	0 mg

I find that peppermint, spearmint, and lemon mint leaves make a refreshing tea after floating in my water bottle for a few hours. Nettles can be cooked. They taste like spinach, only better; and dandelion greens, gathered before the plant flowers, make a great salad. Later in the spring, I look for strawberries, raspberries, and cherries.

From her book, *Walking Home: A Woman's Pilgrimage on the Appalachian Trail.*

KELLY WINTERS "AMAZIN' GRACE"
BAYVILLE, NEW YORK

Shawnee Sage Tea

"The Shawnee is a beautiful 46-mile loop trail in the tree-covered hill country of south-central Ohio where I hiked as a boy and where our kids, James, Michael, and Maria, began their backpacking careers. It was also the place where I experienced a midlife meltdown in July 2000 when I tried to walk the entire loop in one day.

"I clearly recall the beginning of this overly ambitious shot at a personal best when, at 3:00 A.M. sharp, I punched into an exceptionally dark and thick hardwood forest that had just been drenched by a strong thunderstorm. The first 25 or 30 miles went surprisingly well and I felt great. As I headed into the evening hours, though, I was humiliated into reality. By 35 miles, my vision was blurred, my mental state seriously altered, and the lactic acid buildup so heavy that I was down to a stagger. By 40 miles, I couldn't move my legs without using my arms to lift and pull my thighs forward. Other than a drug deal that I stumbled upon at a back-road trail crossing late morning and a group of rowdy college kids at midafternoon, I had seen no one else the entire day. Now, near midnight, and still many miles from my car, I was faced with the unpleasant prospect of having to crawl to the door of a rural homestead to ask for help. My prayers, however, were answered in a more direct way: I very soon crossed paths with an angelic being, cleverly disguised as a raccoon hunter, who hauled my beleaguered carcass out of the dark Ohio wilderness in his late-model pickup truck. Several days passed before I fully recovered. I gained a much-increased appreciation for the ultra-distance folks who are able to do that kind of mileage day after day on the long trails, in lofty mountains, and with significant weight on their backs. I gained an improved appreciation for 'coon hunters as well."

—Tim

AT HOME:

2 standard-size bags black tea
1/4 cup granulated sugar
2 heaping tablespoons dried whole sage leaves

Package ingredients separately for the trail. If the sage leaves are grown fresh, do not water the plant for at least two days prior to picking the leaves.

ON THE TRAIL:

4 cups water

Bring 4 cups of water to a boil, then add 1/4 cup of sugar. (Doing so in this order helps to keep the tea clear.) Remove from heat. Add tea bags and sage leaves. Let simmer for several minutes. Makes 2 servings.

CHRISTINE AND TIM CONNERS
SAVANNAH, GEORGIA

TOTAL WEIGHT: 2 OUNCES
Weight per serving: 1 ounce
Total servings: 2 (2 cups per serving)

Nutritional information per serving:

Calories:	110
Protein:	0 g
Carbohydrates:	18 g
Sodium:	8 mg
Fiber:	0 g
Fat:	0 g
Cholesterol:	0 mg

Goat Dance Brandy

"I learned about this drink from my sister-in-law, who taught climbing on Mt. Rainier. It has great powers of recuperation and relaxation after a hard day of almost anything outdoors. On the trail I have to ration this drink, or the goat-packer's club that I hike with will drink it all the first night."

CAROLYN EDDY
"DANCES WITH GOATS"
ESTACADA, OREGON

AT HOME:

3 tablespoons Hain Superfruit Strawberry Dessert Mix
1 tablespoon peach brandy (or to taste)

Carry each ingredient separately. You can usually find Hain Dessert Mix, a vegetarian gelatin, at your local health-food store.

ON THE TRAIL:

1 cup water

Bring 1 cup of water to a near-boil. Add dessert mix and brandy. Stir until dissolved. This delicious night-cap is sure to have you dancing with the goats!

Weight per serving: 2 ounces
Total servings:1

Nutritional information per serving:

Calories:	138
Protein:	0 g
Carbohydrates:	30 g
Sodium:	15 mg
Fiber:	0 g
Fat:	0 g
Cholesterol:	0 mg

Whopper Malt Bribe

"Once while we were all hiking the AT approach trail in northern Georgia, our daughter, Maria, generally an agreeable little girl, absolutely refused to take another step. With the narrow trail hemmed in high on both sides by a nettle hedge as long as the Great Wall of China, we were out of options. So our two-year-old went to the top of already-heavy backpacks, bulging with two days' worth of her used diapers and extra gear for not only Maria but also her two older brothers, James and Michael. Christine and I both took turns hauling 'Trail Princess' up the mountain from Black Gap to the summit of Springer. With Maria dozing peacefully on top of my pack, I recall stumbling along those last hundred feet of elevation gain in a sweaty daze, neck bent forward like a broken pipe, wanting to have a word with the person who laid out that particular stretch of what seemed at the time to be endlessly meandering trail.

"Since then, we've become much wiser. Now, we stock the larder with a variety of goodies designed solely to move kids' feet from Point A to Point B when they otherwise just don't want to. For those of you who aren't parents of young children, you can call it what you want: bribe, poor parenting, character weakness. For those who are, you'll be happy to learn one of our latest tricks. And, by the way, Whopper Malt Bribe is great for adults too. You just might be able to use it to coerce *your* feet into taking those last few thousand steps of the day!"

—Tim

AT HOME:

1 cup crushed Whoppers

1 cup Ovaltine Chocolate Malt Mix

1 cup nonfat powdered milk

Combine all ingredients in a quart-size ziplock freezer bag.

ON THE TRAIL:

1 cup water per serving

To make 1 serving, add 1/2 cup of mix to 1 cup of either hot or cold water. It works nicely both ways. Stir and serve.

CHRISTINE AND TIM CONNERS
SAVANNAH, GEORGIA

TOTAL WEIGHT: 9 OUNCES
Weight per serving: about 2 ounces
Total servings: 6

Nutritional information per serving:

Calories:	174
Protein:	5 g
Carbohydrates:	31 g
Sodium:	197 mg
Fiber:	0 g
Fat:	3 g
Cholesterol:	2 mg

Panamint Peppermint Cooler

"This drink has the most amazing sequence of aftertastes, all of them intriguing. It starts with the sharp hit of the mint and then smoothly rolls into a series of sweet, fruity nuances. No, it's not wine, but it's not bad, especially considering how easy it is to prepare at home and on the trail."

CHRISTINE AND TIM CONNERS
SAVANNAH, GEORGIA

TOTAL WEIGHT: 10 OUNCES
Weight per serving: 2 ounces
Total servings: 5

Nutritional information per serving:

Calories:	208
Protein:	0 g
Carbohydrates:	78 g
Sodium:	0 mg
Fiber:	0 g
Fat:	0 g
Cholesterol:	0 mg

AT HOME:

1 (4-ounce) package cherry-flavored sweetened Kool-Aid mix
1 (5-ounce) package lemonade-flavored sweetened Kool-Aid mix
1 (20-bag) box Celestial Seasonings Peppermint Tea

Combine cherry- and lemonade-flavored Kool-Aid mixes in a ziplock bag. Carry tea bags separately.

ON THE TRAIL:

4 cups water per serving

To make 1 large serving, bring 2 cups of water to a boil in a pot. Add 4 tea bags and let steep for 6 minutes before removing. While hot, add 1/4 cup of the Kool-Aid mix and stir until dissolved. Allow water to cool, then add 2 more cups of cold water. For an on-the-trail treat, pour into a water bottle for later enjoyment.

Acknowledgments Reprise: Larson's Ultra-Light Leg Cramp Bonanza

"This is a simple, vegetarian—actually vegan—recipe."

TERRY LARSON
TEHACHAPI, CALIFORNIA

Weight per serving: 0 ounces
Total servings: 0

AT HOME:

1 empty water bottle

Regardless of length of trip, bring only 1 water bottle for the trail.

ON THE TRAIL:

Try to ignore your sense of thirst. Stop for the day once leg cramps become unbearable.

AUTHORS' NOTE:

Seriously, folks, we've added this "recipe" as a tongue-in-cheek tribute to legendary outdoorsman and good friend Terry Larson. Never one to follow the latest trends in hiking, and certainly not needing to, Terry's idea of good, on-trail cooking typically involves items requiring only an ax or can opener. In fact, he probably won't have any interest in this book, even though there is an entire page dedicated to him! It wasn't surprising then that he was at a loss when Christine and I asked him to contribute to the cookbook. As a last resort, we encouraged him to submit this one. He has and probably always will view water consumption as an annoying hindrance to a full day of hiking. Perhaps it's a good thing, because the only times I've been able to keep up with Larson have been when his legs eventually cramped late in the day due to dehydration.

Ignoring for the moment his renowned aversion to water, Terry has enormous experience gained from six decades of traipsing around the mountains of California. Ever-patient and good-natured, he was instrumental in teaching me the ways of the wild when I was a novice. We've spent many fine hours together since in the San Gabriel, Tehachapi, and Southern Sierra mountains. To hike with Larson, you must expect the unexpected. I have never met an individual to whom high adventure clung so surely as soon as foot hit the trail. I view Terry as a mentor, a key figure without whom I would not have made it beyond my first backpacking trip let alone all the way to "Lipsmackin' Backpackin'." And, to some respect, had I not become active in the outdoors at the time when I did, it is doubtful that I would have ended up hitched to my trail babe and love, Christine. I suppose I owe even this to Larson.

So here's to you, Terry. Thanks for the never-ending inspiration as well as the path that you helped set me on.

—Tim

Appendix A: Dehydrophobia

Dehydrophobia is the intense and irrational fear of using a food dehydrator. Some of you may suffer secretly from it or know others who do.

This phobia came to my attention after the publication of *Lipsmackin' Backpackin'*. The book, having been written for the long-distance backpacker, often calls for the use of a dehydrator. Although the majority of backpackers recognize the value of dehydration, there was a small contingent that freaked. I realize that "freaked" might be considered a strong word, but that's exactly what happened.

The reaction by these few was so strong that I, as a professional therapist, couldn't help but wonder if there wasn't something more sinister lying beneath the surface. What would cause such an intense reaction? I pondered this for many weeks, until one day it occurred to me. These people were consumed by fear, a fear so gripping and debilitating that it might forever keep them from discovering the joy and fulfillment of dehydration. They were suffering from *dehydrophobia!*

If you are suffering from dehydrophobia, take heart. There is hope. By following my step-by-step, four-week program, you *can* overcome this fear.

Week 1—Educate yourself

The following are the answers to questions frequently asked by dehydrophobics.

What is a dehydrator?

A dehydrator is a big, ugly appliance that takes up most of your counter space and stinks up your house. Its purpose is to dry your food in a slow, even fashion in order to reduce weight, maintain taste, and increase shelf life. People have been drying food since the dawn of civilization. Despite how it may seem, you are not boldly going where no man has gone before. And you don't necessarily need something high tech, either. Tim and I bought ours at a garage sale for fifteen dollars. We tested and developed all of the dehydrated recipes in *Lipsmackin' Backpackin'* and *Lipsmackin' Vegetarian Backpackin'* with it.

Will it burn down my house?

If your dehydrator is operating properly, it shouldn't burn your food much less your house. It is supposed to work more like a crock-pot, with a slow, even operation that, in most cases, doesn't require precise timing. By keeping it at its lowest temperature setting with the door slightly ajar for air circulation, even a basic oven can be used to dry some foods. A good dehydrator, though, is superior to an oven in that it has more drying surface area, a built-in fan, and mesh trays, which allow for better air circulation.

I'm an important person. Why would I waste my time dehydrating?

As a long-distance backpacker, you have special needs. Those needs include reducing your pack weight and having nutritious and tasty food to sustain you physically and emotionally. Commercially available freeze-dried food often tastes odd, with the packages typically containing awkward portions. Dehydration, on the other hand, preserves the taste of your food and allows you to enjoy on the trail many of your favorite, nutritious meals from home, with portions customized to your preference and at a cost lower than freeze-dried.

Do dehydrators come in fashion colors?

Sorry. No.

Week 2—Positive affirmations

Now you are ready for week two! Begin each morning with a deep, cleansing breath. Inhale. Exhale. Perfect! Now repeat the following affirmations six times in front of your mirror each day for the next week: *My dehydrator is my friend. I like to dehydrate. My dehydrator loves me.*

Week 3—Making the purchase

Now it's time to buy! For many of you, being near a real dehydrator may be so anxiety provoking that you will need to make this purchase either via catalog or over the Web. When your dehydrator arrives, place the box in your living room. Each day, as you walk past, repeat the affirmations (see Week 2) while progressively moving closer to it. On the last day of Week 3, take a deep, cleansing breath and touch the box.

Week 4—Dehydrating

This will be most challenging. Find yourself a support buddy. Together, remove the dehydrator from the box and place it in the kitchen. If you panic, repeat your affirmations (see Week 2). Next pour yourself a hot bubble bath, get in, and read your dehydrator instructions (this can be done with or without your support buddy).

Now, plug in your dehydrator and carefully place one frozen pea on a dehydrator tray. With the help of your support person, close the door and switch your dehydrator on. Try not to think about what's really happening. Have a cup of herbal tea, and talk about anything but the pea. After the first hour, take a deep breath and examine the pea. Assure yourself that your pea is doing fine. It's not in pain, just losing a little water. Try not to overidentify with the pea. Remember: Peas are not people. They are just peas.

After about three hours, have your support person help you remove the pea from the dehydrator. Study it. Touch it. Maybe toss it back and forth between the two of you. Now place it in a small ziplock bag along with a teaspoon of hot water. Seal it shut and watch what happens. It's coming back to life! Your pea is alive again! You did it!

Now, move onto other things. Live on the edge and dry a whole bag of peas. Dry a jar of spaghetti sauce. For a special treat, dry your kids' peanut butter sandwiches. Be creative! And always remember... your dehydrator is your friend.

Special thanks to Roberta Cobb and the folks at ALDHA-West, who published a version of this appendix, written by Christine, in the Summer 2002 issue of their newsletter, The Gazette, *and who gave permission for the reprinting above.*

Appendix B: Sources of Dried Foods and Other Ingredients

If you can't locate a necessary ingredient at your local grocery store, you will probably find it through one of the following suppliers.

Adventure Foods
(828) 497–4113
www.adventurefoods.com
Offers a large selection of bulk dried foods and interesting powdered condiment flavors including honey, vinegar, cheese butter, molasses, wine, and sauces.

Be Prepared
(800) 999–1863
www.beprepared.com
Specializes in supplies for emergency situations. Good selection of bulk dried foods.

Blackbird Food Company
(805) 565–4625
www.blackbirdfood.com
Offers a large selection of dried vegetables and fruit.

Bulkfoods
(419) 324–0032
www.bulkfoods.com
A large selection of dried fruit, nuts, spices, and more.

Eden Foods
(888) 441–EDEN
www.edenfoods.com
Interesting selection of Japanese foods, including dried tofu, seaweed, and dried mushrooms, as well as exotic bulk goods.

Fantastic Foods
(800) 288–1089
www.fantasticfoods.com
A popular maker of dried soups, hummus, and the like. Available at most natural food stores and many major grocery stores.

Internet Grocer
www.internet-grocer.com
Many bulk dehydrated basics, including dairy products.

Just Tomatoes, etc!
(209) 894–5371
www.justtomatoes.com
More than just tomatoes, this company sells a large selection of dried fruits, vegetables, and other foods such as tofu, all in reasonably sized quantities.

King Arthur
(800) 827–6836
www.kingarthurflour.com
Not just flour, but a diverse selection of difficult to find ingredients, including dried whole egg powder, tomato powder, and more.

Living Tree Community
www.livingtreecommunity.com
A variety of organic dried nuts, fruits, and nut butters offered in a range of convenient quantities.

Loma Linda Market
(888) 558–7282
www.lomalindamarket.com
Bulk supplier of many products typically found at natural health-food stores, such as fruits and cereals.

Lumen Foods / Heartline Products
(800) 256–2253
www.lumenfds.com
Lumen Foods offers many varieties of meat alternatives.

My Spicer
(903) 553–0800
www.myspicer.com
An exotic selection of dried vegetables, fruit, and other items from throughout the world.

Sun Organic Farms
(888) 269–9888
www.sunorganic.com
A good selection of organic dried fruits and vegetables as well as seasonings, beans, and nuts.

Suttons Bay Trading Company
(888) 747–7423
www.suttonsbaytrading.com
A large selection of dried fruit and vegetables as well as a wonderful assortment of flavored powders, including horseradish, soy sauce, yogurt, wine, and honey.

Taste Adventure
(800) 874–0883
www.tasteadventure.com
A popular supplier of dehydrated beans, soups, and the like. Available at many natural food stores.

United Natural Foods
www.unfi.com
This organization is one of the largest wholesalers of natural and organic food and personal care products in the United States.

Walton Feed Company
(800) 847–0465
www.waltonfeed.com
A very large selection of foods. Good product quality and price.

Special thanks to Jen Schaeffer with ALDHA-West for her assistance in compiling this list.

Appendix C: Measurement Conversions

Standard Conversions

3 teaspoons	1 tablespoon
48 teaspoons	1 cup
2 tablespoons	$\frac{1}{8}$ cup
4 tablespoons	$\frac{1}{4}$ cup
5 tablespoons + 1 teaspoon	$\frac{1}{3}$ cup
8 tablespoons	$\frac{1}{2}$ cup
12 tablespoons	$\frac{3}{4}$ cup
16 tablespoons	1 cup
1 ounce	2 tablespoons
4 ounces	$\frac{1}{2}$ cup
8 ounces	1 cup
$\frac{5}{8}$ cup	$\frac{1}{2}$ cup + 2 tablespoons
$\frac{7}{8}$ cup	$\frac{3}{4}$ cup + 2 tablespoons
2 cups	1 pint
2 pints	1 quart
1 quart	4 cups
1 jigger	$1\frac{1}{2}$ fluid ounces
16 ounces water	1 pound
2 cups vegetable oil	1 pound
2 cups or 4 sticks butter	1 pound
2 cups granulated sugar	1 pound
$3\frac{1}{2}$ to 4 cups unsifted powdered sugar	1 pound
$2\frac{1}{4}$ cups packed brown sugar	1 pound
4 cups sifted flour	1 pound
$3\frac{1}{2}$ cups unsifted whole wheat flour	1 pound
8 to 10 egg whites	1 cup
12 to 14 egg yolks	1 cup
1 whole lemon, squeezed	3 tablespoons juice
1 whole orange, squeezed	$\frac{1}{3}$ cup juice

Metric Conversions

Volume and Weight

English	**Metric**
1/4 teaspoon	1.25 milliliters
1/2 teaspoon	2.50 milliliters
3/4 teaspoon	3.75 milliliters
1 teaspoon	5 milliliters
1 tablespoon	15 milliliters
1 fluid ounce	30 milliliters
1/4 cup	60 milliliters
1/2 cup	120 milliliters
3/4 cup	180 milliliters
1 cup	240 milliliters
1 pint	0.48 liter
1 quart	0.95 liter
1 ounce weight	28 grams
1 pound	0.45 kilogram

Temperature

English (deg F)	**Metric (deg C)**
175	80
200	95
225	105
250	120
275	135
300	150
325	165
350	175
375	190
400	205
425	220
450	230
475	245
500	260

Drying Conversions

The following weights and measures may vary slightly due to a variety of factors, including brand selection, depth of cut, dehydrating method, and equipment.

Undried Item	Dried Volume	Dried Weight
1 tablespoon fresh herbs	1 teaspoon	less than 1 ounce
1 tablespoon mustard	1 teaspoon	less than 1 ounce
1 garlic clove, pressed	1/8 teaspoon powder	less than 1 ounce
1 pound frozen peas	1 cup	4 ounces
1 pound cooked and sliced carrots	1/2 cup	2 ounces
1 pound boiled and sliced potatoes	1 1/2 cups	4 ounces
1 pound diced onions	1 cup	1 ounce
1 pound frozen French-sliced green beans	2 cups	1 1/2 ounces
1 pound diced celery	1/3 cup	1/2 ounce
1 pound sliced fresh mushrooms	2 1/2 cups	1 ounce
1 pound fresh green bell pepper	3/4 cup	1 1/2 ounces
1 pound fresh jalapeño peppers	1 1/3 cups	1 ounce
1 pound frozen mixed vegetables	3/4 cup	3 1/2 ounces
1 (15-ounce) can mixed vegetables	1/2 cup	1 1/2 ounces
1 (6-ounce) can medium diced olives	1/2 cup	1 ounce
1 (15-ounce) can pinto beans	1 cup	2 1/2 ounces
1 (15-ounce) can black beans	1 1/4 cups	3 1/2 ounces
1 (15-ounce) can kidney beans	1 cup	2 1/2 ounces
1 pound steamed and chopped zucchini	1/3 cup	1/2 ounce
1 pound frozen sliced broccoli	1 cup	1 ounce
1 pound sliced Roma tomatoes	1 cup	1 ounce
1 (6-ounce) can tomato paste	Leather roll	1 1/2 ounces
1 pound salsa	1/2 cup	1/2 ounce
1 pound sliced apples	1 1/2 cups	3 ounces
1 pound sliced bananas	1 1/2 cups	4 ounces
1 (20-ounce) can diced pineapple	3/4 cup	2 ounces
1 pound trimmed watermelon	1 cup	1 ounce
1 pound frozen cherries	1/2 cup	2 ounces
1 cup whole milk	1/2 cup powdered	2 ounces

About Our Contributors

Bill Albrecht

Lancaster, California

Bill was born in Flushing, New York, in 1924 and served in the U.S. Army Corps of Engineers during World War II, after which he entered the aerospace industry. He finally settled at NASA's Dryden Flight Research Center in the Mojave Desert of California, where he worked for *five* decades before recently retiring. He has spent many years hiking throughout the High Sierra and the mountains of Southern California, where he stays busy to this day working in a volunteer capacity for the U.S.D.A. Forest Service.

Suzanne Allen

Seattle, Washington

Suzanne grew up day-hiking in the rain forests of Washington's Olympic Peninsula as well as in other places where the navy moved her family. When she realized that she didn't actually want to apply her teaching degree after all, she decided to pursue outdoor education only to realize that she really didn't know anything about it! "I have been using the requirement to learn these skills as an excuse to play in the outdoors as much as possible: climbing, hiking, and exploring as much as I can while managing to stay employed. They say you're never really done learning . . . . "

Emmett Autrey

"Ol' Kooger" Amarillo, Texas

Emmett began backpacking the Pacific Crest Trail in sections, starting at the Mexican border, in June 1992. He has made 9 trips, hiking more than 830 miles to date. He plans to complete the remainder of the trail in a single hike during summer 2005 following his retirement. His trail name comes from his attitude about unnecessary ascents: Why go over if you can go around? Just like an old Cougar with a broken tooth. Emmett is married and has three grown sons and three granddaughters. He is a water production superintendent for the city of Amarillo and from time to time teaches a backpacking basics course at Amarillo Community College. Kooger has a philosophy about the PCT: "Yes, it is 6 million steps, but you only have to take them one at a time."

Ted Ayers

"Trekin' Ted" Rapid City, South Dakota

Ted has nearly thirty years of hiking and backpacking experience exploring much of the southwestern United States, including multiple trips into and around the Grand Canyon. His favorite locale is the Southern Sierra Nevada Mountains, where he has solo hiked for years. Ted has also soloed on the John Muir Trail numerous times. He has explored the highest peaks of the Black Hills of South Dakota, as well as those in Australia, North Wales, and Northern Ireland. In 1999 Ted hiked the Anapurna Sanctuary and Everest Base Camp areas of Nepal, culminating in the summit of Kala Patar at 18,600 feet. He describes himself as a trekker who enjoys spending as many as fifteen to twenty days at a time on the trail. So he "eats to live" and sacrifices food for photo equipment! Many of his trail foods are lightweight, simple, and quick to prepare.

Sherry Bennett

Rochester, New York

Sherry has hiked and paddled throughout the northeast United States and Canada. She loves trail cookery and always has to try out the latest way to cook or bake on the trail. She belongs to the Adirondack Mountain Club.

Liz Bergeron

Sacramento, California

As the executive director of the Pacific Crest Trail Association, of course Liz loves to hike, backpack, and spend as much time outdoors as possible! She lives in Sacramento with her husband, Robert Francisco, as well as her Weimaraner, Floyd.

Larry and Gloria Bright

John Day, Oregon

With a combined 122 years of youth, these newlyweds are still in great health. They love backpacking and exploring the backcountry and are off to new adventures every day with their packs full of good, wholesome food.

Heather Burror

Martinez, California

An avid backpacker, Heather hit the trail for her first overnight adventure at the age of two, armed with a homemade backpack containing only the essentials—cookies! Since then, she has significantly expanded her culinary repertoire during numerous trips throughout the High Sierra, including a recent thru-hike of the John Muir Trail.

Marion Davison

"Llamalady" Apple Valley, California

Llamalady is a schoolteacher. She spends her summers in the High Sierra with her husband and their three pack llamas, hiking long sections of the Pacific Crest Trail and connecting trails. They hope to eventually complete the PCT in California through weekend, weeklong, and monthlong treks.

Alan Dixon

"Adventure Alan"   Arlington, Virginia

Adventure Alan was born in California and was carrying his own backpack into the Sierra at the age of four. Since then he's hiked the Sierra, Cascades, Rockies, Tetons, the deserts and canyons of the southwestern United States, and sections of the Appalachian Trail. He now hikes these same areas with his children and friends. Adventure Alan likes to strike routes cross-country, so his favorite trail is "no trail at all."

Carolyn Eddy

"Dances with Goats"   Estacada, Oregon

Carolyn is an ultralight goatpacker who regularly uses pack goats for trips to Mount Hood in Oregon for the Wilderness Steward Program of the U.S.D.A. Forest Service. She is a writer of books about goatpacking and the publisher of *Goat Tracks Magazine: Journal of the Working Goat.* She typically spends much of her summertime in the mountains performing wilderness patrols for the Forest Service.

Matthew Farnell

Woodland, Washington

Matthew lives on a farm where his family raises llamas, goats, chickens, ducks, and guineas. He is interested in natural health and cooking. He enjoys backpacking, snow sports, unicycling, and spelunking, as well as playing the piano. He runs a Web site business out of his home and is working toward a bachelor's degree. He hopes to become a teacher someday.

Fred Firman

"Greybeard"   Columbia, Maryland

Greybeard was a programmer for the federal government until he retired at the end of 1994. To prove to himself that there was indeed life after retirement, he thru-hiked the Appalachian Trail in 1995. Since then he has continued to backpack a few weeks out of each year. He has completed the Northville-Placid Trail in New York, the Long Trail in Vermont, rehiked half of the AT, and, last summer, hiked the Colorado Trail. Fred volunteers his time at the headquarters of the Appalachian Trail Conference. He maintains a stretch of the AT that he has adopted. Greybeard claims that his cooking is pretty much limited to his hiker breads and an occasional loaf of yeast bread.

Ben Hahn

"The Vegan Super Hero" Corvallis, Oregon

The Vegan Super Hero was raised in the southeastern United States along a desolate stretch of the coast of the Gulf of Mexico. Alas, Alabama has no mountains, so when he moved to the Olympic Peninsula of Washington state, he was immediately awed by the glorious peaks, rivers, and forests. Since then he has hiked throughout the Olympic Range and floated down the Solduk, Elwah, and the mighty Dosewallips. During college, Mount Baker was his home, with beautiful trails and the gorgeous San Juan Islands as a backdrop. Here is where he came into his enlightenment. One day while hiking he encountered a marmot; and as he was about to smack the creature over the head with a rock so that he could eat her, she said to him, "Ben, son of the earth, do not be so quick to consume the living, for their suffering is in vain." And after this interlude with the floating marmot goddess, he vowed never again to consume animal products. From his dedication and conviction, he has gained untold super vegan powers that allow him to bear the drudgery of endless uphill trails and to shoulder heavier packs laden with healthy vegan chow. He carries the torch of the marmot goddess and spreads her wisdom with every fellow hiker.

Richard Halbert

"Ranger Rick" Traverse City, Michigan

Rick does most of his backpacking in the Great Lakes states and Canadian provinces. He believes his vegetarian diet is healthier for himself and the planet. Because his fully loaded pack almost always weighs less than twenty pounds, he is able to enjoy the hike more fully and leave behind a lighter footprint. Rick shares his hiking philosophy and techniques on his Great Lakes Lightweight Backpacking Web site at www.members.tripod.com/halbertri.

Ramona Hammerly

Anacortes, Washington

Ramona is an artist who illustrated *Northwest Trees* and *Timberline* (currently out of print) as well as a portion of *Freedom of the Hills.* She has climbed peaks in the Cascades, the Olympic Range, and the Alaskan Range, and she has even scaled Mexican volcanoes. She has backpacked extensively, including trails throughout California, Oregon, Washington, and Vancouver Island in British Columbia. Her kayaking experience includes the Bowron Lakes Loop and the San Juan Islands of Puget Sound.

Carole Harbison

San Francisco, California

Carole participated in a four-week backpack trip in Alaska's Wrangell Range with the National Outdoor Leadership School. She has also hiked in Arizona, California, Utah, Colorado, Wyoming, Washington, Hawaii, New York, and abroad. Her favorite national park is Mount Rainier.

Ken Harbison

Rochester, New York

Ken and his wife, Judy, are Adirondack 46ers and have also climbed the Catskill 3500. They have completed the Northville-Placid Trail, the Adirondack Quest, and the Adirondack Fire Tower Challenge and are working on the Long Trail. On August 7, 2003, they completed their goal of climbing all of the Northeast 111 peaks. They have hiked in New York, New England, the western United States, and the British Isles. Ken is the director of the Adirondack Mountain Club. He is contributor Carole Harbison's father.

Phil Heffington

"Scodwod" Edmond, Oklahoma

"Scodwod" is what Phil's daddy called him as a kid. In 125 days of hiking from 1998 through 2002, he walked 1,500 miles of the Appalachian Trail, covering the stretch from Springer Mountain, Georgia, to Great Barrington, Massachusetts. He has also walked the Ozark Highlands of Arkansas as well as the Gila Wilderness of New Mexico. He particularly loves long-distance hiking on the AT and has covered as many as 395 miles in one outing.

Dave Hicks

"Chainsaw" Dublin, Virginia

Chainsaw is sixty-three years old and has been camping and hiking since the 1940s. Most of his trips have taken place on the Appalachian Trail and other eastern mountain trails, although he has trekked in the northwestern United States and Alaska as well. Though not an AT thru-hiker yet, he has picked away at it since the 1950s. He has section-hiked more than 700 miles of the AT, covering many of the same miles several times.

Carolyn Hiestand

Seattle, Washington

Growing up near the southern terminus of the Pacific Crest Trail, Carolyn spent her teenage years backpacking along the John Muir Trail near Mount Whitney. Carolyn now lives near the northern end of the PCT, where she and her husband explore the beautiful Cascade Mountains. Pine Valley Couscous has become one of their favorite reasons to hit the trail!

Barbara Hodgin

"Mule 2" Sacramento, California

Mule 2 is a member of the Board of Directors of the Pacific Crest Trail Association and a retired public administrator from Alaska. She now enjoys living in warm, sunny Sacramento, where the hiking season is longer and the Sierra Nevada range is nearby. Why the odd trail name? "My husband is 'Mule 1.' Like mules, we carry heavy loads and move faster as the day goes on because we smell the barn."

Chris Ibbeson

"Flatfoot" Hemet, California

Flatfoot is forty-five years old. He received a degree in chemistry from UC Irvine many years ago and is currently employed as a software engineer in Temecula. He has backpacked throughout the Sierra Nevada mountains. Although he has never hiked the entire John Muir Trail, a future dream of his, he has covered more than half of it in sections. He particularly enjoys ultralight cross-country backpacking. A super treat is meeting people on the trail that use his Backpacking Gear Weight Calculator program! His Web site is members.tripod.com/ibbeson/.

Will Jaynes

"Hayduke" Three Rivers, California

Hayduke is twenty-eight years old and originally from Oregon. He thru-hiked the Appalachian Trail in 1998 and is now employed by the National Park Service. He has worked at Oregon Caves National Monument, Martin Van Buren National Historic Site, Lava Beds National Monument, and Sequoia and Kings Canyon National Parks.

Rachel Jolly

Burlington, Vermont

Rachel was raised in the Pacific Northwest but really didn't start backpacking until she moved east for college and began working in the Green Mountains. She has since hiked and backpacked in Vermont, Maine, New Hampshire, Washington, Nepal, Ireland, Morocco, and Israel. She works as an environmental educator at a hands-on science center.

Peggy Kinnetz

"Mama Llama" Louisville, Kentucky

Growing up car camping, Peggy didn't like all the paraphernalia that went with that type of "luxury" outdoor living. She tried streamlined car camping while in college and inevitably moved into backpacking. Peggy comes from a long line of great cooks and bakers, and she considers good food a "basic," not a luxury. Now a professional clinical counselor, she loves skiing, shade gardening, and working with stained glass when not section-backpacking the Appalachian Trail. Her goals, in no particular order: to make enough money to buy glass and supplies, to not break a leg skiing so as to be able to complete the AT, and to finally rest in a weed-free garden.

Terry Larson

Tehachapi, California

Terry was born in Glendale, California, in 1931 and graduated from UCLA with a degree in meteorology. He contributed to early rocket aircraft research and atmospheric studies at Edwards Air Force Base beginning in the 1950s. He retired from NASA's Dryden Flight Research Center in the 1990s, culminating his career through his work on the Space Shuttle program. He now enjoys writing science fiction and mystery stories, as well as hiking, golfing, and traveling. He and his wife, Jean, have two sons.

Robert Lauterbach

"Red Husky" Rochester, New York

Retired after thirty-five years in the gas and electric utility business, Robert loves to cook, garden, take pictures, and walk his two dogs.

Laurie Ann March

Guelph, Ontario, Canada

Laurie was born and raised in rural Ontario. Growing up in the country gave her excellent opportunities to view wildlife, hike, camp, snowshoe, cross-country ski, and orienteer. A 4-H outdoor-living course taught her basic survival and outdoor skills. After ten years of participating in outdoor activities with her husband, Bryan, she has developed a tolerance to rainy weather after purchasing impenetrable rain gear! Laurie enjoys backpacking, stargazing, and the outdoors in general. Laurie also is the editor of outdooradventurecanada.com and loves to hike on the Bruce Trail. She is most often the last one into camp because she stops to smell every flower, look at every leaf, and photograph every vista.

Traci Marcroft

Arcata, California

Traci is forty-one years old and a single mother of one wonderful daughter. She works, attends school, and enjoys admiring nature, not conquering it.

Alex Messinger

Burlington, Vermont

Alex and his wife, Kim, have hiked extensively throughout the northeastern United States as well as in Hawaii and Bolivia. With the birth of their daughter, Anna, in 1999, their hiking trips became shorter but no less frequent. By age two, Anna already had several overnight trips and dozens of day-hikes to her credit.

Ed Molash

"EZ Ed" *Olympia, Washington*

EZ is a forty-four-year-old environmental engineer for the Washington Department of Transportation. Besides the Pacific Crest Trail, his extended backpacking trips have included the Wonderland Trail, Bailey Range Traverse, Glacier Peak circumnavigation and summit, Eagle Cap Wilderness, Pasayten Wilderness, and the Kalmiopsis Wilderness. Planned for the future: traversing the entire Olympic National Park, backpacking select portions of the Continental Divide and Pacific Northwest trails, traversing the length of New Zealand, and kayaking the Inside Passage to Alaska.

Hannah Morris

Burlington, Vermont

Hanna is a graphic artist, working primarily for a natural-foods grocery store in Burlington as well as doing freelance design and illustration. When she's not working, she's hiking, biking, gardening, cooking, traveling, and drawing. She started camping and backpacking in high school with the Vermont Youth Conservation Corps and went on to college to find great experiences in the woods and on the trails in Maine. She's hiked in the Rockies, along the coast, in the rain forest, and as far away as Machu Picchu, Peru.

Beth Murdock

Portland, Oregon

As a nurse who loves long-distance hiking, Beth has hiked about half of the entire length of the Pacific Crest Trail to date. She actually enjoys preparing for long hikes! Her goals are to finish the PCT and then, eventually, the Continental Divide Trail as well.

Mara Naber

Mountain Ranch, California

Mara has been camping and hiking since her senior year in high school. She really became interested in wilderness backpacking and canoeing after she returned from living overseas. After the addition of two step daughters, it became even more enjoyable as she began introducing them to the pleasures of the woods. Every year she would organize a wilderness backpack or canoe trip with her daughters and their friends. She became proficient at developing recipes that pleased even nonvegan/nonvegetarian children. "After every trip," she said, "we would all sit down and discuss which dishes were winners, which were losers, and which, with help, could be better. My girls still go out each year with us and I am now including my nieces and nephews on trips as they become old enough."

Therése and Michaela Polacca

Mojave, California

Soon after college, Therése traveled via wagon train from Pennsylvania to Corpus Christi, Texas, as a counselor and chaperone for a program designed to help troubled youth. Their trip took them to Native American tribal lands in Arizona, where she fell in love with the country and the people. She returned there some years later as a school instructor on the Hopi Reservation. Therése has since moved to California, where she lives with her daughter, Michaela, and where she continues to teach. Therése and Michaela return to the Hopi Reservation once a year to visit Michaela's grandparents, who live high on a mesa in the traditional lifestyle.

Andreas Raehmi

"Marmoset" Zurich, Switzerland

Andreas was raised in Belgium, where he hiked extensively in the Ardennes and High Fens National Parks. In school he majored in economics, the sciences, Latin, and English. He later moved to South America for a sabbatical, where he lived and worked in the jungle of French Guyana for a year. While there, he thru-hiked from Saül to Bélizon in twenty-three days with no resupply, eating plenty of Bami

Goreng! He is a real-life Swiss banker, so feel free to contact him regarding any "special" financial needs.

Mike and Sue Reynolds

"Spiderman" and "Ground Control" Columbus, Indiana

Spiderman is a college student majoring in outdoor education. At his on-campus job, he teaches rock climbing at the university's indoor climbing gym. Mike has hiked in the Sierra Nevada Mountains in California and lived for three months in a tent in the Colorado Rockies while teaching emergency preparedness to Boy Scouts. Now an Eagle Scout, Mike completed the AT in 2002. Mike's mom, Sue, an educational consultant, greatly enjoys supporting her son's adventures.

Brian Robinson

"Flyin' Brian" Mountain View, California

In 2001 Flyin' Brian became the first hiker in history to complete the entire "Triple Crown" in a single season. His incredible 7,371-mile journey along the Pacific Crest, Appalachian, and Continental Divide Trails covered twenty-two states, traversed the entire lengths of the three major U.S. mountain divides, and took him 300 days to complete. Brian averaged an amazing 30 to 35 miles per day during this time, hence his trail name. He credits much of the success to his "Trail Dad," Roy, who kept Brian well supplied during his trek. Flyin' Brian has a B.S. in electrical engineering and worked for seventeen years at Tandem Computers—now Compaq.

Jason Rumohr

Seattle, Washington

Jason has been hiking, backpacking, and climbing for fifteen years. Most of his trips have been in the Cascade Mountains, in eastern and western Washington, and in northern Oregon, but he has also backpacked on Kauai, Hawaii. He started out as a heavyweight backpacker, is now "lightweight," and is working toward ultralight. His three-season basic pack weight now averages sixteen pounds. Jason also enjoys rock climbing and mountain biking and is considering hiking the entire Pacific Crest Trail someday.

Katarina Sengstaken

"Katgirl" Hollis, New Hampshire

Katgirl is eighteen years old, a high school senior, and afflicted with a nasty travel bug. She took a trip through Europe in 2001, and it stuck with her. She hikes the White Mountains of New Hampshire all the time. Katgirl is a skier and painter who is always looking for the next adventure.

Rich Simmons

"Richman-Poorman" Plymouth, Michigan

Rich recently graduated from Eastern Michigan University with a degree in construction management. In summer 2000, he biked cross-country from San Francisco to Washington, D.C. He states, "Like many of the people that read this book, I have an incredible love for the outdoors." In 2002 he completed a thru-hike of the AT.

Rebecca and Jim Spencer

Albany, California

Rebecca is a researcher in neuroscience at UC Berkeley while her husband, Jim, is a research scientist in pharmaceutical chemistry at UC San Francisco. They began backpacking in Rebecca's home state of Michigan. After obtaining their doctorate degrees, they moved to California, where they backpack as much as possible: the Sierra, the Pacific Coast, or wherever their dog Zazu is allowed.

Brandon Stone

"Uluheman" Honolulu, Hawaii

Uluheman is a longtime Honolulu resident, vegan, juggler, hiker, seeker of island waterfalls, and native Hawaiian plant and moss enthusiast.

Rosaleen Sullivan

Hudson, Massachusetts

Rosaleen is married and the mother of three adult sons. She has been family camping since childhood and backpacking for more than fifteen years. She started cooking and studying food preparation as a child. Proper nutrition for her and her family has always been important to her. "Keeping to a standard of nutrition is just part of the backpacking challenge."

Craig Turner

"Nigal" Piqua, Ohio

Nigal is a simple hiker who enjoys walking off the beaten trails of Ohio. His walking style can be described as "dirt bagging," so it should come as no surprise that his recipes would be as simple as he is. No chopping. No dicing. No mess. Just keep your hands and feet away from his mouth when he is eating and no one will get hurt! Nigal's Web site at www.dirtbagsdeluxe.natureavenue.com/ encapsulates his collection of hiking and backpack cooking experiences from throughout the years.

Dean Webb

"Dinuba Wolf" aka "El Lobo" Lancaster, California

The Wolf was born in Dinuba, California, the raisin capital of the world, where he was raised on a farm. El Lobo received degrees in physics and math from Fresno State, joined NASA's Dryden Flight Research Center in 1960, and worked on the X-15 rocket plane. The Dinuba Wolf eventually retired from NASA in the mid 1990s, but he stays as active as ever. Besides food in general, he has many interests, including nature photography, particularly in the Mojave Desert and the Eastern Sierra. He has enjoyed following the careers of such master photographers as Ansel Adams, Edward Weston, Imogen Cunningham, and Doctor Figburger. In his younger days he would do long hikes in the Sierra and camp frequently in the Death Valley area. Dean continues to stay involved in many outdoor activities and devotes his time to numerous environmental causes.

Kelly Winters

"Amazin' Grace" Bayville, New York

Kelly hiked most of the AT in 1996 and is the author of *Walking Home: A Woman's Pilgrimage on the Appalachian Trail.*

Jack Young and Jo Crescent

Winters, California

Jack began ultralight backpacking in 1968 at the age of seven with his father in the deserts of Arizona. In those days they had to design and make their own lightweight gear. Jack is a second-generation Scoutmaster and feels strongly that kids need to learn the ultralight approach to backpacking. Jo Crescent also experienced her first backpack adventure in the Arizona desert, only several decades later than Jack's! Jack and Jo's first backpacking trip together was in 1999 in southern New Mexico—essentially an eighteen-year reunion of college sweethearts. In 2001, on their honeymoon, they backpacked for eight days into the wilderness of Yellowstone National Park, where Jack had previously lived and backpacked for two years. That trip reinforced their realization that all calories are not created equal. It inspired their recipes presented in this book as well as others available on Jack's light trail food Web site at www.geocities.com/lighttrailfood/, where food-savvy backpackers share their ideas about making food as nutritious as possible so that they can carry less of it.

Index

A

Absaroka Sweet & Sour, 85
Adirondack Apricot Oatmeal, 29
Agar-agar Powder, using, 78
Alaskan Winter Coffee, 177
Algonquin Apple Leather, 157
Altitude Bread, 148
Anasazi Trail Food, 68
Apricot
  Almond Bread, Greybeard's, 149
  Oatmeal, Adirondack, 29
Apple(s)
  Firehouse, 156
  Granola, Rockhouse Basin, 42–43
  Leather, Algonquin, 157
  Pancakes, Arapaho, 35
Applesauce Leather, 160
Arapaho Apple Pancakes, 35

B

Back Rock Bami Goreng, 124
Baja Burritos, 65
Baked Goods
  Cabin Fever Cookies, 62
  Cheese Coins, 56
  Jenkins Journey Cakes, 15
  Lembas Waybread, 63
  Sasquatch Scones, 14
  Wood Gnome Cobbler, 36
  See also Bars, Breads
Balls
  Energy, 46
  Northville-Placid Trail, 46
Bami Goreng, Back Rock, 124
Banana Puddin', Skidaway, 165
Bars
  Dodie-Kakes, 64
  Niagara, 37
  Oasis Fruit, 142
  Spirit Lifters, 47
  Whole-Food Granola, 61
Basic Backpacker's Sushi, 70
Beans
  in Anasazi Trail Food, 68
  in Black Bear Hummus, 72
  in Black Mountain Potatoes, 97
  in Brunswick Stew, 106
  in Chiwaukum Quinoa, 111
  in Dinner in Denali, 131
  in EZ Ed's Burritos, 92
  in Lost Cowboy Chili, 126
  in Mexican Volcano, 123
  Peaks of Dolomiti Rice and, 136
  in Soul Food, 130
  in Soup of Mount Inthanon, 103
  in Vegan Super Hero Burritos, 90
Beans, Refried
  in Baja Burritos, 65
  in Burrito Olé for Two, 91
  in Pacific Crest Tortillas, 96
Bear Bait, 58
Berry Fruit Leather, Wild, 159
Beverages
  Goat Dance Brandy, 182
  Larson's Ultra-Light Leg Cramp Bonanza, 185
  Panamint Peppermint Cooler, 184
  Whopper Malt Bribe, 183
  See also Coffee, Hot Chocolate, Smoothie, Tea
Black Bear Hummus, 72

Black Mountain Potatoes, 97
Blue Bear Mush, 24
Blueberry(ies)
in Blue Bear Mush, 24
Leather, 159
Nian-Gao Rice Cake, 167
Blue Blazer's Soup, 102
Boot-Stomped Spuds, 98
Boundary Waters Hummus on Rye, 74
Boysenberry Leather, 159
Bragg's Liquid Aminos, using, 88
Bragg's Tofu Jerky, 80
Brandy, Goat Dance, 182
Bread(s)
Altitude, 148
Brooks Range Bannock, 143
Dusty Roads Date-n-Walnut, 150
Ginger Kick, 147
Greybeard's Apricot-Almond, 149
Hardtack, 141
Hopi Fry, 144
Kentuckiana Logan, 140
Lembas Waybread, 63
Mama Llama's Fruit, 152
Oasis Fruit Bars, 142
Poppy Field, 146
Sacagawea Corn, 145
Sasquatch Scones, 14
Traveler's Tahini-Lemon, 151
Breakfast, Omega, 26
Brooks Range Bannock, 143
Brownies, Fabulous Fry, 154
Brunswick Stew, 106
Bulgur, Chewonki Morning, 17
Burrito(s)
Baja, 65
EZ Ed's, 92
Four-Corners Fiesta, 21
Olé for Two, 91
Saucy Summer Breakfast, 20
Vegan Super Hero, 90

C

Cabin Fever Cookies, 62
Candy
Firehouse Apples, 156
Wendjidu Zinzibahkwud, 166
Carrot Salad, Walking, 78
Carter Notch Coleslaw, 75
Cashew Butter, in Bear Bait, 58
Cedar Grove Couscous Risotto, 84
Cereal
Blue Bear Mush, 24
Kalalau Quinoa, 23
Mountain Muesli, 22
Mule Fuel, 25
Omega Breakfast, 26
See also Granola, Oatmeal
Chainsaw's Pumpkin Pleaser, 133
Cheese
in Blue Blazer's Soup, 102
in Burrito Olé for Two, 91
in Chewonki Morning Bulgur, 17
Coins, 56
in Dirt Bagger's Pasta Parmesan, 112
in EZ Ed's Burritos, 92
in Four Corners Fiesta Burritos
in Red Husky, 57
in Rib-Stickin' Ramen, 122
in Saucy Summer Breakfast Burritos, 20
Soup, Trail-Angel, 105
in Wasatch Tomato Parmesan, 117
See also Feta cheese, Goat cheese
Cheesy Breakfast Grits, 19
Cheesy Rice, Taconic Mountain, 132
Cherry Leather, 159
Chewonki Morning Bulgur, 17

Chili
Death Valley, 128–29
Kilauea, 127
Lost Cowboy, 126
Chiwaukum Quinoa, 111
Chocolate Chip
Fry Cookies, 155
Pancakes, Chuckwalla, 34
Chocolate Raspberry Indulgence, 163
Chuckwalla Chocolate Chip
Pancakes, 34
Cleo's Coleslaw, 76
Cloudy Mountain Latte, 178
Cobbler
Dirty Socks Peach, 164
Wood Gnome, 36
Coffee
Alaskan Winter, 177
Cloudy Mountain Latte, 178
Lightning, 176
Vanilla, 177
White Bear Mocha, 175
Coleslaw
in Back Rock Bami Goreng, 124
in Baja Burritos
Carter Notch, 75
Cleo's, 76
in Heavenly Hummus, 73
in North Mountain
Okonomiyaki, 108
Cookies
Cabin Fever, 62
Chocolate Chip Fry, 155
Half Domes, 168
Corn Bread, Sacagawea, 145
Couscous
Ketchikan, 16
Pine Valley, 83
Risotto, Cedar Grove, 84
Triple Crown Curry, 82
Crimson Skies Oatmeal, 27
Curry Couscous, Triple Crown, 82

D

Date-n-Walnut Bread, Dusty Roads, 150
Death Valley Chili, 128–29
Dehydrator, using, 5, 9–12, 186–88
Desert Gruel, 32
Dinner in Denali, 131
Dips
Anasazi Trail Food, 68
Heavenly Hummus, 73
See also Spreads
Dirt Bagger's Pasta Parmesan, 112
Dirty Socks Peach Cobbler, 164
Dodie-Kakes, 64
Dried foods, buying, 189–90
Dumplings, Lone Pine Lentils and, 100
Dusty Roads Date-n-Walnut Bread, 150

E

Earth Smoothie, 172
Eastern Sun Miso Soup, 104
Eggplant, in Fuji Feast, 88
Electro-C, using, 179
Electro-Tea, 179
Energy Balls, 46
EZ Ed's Burritos, 92

F

Fabulous Fry Brownies, 154
Feta cheese, using, 119
Firehouse Apples, 156
Flyin' Brian's Garlic Potatoes, 99
Four-Corners Fiesta Burritos, 21
Fruit Bread, Mama Llama's, 152

Fruit, dehydrated, 19
    See also specific varieties
Fuel
    Mule, 25
    Trekin', 48
Fuji Feast, 88

G

Gado-Gado, Golden Bear, 114
Ginger Kick Bread, 147
Goat cheese, using, 94
Goat Dance Brandy, 182
Golden Bear Gado-Gado, 114
Gorp
    Horse Thief, 49
    Hula, 53
    Just, 51
    Logger's, 52
    Oregon Rain, 50
    Red Husky, 57
    Spiderman, 55
    Trekin' Fuel, 48
    Zion, 54
Granola
    Bars, Whole-Food, 61
    Grizzly Berry, 41
    Koolau Ridge, 39
    Ol' Kooger's Mountain High, 38
    Orange Sky, 40
    Rockhouse Basin Apple, 42–43
    See also Cereal, Gorp
Greek Wayfaring Tortilla, 66
Green Dragon Pad Thai, 87
Green Mountain Grasshopper, 161
Greybeard's Apricot-Almond Bread, 149
Grits, Cheesy Breakfast, 19
Grizzly Berry Granola, 41
Grooovy Smooothie, 171
Gruel, Desert, 32
Grunch, 60
Guitar Lake Melody, 121

H

Half Domes, 18
Hardtack, 141
Heavenly Hummus, 73
Hopi Fry Bread, 144
Horse Thief Gorp, 49
Hot Chocolate
    Moo-Less, 174
    Hurricane Hill, 173
Hula Gorp, 53
Hummus
    Black Bear, 72
    Boundary Waters, on Rye, 74
    Heavenly, 73
Hurricane Hill Hot Chocolate, 173

I

Inka, 173

J

Jenkins Journey Cakes, 15
Jerky
    Bragg's Tofu, 80
    Teriyaki Tofu, 79
Journey Cakes, Jenkins, 15
Just Gorp, 51

K

Kalalau Quinoa Cereal, 23
Kearsarge Pass Oatmeal, 31
Kentuckiana Logan Bread, 140
Ketchikan Couscous, 16

Kilauea Chili, 127
Kincora Rice, 135
Kohlrabi Jerky, 80
Koolau Ridge Granola, 39

L

Larson's Ultra-Light Leg Cramp
  Bonanza, 185
Latte, Cloudy Mountain, 178
Leahi Trail Rice, 137
Leather, 119
  Algonquin Apple, 157
  Applesauce, 160
  Blueberry, 159
  Boysenberry, 159
  Cherry, 159
  Loganberry, 159
  Mountain Mango, 160
  Nectarine, 158
  Pear, 158
  Plum, 158
  Point Pelee Peach, 158
  Spaghetti Sauce, 112
  Switchback Smoothie, 170
  Walking Carrot Salad, 78
  Wild Berry Fruit, 159
Lentils
  Lone Pine, 100
  Secret Lake Garlic, 109
Lightning Coffee, 176
Loganberry Leather, 159
Logger's Gorp, 52
Lone Pine Lentils and Dumplings, 100
Lost Cowboy Chili, 126

M

Mama Llama's Fruit Bread, 152
Mango Leather, Mountain, 160
Maple Syrup, in Wendjidu
  Zinzibahkwud, 166
Measurement conversions, 191–93
Mexican Volcano, 123
Miso
  Madness, 89
  Soup, Eastern Sun, 104
Mocha, White Bear, 175
Moo-Less Hot Chocolate, 174
Moonlight Mint Tea, 180
Mountain Goat Quesadillas, 94
Mountain Mango Leather, 160
Mud, 59
Muesli, Mountain, 22
Mule Fuel, 25
Mush, Blue Bear, 24
Mushrooms
  in South Sister Stroganoff, 113

N

Nectarine Leather, 158
Nestlé Nido, using, 178
Niagara Bars, 37
Nori, using, 77
North Mountain Okonomiyaki, 108
Northville-Placid Trail Balls, 46
North Woods Oatmeal, 28

O

Oasis Fruit Bars, 142
Oatmeal
  Adirondack Apricot, 29
  Crimson Skies, 27
  Kearsarge Pass, 31
  North Woods, 28
  Olympus, 30
Okonomiyaki, North Mountain, 108
Olancha Sweet Pepper Pasta, 116
Ol' Kooger's Mountain High
  Granola, 38

Olympus Oatmeal, 30
Omega Breakfast, 26
Orange Sky Granola, 40
Oregon Rain Gorp, 50

P

Pacific Crest Tortillas, 96
Pad Thai, Green Dragon, 87
Panamint Peppermint Cooler, 184
Pancakes
  Arapaho Apple, 35
  Chuckwalla Chocolate Chip, 34
  Pikes Peak Pineapple, 33
Pasta
  in Back Rock Bami Goreng, 124
  in Golden Bear Gado-Gado, 114
  Olancha Sweet Pepper, 116
  Parmesan, Dirt Bagger's, 112
  Pindos Mountain, 119
  in South Sister Stroganoff, 113
  in Springer Mountain Pesto, 118
  in TrailDad's Spaghetti, 115
  in Wasatch Tomato Parmesan, 117
  See also Ramen
Peach
  Cobbler, Dirty Socks, 164
  Leather, Point Pelee, 158
Peaks of Dolomiti Rice and Beans, 136
Pear Leather, 158
Pero, 173
Pesto, Springer Mountain, 118
Pie, Whitewater Moon, 162
Pikes Peak Pineapple Pancakes, 33
Pindos Mountain Pasta, 119
Pineapple Pancakes, Pikes Peak, 33
Pine Valley Couscous, 83
Plum Leather, 158
Point Pelee Peach Leather, 158
Polenta, in Mexican Volcano, 123
Poppy Field Bread, 146
Potato(es)
  Black Mountain, 97
  in Boot-Stomped Spuds, 98
  Flakes, Instant, using, 99
  Flyin' Brian's Garlic, 99
Procrastinator's Deliverance, 134
Pudding
  Chocolate Raspberry Indulgence, 163
  Green Mountain Grasshopper, 161
  Skidaway Banana, 165
  Trailside Breakfast Rice, 18
  Whitewater Moon Pie, 162
Pumpkin Pleaser, Chainsaw's, 133

Q

Quesadillas, Mountain Goat, 94
Quinoa
  Cereal, Kalalau 23
  Chiwaukum, 111

R

Ramen
  in Guitar Lake Melody, 121
  Range Rovin' ,120
  Rib-Stickin', 122
Range Rovin' Ramen, 120
Raspberry Indulgence, Chocolate, 163
Red Husky, 57
Rib-Stickin' Ramen, 122
Rice
  in Absaroka Sweet & Sour, 85
  in Basic Backpacker's Sushi, 70
  and Beans, Peaks of Dolomiti, 136
  in Burrito Olé for Two, 91
  in Chainsaw's Pumpkin Pleaser, 133
  in Dinner in Denali, 131
  in EZ Ed's Burritos, 92
  Instant, about, 85

in Kilauea Chili, 127
Kincora, 135
Leahi Trail, 137
in Miso Madness, 89
in Procrastinator's Deliverance, 134
in Soul Food, 130
Taconic Mountain Cheesy, 132
in Thunder & Lightning Stir-Fry, 86
Trailside Breakfast, 18
in Vegan Super Hero Burritos, 90
Rice Cake, Blueberry Nian-Gao, 167
Rockhouse Basin Apple
Granola, 42–43

S

Salad
Tabouli, 77
Walking Carrot, 78
See also Coleslaw
Sasquatch Scones, 14
Saucy Summer Breakfast Burritos, 20
Scones, Sasquatch, 14
Secret Lake Garlic Lentils, 109
Shawnee Sage Tea, 180
Skidaway Banana Puddin', 165
Smoothie
Earth, 172
Grooovy, 171
Switchback, 170
Soul Food, 130
Soup
Blue Blazer's, 102
Brunswick Stew, 106
Eastern Sun Miso, 104
of Mount Inthanon, 103
Trail-Angel Cheese, 105
Tueeulala Thai, 101
South Sister Stroganoff, 113
Spaghetti Sauce Leather, 112
Spaghetti, TrailDad's, 115
Spiderman Gorp, 55
Spinach
in Blue Blazer's Soup, 102
in Dinner in Denali, 131
in Kincora Rice, 135
Spirit Lifters, 47
Spreads
Bear Bait, 58
Black Bear Hummus, 72
Grunch, 60
Mud, 59
Tapenade, 67
See also Dips
Springer Mountain Pesto, 118
Stew, Brunswick, 106
Stir-Fry, Thunder & Lightning, 86
Strawberries, in Wild Berry Fruit
Leather, 159
Stroganoff, South Sister, 113
SuperFood, using, 172
Sushi, Basic Backpacker's, 70
Sweet & Sour, Absaroka, 85
Sweet Pepper Pasta, Olancha, 116
Switchback Smoothie, 170

T

Tabouli Salad, 77
Taconic Mountain Cheesy Rice, 132
Tahini-Lemon Bread, Traveler's, 151
Tamale, Time-Traveler's, 95
Tapenade, 67
Tea
Electro, 179
Moonlight Mint, 180
Rooibus, 173
Shawnee Sage, 181
Teriyaki Tofu Jerky, 79
Thanksgiving on the Hoof, 110
Thunder & Lightning Stir-Fry, 86
Time-Traveler's Tamale, 95

Tofu
in Eastern Sun Miso Soup, 104
Jerky, Bragg's, 80
Jerky, Teriyaki, 79
Tomatoes, dehydrating, 93
Tomato Parmesan, Wasatch, 117
Tortilla(s)
Greek Wayfaring, 66
Pacific Crest, 96
Trail-Angel Cheese Soup, 105
TrailDad's Spaghetti, 115
Trailside Breakfast Rice, 18
Traveler's Tahini-Lemon Bread, 151
Trekin' Fuel, 48
Triple Crown Curry Couscous, 82
Tueeulala Thai Soup, 101

V

Vacuum-sealing oils, 69
Vanilla Coffee, 177
Vegan Super Hero Burritos, 90
Vegetables. *See specific varieties*

W

Walking Carrot Salad, 78
Wasatch Tomato Parmesan, 117
Wendjidu Zinzibahkwud, 166
White Bear Mocha, 175
Whitewater Moon Pie, 162
Whole-Food Granola Bars, 61
Whopper Malt Bribe, 183
Wild Berry Fruit Leather, 159
Wood Gnome Cobbler, 36

Z

Zion Gorp, 54
Ziplock bags, caution with, 7

About the Authors

Christine and Tim Conners have been hiking together since they first started dating. Marriage and four children later, they are still chasing each other down the trail! Their fondness for the long trails eventually led to their first publication together, *Lipsmackin' Backpackin'*, the prequel to this book.

Christine's love for hiking began in her youth in Hawaii, where she would frequently take long walks alone in the mountains behind her home in Oahu's Niu Valley. After completing a three-week Outward Bound backpacking and white-water course in Oregon, she became involved in longer duration trail trips and is now an accomplished backpacker with many weeks spent hiking the Sierra Nevada mountains. In addition to being a mother and author, Christine also works occasionally as a children's mental health therapist and as an instructor of psychology at local colleges. She is currently pursuing an advanced degree in illustration to complement her work as an author.

Tim's entry into the world of backpacking was more arduous. A bungled trip in Ohio as a young boy left him wondering for many years afterwards why anyone would want to put a heavy pack on his or her back and climb incredibly steep mountains. An extraordinary excursion into the Domeland Wilderness of the Southern Sierra in late 1992 answered the question with finality. Tim has since walked more than 1,000 trail miles in the ranges of California, the hills of Ohio, and, more recently, the Appalachians and Atlantic coastal lowlands. He is employed as a propulsion engineer specializing in advanced aircraft design.

Tim and Christine live in Savannah, Georgia, with their four children, James, Michael, Maria, and David, the newest member of the Conners family. While they keep busy with hiking and camping opportunities in the nearby coastal flatlands, the call of the mountains remains strong. They continue to look forward to the time when they can, as a family, hit the long, high trails for weeks on end.

Packable Trailside Cooking Instructions

The following section contains the on-the-trail cooking instructions for each recipe in the book that requires final preparation in the backcountry. This section is intended to be removed from the book and carried along on the trip. You can either tear out the entire section and create your own lightweight, packable book of trail-side cooking instructions or cut out individual instructions and place the slips of paper in your bag of ingredients or other convenient place in your pack. Reference the Packable Trailside Cooking Instructions by recipe name. They are listed in the same order in which the recipes are presented in the main body of the book.

To preserve your book, the Packable Trailside Cooking Instructions are also available online in PDF format at www.falconbooks.com/lipsmackin.

Sasquatch Scones

To make 1 serving, add 1 teaspoon of oil and 1/4 cup of water to 1 bag of scone mix. Knead the bag until the dough becomes stiff. Warm 1 tablespoon of oil in a nonstick pan at low heat. Spoon 3-inch blobs of dough into the pan and cook on very low heat until the bottoms are browned and the tops begin to lose their shine. Flip and continue cooking until the bottom sides are lightly browned.

Jenkins Journey Cakes

To prepare 1 serving, add 1/3 cup of water to 1 bag of cake mix. Knead contents thoroughly. Melt 1 tablespoon of butter in a pan. Cut a corner from the bottom of the bag and squeeze several dollops of the mixture into the pan. Cook both sides as you would a pancake.

Ketchikan Couscous

To prepare 1 serving, heat 2/3 cup of water to boiling. Stir in the mix and cook for 2 minutes. Remove from heat. Allow the pot to stand covered until the liquid is absorbed and the couscous is tender, approximately 5 minutes.

Chewonki Morning Bulgur

For optimum hydration, presoak the single serving of bulgur mix in 1 cup of water beginning the prior evening. In the morning, warm a pan and scramble the bulgur mix in 1 tablespoon of olive oil. Remove from heat and add small pieces of the stick of string cheese to the top of the mixture, allowing the cheese to melt into the scramble before serving.

Trailside Breakfast Rice

To make 1 serving, bring 1 3/4 cups of water to a boil. Add the bag of rice and heat for approximately 10 minutes until rice is fully cooked. Next, add the bag of mix containing the pudding. Remove from heat. Stir and serve.

Cheesy Breakfast Grits

To make 1 serving, stir the contents of the bag into 1 cup of water and heat to boiling while stirring. Remove from heat and add cheese, chopped into small pieces. Continue to stir until blended, then serve.

Saucy Summer Breakfast Burritos

To make 2 servings, add 3/4 cup of boiling water to the salsa bag to rehydrate. Next, add 3/4 cup of cold water to the egg mix and shake well to reconstitute. Melt 1 tablespoon of butter or pour 1 tablespoon of vegetable oil in a warmed pan and add both the rehydrated salsa and the egg mix. Scramble. Shred 2 ounces of cheese (about 1/2 cup) and divide onto each of the 2 tortillas. Add scrambled-egg mix to both. Roll and serve.

Four-Corners Fiesta Burritos

To make 2 servings, add 3/4 cup boiling water to the bag of dried vegetables to rehydrate. Next, add 3/4 cup cold water to the egg mix and shake well to reconstitute. Melt 1 tablespoon of butter or pour 1 tablespoon of vegetable oil in a warmed pan and add both the rehydrated vegetables and the egg mix. Scramble. Shred 2 ounces of cheese (about 1/2 cup) and divide onto each of the 2 tortillas. Add scrambled-egg mix to both. Roll and serve.

Mountain Muesli

Add 1 cup of muesli mix to your favorite dairy or soy milk.

Kalalau Quinoa Cereal

To make 1 serving, bring 3/4 cup of water to a boil and add to the bag of cereal mix. Allow the contents to rehydrate for several minutes before serving.

Blue Bear Mush

For each serving, bring 1 1/2 cups of water to a boil and add to the bag of cereal mix. Stir and let cool before serving.

Mule Fuel

To prepare 1 serving, add 1 cup of hot or cold water to the cereal mix and serve.

Omega Breakfast

Bring 1 cup of water to a boil and pour into a single-serving bag. Seal and let stand for 5 minutes before eating.

Crimson Skies Oatmeal

Bring 1¼ cups of water to a boil. Add mix from the single-serving ziplock bag and reduce heat. Cook for a few additional minutes, stirring occasionally, then cover and remove from heat. Let stand momentarily before serving.

North Woods Oatmeal

To prepare 1 serving, add bag of oat mix to 1½ cups of boiling water and stir. Remove from heat and allow to stand for 5 minutes. Crumble up 2 granola bars and sprinkle on top before serving.

Adirondack Apricot Oatmeal

Add 1½ cups of boiling water to the single-serving bag of oatmeal mix and stir. Allow to stand for 5 minutes before serving.

Olympus Oatmeal

To make 1 serving, add dried fruit to 2 cups of water and bring to a boil. Add oats when the water begins to boil vigorously. Stir and simmer for 5 minutes. Add powdered milk and any optional ingredients. Stir and serve. Note that adding oats to the water before it is really boiling can result in a gluelike texture that tastes flat.

Kearsarge Pass Oatmeal

For 1 serving, bring a little more than 1 cup of water to a boil. Remove from the stove, and pour over the dry mix. Stir. You should strive for the consistency of ordinary cooked oatmeal, but don't cook *this* mix! You will be wasting your time and reduce the texture to mush.

Desert Gruel

To prepare 1 serving, mix dry ingredients together in a cook pot along with 1 tablespoon of olive oil and 1½ cups of water. Heat, ensuring that the bouillon cube dissolves before serving.

Pikes Peak Pineapple Pancakes

To make 1 serving, add ⅔ cup of water to 1 bag of pineapple pancake mix. Knead the mix inside the bag to eliminate large chunks from the batter. Wait approximately 20 minutes, giving the pineapple a chance to rehydrate. Heat ½ tablespoon of vegetable oil in a pan. Cut a corner from the bottom of the bag and squeeze pancake batter onto pan. Cook as you would plain pancakes.

Chuckwalla Chocolate Chip Pancakes

Add 1/2 cup of cold water to the dry ingredients in the single-serving bag. Knead the mixture well enough to break up the larger lumps. Do not overwork the batter as this will make the pancakes less tender. Grease a pan with 1 teaspoon of vegetable oil. Warm the pan on medium heat until drops of water sizzle and disappear quickly. Pour or spoon approximately 1/4 of the batter at a time into the heated pan. Cook until the top bubbles and the bottom is golden brown. Flip with a spatula and cook until the remaining side becomes golden brown as well. Add additional oil to the skillet, if needed, for subsequent pancakes. Serve with syrup.

Arapaho Apple Pancakes

To prepare 1 serving, place 1 tablespoon of oil on a frying pan and warm over low heat. To 1 bag add 1/2 cup of water. Knead the mixture by breaking apart large clumps. Cut a hole in 1 corner of the bag and squeeze enough batter into the pan to make 1 manageable pancake. Fry and flip the pancake once it is browned on the bottom. Brown the other side and serve. Repeat for the remainder of the batter.

Wood Gnome Cobbler

To prepare 1 serving, bring 1 cup of water to a boil and add the bag of fruit mix. Place 3 tablespoons of water in the bag of Bisquick and knead the mixture. Cut a bottom corner from the Bisquick bag and drop spoonful-size dollops into the soup, pushing down the dumplings so that they are immersed. Cover the pot to steam the mixture for about 5 to 7 minutes, with the heat just high enough to keep the liquid boiling. Check occasionally, adding more water if needed to prevent scorching. The cobbler is ready once the dumplings are fully cooked.

Ol' Kooger's Mountain High Granola

Add 1 cup of hot or cold water to 1 serving of cereal and serve.

Koolau Ridge Granola

To make 1 serving, mix 1 cup of cereal with your favorite milk or soy powder and water, or eat straight out of the bag. Serve either hot or cold.

Orange Sky Granola

To make 1 serving, mix 1 cup of cereal with your favorite milk or soy powder and water, or eat straight out of the bag. Serve either hot or cold.

Grizzly Berry Granola

To prepare 1 serving, mix 1 cup of cereal with your favorite milk or soy powder and water, or eat straight out of the bag. Serve either hot or cold.

Rockhouse Basin Apple Granola

To prepare 1 serving, mix 1 cup of cereal with your favorite milk or soy powder and water, or eat straight out of the bag. Serve either hot or cold.

Trekin' Fuel

Eat straight out of the bag like gorp or add milk to make a cereal. Serving size is 1 cup.

Red Husky

To make 1 serving, cut 2 ounces of cheese into bite-size pieces. Combine with 1/4 cup of almonds and eat.

Bear Bait

Eat straight from the tube or use on crackers, tortillas, or pita bread.

Mud

Eat straight from the container or use as a delicious spread on crackers or bagels.

Grunch

Eat straight from the container or use as a spread on crackers or bread.

Baja Burritos

To prepare 1 serving, pour 1/2 cup of boiling water into the bag of beans and salsa early in the day. Add 1/4 cup of cool water to the vegetable mix. By midday, the foods will be rehydrated and ready to eat. Cut a corner from the ziplock bag containing the rehydrated bean and salsa mix. Squeeze 1/2 of the contents onto 1 tortilla. Next, add 1/2 of the coleslaw mix to the tortilla and roll it up to serve. Repeat for the other tortilla.

Greek Wayfaring Tortilla

To prepare 1 serving, crumble the feta cheese. Add it, along with 1 tablespoon of olive oil, to the bag of dried tomato-basil. Shake the bag, then place the mixture on the tortilla. Roll and serve.

Tapenade

Preferably several hours before lunch, but no less than 15 minutes prior, add 2 tablespoons of water to the 1-serving bag of dry mix and knead into a thick paste. Spread the cheese into the pita shells, then add the now-rehydrated tapenade and serve.

Anasazi Trail Food

To rehydrate 1 serving, cover the contents of the bag with about 1 cup of water. Hike on for a couple of miles, then stop and serve your bean dip. Anasazi Trail Food goes great naturally with crackers or tortillas.

Basic Backpacker's Sushi

To make 1 serving, bring 1 cup of water to a boil early in the day. Pour it into 1 bag of sushi rice mixture. Carefully knead the bag to further break apart remaining clumps of rice mix. Insulate the bag to retain heat as long as possible, and place it in your pack. By midday the rice should be fully rehydrated. At lunchtime, lay 1 sheet of nori flat with the shiny side down and the perforations running perpendicular to you. Moisten lightly with your fingers. Scoop half of the rice from your bag and place on the sheet of nori. Form a band of rice side to side across the length of the sheet about 1 inch from the end closest to you. Carefully roll the nori away from you as you might a fat cigar. The roll can be cut into traditional sushi slices or served like a burrito.

Black Bear Hummus

To make 1 serving, bring ½ cup of water to a boil early in the day and add to the bean mixture, along with 1 teaspoon of optional oil, if desired. Knead the mixture in the bag and stash away in your pack until lunch. When you stop later in the day, eat the hummus as is or add as a topping to your favorite crackers.

Heavenly Hummus

To make 1 serving, pour ½ cup boiling water into a bag of hummus-salsa mix early in the day. Add ¼ cup cool water to the vegetable mix. By midday the foods will be rehydrated and ready to eat. Combine the vegetable mix with the hummus. Can be served as is or used as a dip for crackers, celery, or carrots.

Boundary Waters Hummus on Rye

To prepare 1 serving, add ½ cup cool water to 1 bag of hummus and knead the mixture in the bag. Let stand for a few minutes. Snip the corner from the bottom corner of the bag and squeeze the hummus onto each of your 6 pieces of crispbread.

Carter Notch Coleslaw

To make 1 serving, add ⅔ cup of water to one bag of slaw. Allow to rehydrate for at least 30 minutes.

Cleo's Coleslaw

For 1 serving, add ⅓ cup of cool water to rehydrate. Allow to stand 10 minutes before serving.

Tabouli Salad

Add 1 cup of cold or warm water to the ziplock bag and allow the contents to rehydrate for about 15 minutes before serving. Can be eaten straight from the bag. Makes 1 serving.

Triple-Crown Curry Couscous

To prepare 1 serving, bring 1½ cups of water to a boil. Stir in all ingredients, remove from heat, cover, and let stand until liquid is absorbed. Let cool, then fluff the dish before serving.

Pine Valley Couscous

To prepare 1 serving, place 1 cup of boiling water directly into a ziplock bag of Pine Valley Couscous mix. Allow to rehydrate for 10 minutes before serving.

Cedar Grove Couscous Risotto

To make 1 serving, bring 3 cups of water to a boil. Add the mix from 1 bag labeled "Risotto A." Return to a boil and allow vegetables to become tender. Next, add 1 serving of couscous from a bag labeled "Risotto B." Stir, then cover and remove from heat. Let stand for about 5 minutes before serving.

Absaroka Sweet & Sour

To prepare 1 serving, bring 1½ cups of water to a boil. Add dry mixture to water and cook. Occasionally stir for 5 minutes before serving.

Thunder & Lightning Stir-Fry

To make 1 serving, bring 2¼ cups of water to a boil. Add hot water to the ziplock bag and wait 10 to 15 minutes for the mixture to rehydrate. Can be eaten directly from the bag.

Green Dragon Pad Thai

To make 1 serving, add ¼ cup of cold water to the bag of egg powder and knead into a batter. Bring a pot of water to a boil. Pour ¼ cup of the hot water into the bag labeled "Green Dragon Sauce Mix" and knead until an even consistency. Add Thai noodles to the remaining water in the pot and cook for 2 minutes. Drain noodles. Next, pour both the reconstituted sauce and egg batter into the noodle pot. Stir, cover, and let sit for 3 to 4 minutes before serving.

Fuji Feast

To make 1 serving, bring a pot of water to a boil. Pour 1 cup of hot water into the vegetable-mushroom-spice-mix bag and allow contents to rehydrate. In the meantime, bring 4 ounces of noodles to a boil in the remaining water. Once the noodles are thoroughly cooked, drain water and add the eggplant mixture from the ziplock bag. Stir thoroughly and serve.

Miso Madness

To make 1 serving, bring 2½ cups of water to a boil. If using a garlic clove, cut into small pieces and toss back into the bag. Carefully pour the hot water into the bag and allow to stand 8 to 10 minutes, kneading occasionally to help ensure that all ingredients are evenly hydrated. Serve straight from the bag.

Vegan Super Hero Burritos

To make 2 servings, add 2 cups of corn, 1 package of rice mix, and 1 tablespoon of vegetable oil to 3¼ cups of water and bring to a boil for 5 minutes. Reduce heat, cover, then simmer. Once fully cooked, scoop onto 4 tortillas, fold, and serve.

Burrito Olé for Two

To prepare 2 servings, bring 4 cups of water to a boil. Pour 1¾ cups of the boiling water into a bowl containing the beans. Mix and let sit. Pour rice into the remainder of the boiling water and let simmer until fully rehydrated. Once the beans and rice are ready, fill 4 tortillas. Add 8 ounces of cheese and optional hot sauce.

EZ Ed's Burritos

Bring 1½ cups of water per serving to a boil. Pour water into a 1-serving ziplock bag. Knead the mixture thoroughly. Insulate so that the bag will hold the heat. Allow to sit at least 10 minutes, continuing to periodically knead the contents. Once ready, cut off 1 corner of the bag and squeeze the contents into each of 2 tortillas. Roll to form burritos.

Mountain Goat Quesadillas

To make 2 servings, add ¼ cup of boiling water to the dry mix and allow to rehydrate for a couple of minutes. Add ¼ of the cheese and ¼ of the rehydrated vegetable mix to 1 tortilla shell. Fold the shell to enclose the mix and cheese. Put ½ tablespoon of oil on each tortilla shell. Fry on both sides of the tortilla until the cheese has melted. Repeat for the remaining 3 tortillas.

Time-Traveler's Tamale

To prepare 1 serving, bring 1¾ cups of water to a boil. If using a garlic clove, cut into small pieces and toss back into the bag. Carefully pour the hot water into the bag and allow to stand 8 to 10 minutes, kneading occasionally to help ensure that all ingredients are evenly hydrated. Serve straight from the bag.

Pacific Crest Tortillas

To make 1 serving, bring 1 cup of water to a boil and add to a bag of bean and seasoning mix. Seal bag and carefully knead contents. Once rehydrated, cut a corner from the bag and squeeze onto 2 tortillas. Roll them up and serve.

Black Mountain Potatoes

To prepare 1 serving, bring 2½ cups of water to a boil. Pour about 1 cup of the boiling water into the soup cup (don't fill it to the top!). Stir the soup and let sit 5 minutes. Add potato-cheese-garlic blend to the remaining water in the pan. Stir until the mix fully thickens. Once the bean soup is ready, pour it on top of your potato mountain and serve.

Boot-Stomped Spuds

Add 1 cup of hot water to the single-serving bag of spud mix. Knead the contents thoroughly. Serve immediately from the bag.

Flyin' Brian's Garlic Potatoes

To make 1 serving, bring 2 cups of water to a boil. Stir in all ingredients and immediately remove from heat. Let stand until cool enough to serve.

Lone Pine Lentils and Dumplings

In a pot, pour the lentil mix into 2 cups of water. Bring to a boil, stirring occasionally, then reduce to a simmer. Meanwhile, add 1 tablespoon oil and about ¼ cup of water to the flour mixture. Thoroughly mix, then spoon the batter onto the simmering lentils in 5 or 6 globs. They will be touching but should stay distinct. Cover the pot and simmer for about 20 minutes until the lentils and dumplings are cooked through. Additional time may be required at very high altitudes. Hydrate the lentil mix with small additions of water if in danger of drying out and burning. Makes 1 serving.

Tueeulala Thai Soup

To prepare 1 serving, bring 2½ cups of water to a boil. Add 1 package of vegetable mix and 1 package of Thai noodles along with the contents from its spice packet. Return to a boil for about 3 minutes. Remove from heat, cover, and let sit for an extra minute, giving time for the vegetables to rehydrate before serving.

Blue Blazer's Soup

To make 1 serving, bring 2½ cups of water to a boil. Add 1 bag of soup mix. Return to a boil for 3 to 5 minutes, stirring occasionally. Soup is ready to serve once noodles are soft.

Soup of Mount Inthanon

Bring 2 cups of water to a boil. Add seasonings and hot water to the 1-serving bag. Set aside for a few minutes, allowing the beans to rehydrate before serving.

Eastern Sun Miso Soup

Bring 1½ cups of water to a boil and add to the mix in the single-serving ziplock bag. Let sit about 5 minutes. Can be eaten directly from the bag.

Trail-Angel Cheese Soup

To make 1 serving, cut ½ of the Velveeta log into small cubes. Add cheese to 2 cups of water and bring to a boil. Remove from heat. Add bag of potato contents a little at a time while stirring. Let stand for 5 minutes. Add crackers then serve. The extra Velveeta can be used the next day to make a second pot of soup or served with crackers for lunch.

Brunswick Stew

To make 1 serving, bring 2½ cups of water to a boil. Pour 1 bag of "Brunswick Stew A" into the boiling water and continue to cook until vegetables soften. Remove from heat and add 1 bag of "Brunswick Stew B." Stir, cover, and allow to stand until the vegetables fully soften and the flavor develops. Note that if Bag "B" is added prior to removing from heat, the mix may scorch.

North Mountain Okonomiyaki

To make 1 serving, add ⅓ cup of water to 1 ziplock bag of coleslaw mix and allow to rehydrate for about an hour. Ensure that bouillon cube dissolves evenly. Add ¾ cup of water to 1 bag of the flour mix and knead. Add rehydrated coleslaw mix to the bag and knead again. Place 1 tablespoon of oil in pan. Pour about ¼ cup of dough at a time into a heated pan as you would for a pancake (exact amount depends upon your pan size). After the edges are cooked, flip. Remove patty from pan and repeat as required for the remainder of the mix. Sprinkle with 1 tablespoon of soy sauce and serve.

Secret Lake Garlic Lentils

To prepare 1 serving, heat 2 tablespoons of vegetable oil in a pan, then add lentil mixture. Stir to coat mixture with oil. Add 1¼ cups of water and bring to a boil for a few minutes. Cover and reduce heat. Simmer on low heat for about 30 minutes before serving.

Thanksgiving on the Hoof

To make 1 serving, add 1 bag of Prosage mix and 1 tablespoon of butter to 1½ cups of water. Bring to a boil until the Prosage softens, typically a couple of minutes. Next add 1 bag of potatoes and stuffing mix. Stir well. Remove from the stove and allow to rehydrate for several more minutes. Add optional salt to taste.

Chiwaukum Quinoa

To prepare 1 serving, bring 2½ cups of water to a boil. Tear the spaghetti leather into small pieces. Place sauce leather in boiling water along with 1 bag of mix and 2 tablespoons of oil. Chop the garlic clove and add to the pot as well. Cook, stirring occasionally, until the beans rehydrate.

Dirt Bagger's Pasta Parmesan

Cook the pasta in 2½ cups of boiling water. Most of the water should be absorbed by the time the pasta is soft. Remove from heat. Stir in 3 tablespoons of parsley flakes and 3 tablespoons of olive oil. Top with ¼ cup of Parmesan cheese. Add optional seasonings, if desired. Makes 1 serving.

South Sister Stroganoff

To prepare 1 serving, put a little water into 1 bag of dried sauce mix, enough to barely cover the contents, about 1 hour prior to dinner. Bring 2 cups of water to a boil and add the contents of 1 bag of noodles. Once the noodles are fully cooked, drain. Add the rehydrated sauce mix and stir. Let the pot sit, covered, for a few minutes before serving.

Golden Bear Gado-Gado

Add the wet ingredients to the bag of dry ingredients, reseal, and knead bag to mix the contents. Bring a pot of water to a boil and add 4 ounces of pasta. Heat until tender, then drain excess water. Add sauce mix to the pasta and stir. Makes 1 serving.

TrailDad's Spaghetti

For 1 serving, crumble dried spaghetti sauce into 2½ cups of cold water and heat to boiling. Add 2 tablespoons of olive oil and 4 ounces of pasta. Stir quickly for a few minutes. Simmer if your stove will permit; otherwise, remove from heat to prevent burning, keeping the contents hot as long as possible. The pasta should soak up the liquid so that there is no need to drain the pot. Add ¼ cup of Parmesan cheese, stir, and serve.

Olancha Sweet Pepper Pasta

To make 1 serving, bring a pot of water to a boil. Pour ½ cup of hot water into 1 bag of sauce mix and allow to rehydrate. Add 4 ounces of noodles to the remainder of the boiling water. Continue on high heat until the noodles are tender. Drain and add the sauce mix and 1 tablespoon of olive oil. Stir well and serve.

Wasatch Tomato Parmesan

To prepare 1 serving, put a little water into 1 bag of dried sauce mix, enough to barely cover the contents, about 1 hour before dinner. Bring 2 cups of water to a boil and add the contents of 1 bag of noodles. Once the noodles are fully cooked, drain. Add the rehydrated sauce mix and stir. Let the pot sit, covered, for a few minutes before serving.

Springer Mountain Pesto

For 1 serving, bring 2½ cups of water to a boil. Cook pasta thoroughly. Most of the water should be absorbed, requiring little draining. Add ¼ cup olive oil and pesto mix to the pasta, toss, and serve.

Pindos Mountain Pasta

To prepare 1 serving, add a small amount of water to the tomato-basil mix to begin rehydration. Next, bring 2½ cups of water to a boil. Cook pasta thoroughly. Most of the water should be absorbed, requiring little draining. Add the remainder of the ingredients to the pasta, then toss and serve.

Range Rovin' Ramen

To prepare 1 serving, crush the ramen noodles and pour them, along with the dried vegetables, into 2½ cups of water. Bring to a boil, being careful to prevent the ramen from becoming mushy. Serve once the vegetables rehydrate.

Guitar Lake Melody

To prepare 1 serving, bring 2½ cups of water to a boil, add contents from the ziplock bag, stir well, then cover. Remove from heat and let stand for 20 minutes before serving.

Rib-Stickin' Ramen

To make 1 serving, bring 2 cups of water to a boil and add noodles. Do not include the ramen seasoning packet, which often contains meat by-products. Once noodles are soft, remove from heat and add the flour-seasoning mix, 1 tablespoon butter, and 2 ounces of cheese. Stir until cheese melts.

Mexican Volcano

To prepare 1 serving, bring 1½ cups of water to a boil. Pour ½ cup of the heated water into the bean mix and set aside to rehydrate. Add polenta to the remainder of the hot water. Once the polenta and beans are rehydrated, pour the bean mix directly onto the polenta and serve.

Back Rock Bami Goreng

To make 1 serving, add ⅓ cup of filtered water to 1 bag of vegetable-mushroom mix and allow to rehydrate for approximately 1 hour. Once rehydrated, bring 1 cup of water to a boil along with 1 dissolved bouillon cube. Add the noodles, allowing them to cook for about 3 minutes. Drain off the broth from the noodles and pour into a cup as a hot drink on the side. Add the cooking oil from the Thai noodle package and stir-fry the cooked noodles for about 1 minute. Now open the seasoning packet from the Thai noodle package and pour over the noodles in the pot. Add the veggie-mushroom mix and stir-fry once again for an additional minute. Remove from heat and add the soy sauce before serving.

Lost Cowboy Chili

To make 1 serving, bring 2 1/4 cups of water to a boil. Tear the chili leather into small pieces and add to the boiling water. Stir occasionally until fully rehydrated.

Kilauea Chili

For 1 serving, bring 1 3/4 cups of water to a boil. If using a garlic clove, cut into small pieces and toss back into the bag. Carefully pour the hot water into bag and allow to stand 8 to 10 minutes, kneading occasionally to help ensure that all ingredients are evenly hydrated. Serve straight from the bag.

Death Valley Chili

Tear chili leather into small pieces and return to the ziplock bag that it came from. Add 1 1/2 cups of water to the bag and let the chili mix rehydrate for a while. Kneading the bag occasionally will help accelerate the process. Pour mixture into a pan and bring to a low boil. Heat until the chili finishes rehydrating, stirring occasionally to prevent burning. Serve as is or use as a topping on optional cooked spaghetti noodles. Makes 1 serving.

Soul Food

For 1 serving, bring 2 cups of water to a boil, add contents from the ziplock bag, stir well, then cover. Remove from heat and let stand for 20 minutes before serving.

Dinner in Denali

To prepare 1 serving, bring 1 1/2 cups of water to a boil. Pour water into 1 bag of mixture. Seal, insulate to preserve heat, and allow to sit for about 10 minutes. Can be eaten straight out of the bag.

Taconic Mountain Cheesy Rice

Bring 1 1/4 cups of water to a boil. Add all the ingredients including 1 tablespoon of butter and 2 ounces of string cheese. Stir until rice is rehydrated and cheese is melted. Makes 1 serving.

Chainsaw's Pumpkin Pleaser

To make 1 serving, bring 2 cups of water to a boil and add the contents from 1 bag of pumpkin-rice mix. As an option, olive oil or ghee can also be added at this time. Serve once ingredients have fully rehydrated.

Procrastinator's Deliverance

To prepare 1 serving, bring 1 1/2 cups of water to a boil. Add hot water to the ziplock bag and allow to rehydrate for about 5 minutes. Can be eaten directly from the bag.

Kincora Rice

To make 1 serving, bring 1 1/4 cups of water to a boil. Add water to the ziplock bag, reseal, and allow to sit until rice is fully rehydrated. Can be eaten directly out of the bag.

Peaks of Dolomiti Rice and Beans

To make 1 serving, bring 2 cups of water to a boil, add contents from the ziplock bag, stir well, then cover. Remove from heat and let stand for 20 minutes before serving.

Leahi Trail Rice

To prepare 1 serving, bring 3/4 cup of water to a boil. If using a garlic clove, cut into small pieces and toss back into the bag. Carefully pour the hot water into the bag and allow to stand 8 to 10 minutes, kneading occasionally to help ensure that all ingredients are evenly hydrated. Serve straight from the bag.

Brooks Range Bannock

Being careful not to use too much, add 1/4 cup water to mixture, adjusting the amount as required to make a soft dough. First cooking method: flatten dough with the palm of your hand and fry in 1 tablespoon of vegetable oil, turning once. Second cooking method: Forgoing the oil, wrap dough around a stick and bake over a campfire. Makes 1 serving.

Hopi Fry Bread

To make 1 serving, slowly add 1/2 cup of warm water to the bag. Seal the bag, then knead the mixture. Remove the dough from the bag once the consistency thickens, then continue kneading until the mixture forms an elastic ball of dough. Elasticity will improve further if the dough is left in the open air for a brief period of time. Meanwhile, heat half of the oil (1 tablespoon) until sizzling hot. Split the ball of dough in two, take half, roll it and then knead it into a flat, waferlike tortilla approximately 1/2-inch thick. This can be done by repeatedly pinching the dough in circles in your hand or using a water bottle as a rolling pin. Once the dough has been thoroughly stretched, pinch a hole in the middle—like a flat doughnut. Place it carefully in the hot oil. Flip over once the sides begin to brown. Pour half of the contents of the bag of seasoning mix onto the fry bread. Repeat with the remainder of the dough.

Sacagawea Corn Bread

Cube 1 ounce of cheese into small pieces. Add 1 tablespoon of oil and 1/3 cup of water along with the cubed cheese to the mix in the ziplock bag and thoroughly knead until a very stiff dough forms. Note that if too much water is added, the corn bread will fall apart while cooking. Heat 1 tablespoon of vegetable oil on low flame in a nonstick pan and spread 1/2-inch-thick rounds of batter onto the cooking surface. Rounds can be of any manageable diameter. Continue to cook on low heat until the bottom of the bread is browned and the top begins to lose its shine. It is very important that the stove heat remains low; otherwise, the bread will burn. Flip the bread, flatten slightly, and continue cooking until the remaining side is browned. Makes 1 serving.

Fabulous Fry Brownies

To make 1 serving, heat 1 teaspoon of oil in a pan at low heat. Add a second teaspoon of oil and 2 tablespoons of water to 1 bag of brownie mix. Knead the mixture in the bag. Once the pan is hot, scoop small, spoon-size mounds into the pan or cut a corner from the bag and squeeze out small brownie batter blobs. Cook until the bottoms are browned and the tops are no longer shiny. Flip, flatten, and brown the other sides.

Chocolate Chip Fry Cookies

To make 1 serving, heat 1 teaspoon of oil in a pan at low heat. Add 2 tablespoons of water to 1 bag of cookie mix. Knead the mixture in the bag. Once the pan is hot, scoop small, spoon-size mounds into the pan or cut a corner from the bag and squeeze out small cookie batter blobs. Cook until the bottoms are browned and the tops are no longer shiny. Flip, flatten, and brown the other sides.

Green Mountain Grasshopper

To make 1 serving, add $\frac{1}{2}$ cup cold water to 1 bag of pudding mixture. Shake vigorously for 1 to 2 minutes. Allow to set for at least 5 minutes. Impress your friends by artistically topping your pudding with three broken Oreo cookies and 2 teaspoons of crème de menthe.

Whitewater Moon Pie

To make 1 serving, add 1 cup of cold water to 1 bag of the pudding mix and shake vigorously until the mixture thickens. This may take a couple of minutes. Next add 1 serving of wafer mix to the bag and knead. Serve straight from the bag.

Chocolate Raspberry Indulgence

To make 2 servings, combine 2 cups of water with the powdered milk and pudding mix in a pot. Heat until the mixture comes to a full boil, stirring constantly. It is helpful to use a heat disperser between the pot and some stoves to minimize scorching. Divide the raspberries between 2 bowls, cups, or ziplock bags. Pour the cooked chocolate pudding over the raspberries. Serve warm or cold. If not eaten immediately, cover or close the bag to prevent a crust from forming.

Dirty Socks Peach Cobbler

To prepare 2 servings, pour $\frac{1}{4}$ cup of water and the peaches into a nonstick cook pan. If not using a nonstick pan, spread a little butter or oil within the pan to prevent sticking. Bring to a boil, then reduce heat. Add $\frac{1}{4}$ cup of water to the bag containing the Bisquick mix and knead. Cut a corner from the bottom of the bag and squeeze the mixture onto the peaches. Continue to scramble the mixture in the pan until the batter is fully cooked.

Skidaway Banana Puddin'

To produce 1 serving, add 1 cup of cold filtered water to 1 bag of the pudding-milk mix. Shake vigorously for about 1 minute. The pudding will thicken within a couple of minutes. At this point, add the wafer-banana mix to the pudding bag and knead. Can be served straight from the bag.

Switchback Smoothie

Tear 1 serving of leather into very small pieces and place in a widemouthed bottle containing 1 cup of cold water. Allow mixture to dissolve for about 30 minutes, periodically shaking vigorously to help speed the process. The fruit leather itself is also very tasty and can be eaten as is.

Grooovy Smooothie

Add 3 tablespoons of drink mix to 1 cup cold water. Stir or shake.

Earth Smoothie

To make a single serving, add mixture from a single bag to a widemouthed water bottle. Add 2 cups of water and shake vigorously until well mixed.

Hurricane Hill Hot Chocolate

For 1 serving, bring 1 cup of water to a boil. Place 1/3 cup of mixture into your mug. Add boiling water and stir well.

Moo-Less Hot Chocolate

For 1 serving, bring 1 cup of water to a boil. Place 1/4 cup of mixture into your mug. Add boiling water and stir well.

White Bear Mocha

Boil 1 cup of water and pour into your mug. Add 2 tablespoons of White Bear Mocha mixture and stir.

Lightning Coffee

Boil 1 cup of water and pour into your mug. Add 3 tablespoons of Lightning Coffee mixture and stir.

Alaskan Winter Coffee

Boil 1 cup of water and pour into your mug. Add 3 tablespoons of Alaskan Winter Coffee mixture and stir.

Cloudy Mountain Latte

Pour 1 cup of water into a rigid widemouthed bottle. The bottle should be large enough to accommodate at least 20 fluid ounces to provide adequate additional volume for shaking. Add mix. Shake vigorously for about 10 seconds once per minute for 3 to 5 minutes, at which point the coffee and milk will have dissolved. Add remaining cup of water and shake again.

Electro-Tea

Heat 1 cup of water and add 1 teaspoon of tea mix. Stir well.

Moonlight Mint Tea

Bring 4 cups of water to a boil, then add 1/4 cup of sugar. (Doing so in this order helps to keep the tea clear.) Remove from heat. Add tea bags and mint or peppermint leaves. Let simmer for several minutes. Makes 2 servings.

Shawnee Sage Tea

Bring 4 cups of water to a boil, then add 1/4 cup of sugar. (Doing so in this order helps to keep the tea clear.) Remove from heat. Add tea bags and sage leaves. Let simmer for several minutes. Makes 2 servings.

Goat Dance Brandy

Bring 1 cup of water to a near-boil. Add dessert mix and brandy. Stir until dissolved.

Whopper Malt Bribe

To make 1 serving, add 1/2 cup of mix to 1 cup of either hot or cold water. It works nicely both ways. Stir and serve.

Panamint Peppermint Cooler

To make 1 large serving, bring 2 cups of water to a boil. Add 4 tea bags and let steep for 6 minutes before removing. While hot, add 1/4 cup of the Kool-Aid mix and stir until dissolved. Allow water to cool, then add 2 more cups of cold water. For an on-the-trail treat, pour into a water bottle for later enjoyment.